An engraving by Howard Pyle.

Mysterious New England

Edited by

AUSTIN N. STEVENS

Design and Production by

MARGO LETOURNEAU

Editorial Consultant

REED ALVORD

PUBLISHED BY YANKEE PUBLISHING INCORPORATED
DUBLIN, NEW HAMPSHIRE

Second Edition, 1979
Fourth Printing, 1986

Library of Congress Catalog
Card Number 74-172976
ISBN No. 0-911658-86-6

Manufactured in the United States of America

FOREWORD

For many, an interest in ghosts, witches, and vampires is something less than the hallmark of enlightenment. The "educated" man is steadfast in his contempt for all things related to the occult. Indeed, he wouldn't believe in a ghost if one knocked him down, sat on his chest, and beat him over the head with an ectoplasmic chain.

By his own admission, the "educated" man can only accept the part of reality that can be tested in a laboratory by a test which is administered with only the portion of his mind that is analytical. And what a pity, too, for like the part of the iceberg we see above the line of water, laboratory realities are supported by another part — vague, mysterious, menacing and nine times the size of the part we see.

It is in this dark underworld that men see ghosts, develop legends, and create our myths, and in so doing describe their sense of the unknown . . . that sleeping giant whose dreams, in turn, haunt men. We catch his breath in the winter wind, feel him beckon in an ocean swell, sense his essence in an ancient and deserted house. And yet, if we're enlightened enough, we can ignore all that.

What is, of course, hard to ignore is the work of artists and poets and great musicians who draw much of their inspiration from the same unconscious source and who describe in other terms, less distorted by fear and guilt, the same magnificent and mysterious silhouette. The great religions marry myth and art and serve their own times as cultural cornerstones.

The educated man should no more turn his back on a legend or a good ghost story than he should on a good painting. Neither will stand up too well under analysis. Both will prove full of faults under the hard white light of a laboratory, and yet somehow they are among the vital elements of our sense of wholeness . . . both assuredly more important to our psychic well-being than a transistor radio or an atomic bomb.

Many of the stories in this book challenge credibility. So if "rationalism" has become such a habit with you that you insist on distilling this book's fact from its fancy, reading it will probably be a frustrating experience.

If, on the other hand, you can accept the premise that "there are more things in heaven and earth" than you have complete knowledge of, you should receive your full measure of enjoyment. In fact, it may even make you think twice about the time you *felt* somebody staring at you, *before* you caught him at it, or the day you *knew* that "this has all happened before . . ."

However you read this book, we'll promise you this: henceforth, your investigations of things that go "BUMP" in your attic will most certainly be a hell-of-a-lot more exciting.

The Editor

CONTENTS

Section I

The Yankee Disposition

Hanging at Wassaguscus

by Lewis A. Taft

> *Justice gives sentence many times*
> *On one man for another's crimes.*
> *Our brethren of New England use*
> *Choice malefactors to excuse,*
> *And hang the guiltless in their stead,*
> *Of whom the company have less need.*
> *Samuel Butler in "Hudibras."*

With many misgivings, tall gentlemanly Edward Johnson stood under the bare, spectral branches of the white oak tree on Hunt's Hill, overlooking the small settlement of Wassaguscus (Weymouth, Massachusetts). The members of the colony were grouped in front of him, shivering in the cold wintry wind that swept over the hill. A sorry dispirited company, he thought. Weak, cold and half-starved, they could put up little resistance if the Indians were to attack them.

Savagely he kicked at a stone, then raised his eyes to glance at the group of Indian warriors clustered at the edge of the clearing, watching the small band of colonists. The threat of an Indian attack hovered over the settlement and only judicial action by the company could avert it.

Fate had placed Edward Johnson in an unenviable position, for in this dangerous situation he was the judge and temporary leader of the Wassaguscus Colony. And this day he must sentence a member of the company to the gallows. A man must hang for stealing from their Indian neighbors. It was late winter in the year 1623.

A short time after the Pilgrims landed at Plymouth, a wealthy London merchant named Thomas Weston had organized a group of colonists and sent them to America in two small ships. Thomas Weston had been instrumental in dispatching the Pilgrims to New England in the *Mayflower* and there are reasons to believe that the colonists were sent to New England in 1622 to re-enforce the depleted manpower of the Plymouth Colony.

The Pilgrims objected to the newcomers landing at Plymouth, so the Weston colonists landed north of Plymouth at a place then known by the Indian name of Wassaguscus. They exchanged gifts with the local Indian Sachem, then selected a site for their settlement on a peninsula at the mouth of the Monatiquot River. Industriously the new colonists constructed a blockhouse, some buildings for storing goods and cabins to live in and surrounded the whole thing by a stockade.

The company had landed in August, too late to plant crops, so they were forced to depend on what stores the ships had left for them. Few of them were proficient in hunting or fishing so they soon needed food.

The new colony had an able and resourceful leader in Richard Green, a counterpart of energetic Myles Standish. Green led two expeditions, comprised of men from Plymouth and Wassaguscus, to trade with the Indians and thus obtain food. The friendly Indian Squanto went with them as an interpreter.

They were moderately successful on the first expedition but on the second trip the shallop they sailed in was capsized, throwing them into the water. Richard Green and Squanto died after this experience, probably from pneumonia.

The leadership of the Wassaguscus Colony now devolved on an irresolute gentleman by the name of John Saunders or Sanders, who was unable to provide the kind of leadership that was needed.

The winter advanced and the plight of the little colony became desperate. The colonists bartered most of their personal possessions to the Indians for food until they had little left but their weapons. Without trade goods the natives refused to give them anything.

As the colonists became weakened by hunger, the Indians, losing their fear of white men, became bolder. One Indian warrior threatened to kill a woman of the colony and went unpunished, but any colonist who stole from the Indians was publicly flogged. To curb the starving settlers, John Saunders decreed that the next man who stole from the natives would be hanged by the neck until dead.

The Indians became so threatening that it was decided to send to Plymouth for military assistance. The colony became a haven of fear. Fear of death at the hands of their savage neighbors even transcended their fear of death from starvation. The men stayed close to the blockhouse, too frightened to dig for shellfish or to go hunting in the forest.

John Saunders, in spite of the danger of winter seas and the threat of an Indian attack on the settlement, embarked in a small ship and sailed for the Maine coast in the hope of obtaining food from the fishing settlements. He left Edward Johnson as the leader of the unhappy colonists.

A short time later one of the bravest men in the Wassaguscus Colony ventured into the forest to hunt for deer and found a large Indian storage pit filled with corn. He took the corn, brought it into the settlement and divided it amongst his fellow colonists.

When the Indians discovered the rifled storage pit they hurried to the blockhouse and demanded that the thief be handed over to them for punishment. Edward Johnson refused but promised the angry natives that the culprit would be punished speedily by the colonists. Quickly he ordered the drummer to drum the men to an assembly.

The men assembled on Hunt's Hill. Indians from the nearby village assembled also and grouped on the edge of the clearing, their attitude both angry and truculent.

Johnson explained to the company the reason for calling an assembly, and requested the guilty person to step forth that his actions might be judged.

A strong young man of the company, a cobbler by trade, stepped forth and in a loud voice admitted that he had taken the corn from the Indian storage pit.

"I took the corn and distributed it to our people that they might not die of hunger," he said. "Why worry you about the Indian corn when your people are hungry. Only two men of our company have dared to go into the forest to hunt the deer. Unless more diligence is shown in procuring food our people will all die before the ships arrive in the Spring."

"What you say about our lack of diligence is true," Johnson answered him. "But the thievery of the Indian corn has jeopardized the lives of everyone in our company. The savages are many and we are few. They can easily overwhelm us and take our lives. Under these circumstances to send hunters into the forest would be folly. The Indians are demanding a victim for the loss of their corn. If one is not soon forthcoming, I am afraid that they will attack us."

"Find your victim then but do not expect me to sacrifice myself," the young man said angrily. "I took the corn from the heathen and I do not feel at fault." Sturdily he walked to the huge oak tree and leaned his back against it, glaring defiantly at Johnson.

His fellow colonists looked with troubled countenances from their leader to the cobbler and murmured to each other uneasily. They hoped that the judge would not ask them to disarm the malefactor for he was a person that could be a Samson in his wrath. Moreover, many of them had eaten some of the stolen corn and felt a kinship in guilt with the young cobbler.

In their dilemma a young carpenter stood forth from his fellows and urged the judge and assembly not to allow the complaint against their fellow for they could ill afford to lose the services of the only cobbler in the colony.

Now there was in the assembly a certain wool sorter, a widower and childless, an argumentative, contentious man who had always been loud in his criticisms of those in authority but short in the performance of his duties to the company. He now stood forth from the assembly and branded the members as a group of ungodly sinners who would condone acts of thievery against their brothers and neighbors, the poor Indians. The cobbler had sinned and should hang, he argued, otherwise the Indians would become angered by the dilatory actions of the assembly and might kill all of them.

Other members of the assembly stepped forward, the majority of them in favor of showing mercy to the accused, but as soon as one would finish his speech the wool sorter would cry out, calling them sinners and demanding that the company should hang the cobbler.

Then a gentleman of the company, a droll quick-witted rogue named Thomas Morton, stepped from the group and bowed to Edward Johnson. He spoke somewhat as follows: "It has been proved by many that this cobbler is exceedingly valuable to this company but this wool sorter is also right in one respect. If we do not punish anyone the natives are likely to attack us. We must produce a victim to mollify the savages. I propose that we forget the guilt of our friend the cobbler. Let us pick for a victim a man without kith or kin, a man who eats much but provides little, a person of no value to our company. Gentlemen, I gaze upon this assembly and I see hunters and fishermen, carpenters and coopers, a cobbler, a tanner, a tailor, a smith, all valuable to our company. We also have this fellow a wool sorter but alas, we have no wool. He hath no kith or kin nor has he dependents. Gentlemen, I urge that this man be hanged. Not because of any guilt on his part but because he will occasion us little loss. We have little time left for debate. The savages are waiting for a victim."

At the end of Morton's speech there was a chorus of Amens. A few members of the assembly laid hold of the poor wool sorter and looked toward their judge Edward Johnson for confirmation.

This was Edward Johnson's moment of decision but like Pontius Pilate he washed his hands of the proceedings by turning his back on the assembly.

I somehow picture Edward Johnson standing alone on Hunt's Hill, long after the colonists and Indians had left. I wonder what bitter thoughts passed through his mind as the cold wind whistled sadly in the branches of the oak tree, fluttering the clothes on the stiffening body of the wool sorter. Then I picture Edward Johnson, a sad and lonely man, an appeaser, walking slowly down the hill and out of the realm of recorded history, leaving behind him little more than contempt for a leader who had let expediency overrule justice.　　□□

Cling-Clang
The Vaulting Peddler

by Alton Hall Blackington

*He was a tin knocker and clock fixer. He would
drink his tea first, straight and clear, and then
eat two spoonsful of sugar . . . but the strangest
thing about him was the way he got around.*

Rambling 'round New England as I have for the past quarter century with camera, notebook and an insatiable curiosity, I have come across some mighty interesting anecdotes concerning the odd and interesting characters who used to be familiar figures on the highways and byways.

Usually, they travelled on foot and alone unless accompanied by a dog. If they were not invited to curl up in the hay, or sleep in the shed, they'd find a comfortable spot alongside the stone wall, or under a tree and with leaves for a blanket, they'd snooze thru the starry night. Only when a line storm or freezing blizzard raged would they ever consent to occupy the bliss of a feather bed inside the farm house.

If one of these itinerant travellers did condescend to have supper with the family, then curl up on the living room couch, you can be sure his every move and word was remembered and talked about, for many moons thereafter.

A classic example of this type of "tramp" was old Cling Clang, tin knocker and clock fixer who frequented the coastal towns of Maine, sometimes jumped over into New Hampshire and once, every few seasons larruped up into King's County, Nova Scotia. It was there, about 90 years ago, that Cling Clang sought shelter under the hospitable roof of Daniel Sanford, providing unexpected entertainment for the big family of boys and girls. Mrs. Sanford made the kids eat first, then packed them off upstairs to bed. For the next hour, they lay on their tummies, pressing close to the cracks in the floor boards, to watch Cling Clang eat the first good-sized meal he'd had in weeks. One of those children's children, now Emily Sanford Henniker, tells me: "My dad and uncles still talk about old Cling Clang. They never forgot how they spied on him through the cracks of the ceiling and watched him eat. Always, he finished one part of his meal before tackling another. First, he'd eat all of his potato, then his squash or onions. Then he'd eat several biscuits, or slices of bread, then eat the butter and lap up the gravy. Never did he mix them. They watched him drink his tea, straight and clear and then eat two spoonfulls of sugar."

After he'd satisfied his hunger, Cling Clang would reach in the enormous bag he carried over his back and fish out a well-worn and unpainted barrel head. He used this as a cushion, while he sat and worked on the clocks and every night of his life it became his pillow. When he was asked to sleep in the main house, where it was warm beside the coal stove, he'd shake his long hair and point to the shed, and out there he would go with his barrel head for a pillow and curl up in a corner, where it was nice and cool. They say he brought that barrel head from Europe, and once it was under him, he'd sleep like a log. But—he was always up and gone before the crack of dawn next morning.

When he stopped over at farm houses he would always ask the farmer if there was a rooster on the place and if told "Yes" he would look distracted, then say, plaintively, "Would you put a basket over him, so he won't crow in the morning?" For some strange reason, the crowing of a rooster and the crying of a baby so completely upset Cling Clang he'd go almost out of his mind.

All over Hancock County, Maine, there are farm folks who remember his allergy to crowing roosters, and when the clock fixer stopped one night at Swan's Island some mischievous boys let their Plymouth Rock rooster loose, about 4 A.M., and he crowed lustily. Cling Clang dashed out of the shed, bag and barrel head hugged close to him and mounting his poles went leaping down the road, screaming as if in pain. He was never seen at Swan's Island again.

I first heard of this odd character from "Chief" Stanwood, who runs the Big Chief hunting camps at Tunk Lake in East Sullivan, Maine. He was just a boy when Cling Clang covered the country but he remembers seeing him as he "poled" it down the long hill in Ellsworth. He had two long, brass-tipped poles and by grasping them as high as he could reach, he could leap ahead, ten to twelve feet at a bound, and in this way he could cover the country six or seven miles an hour. Swinging over fences and ditches was easy for Cling.

As he carried all his equipment, as well as new pots and pans, in the bags on his back, they naturally rattled and banged when he leaped, giving him the nickname of Old Cling Clang. He could be heard coming a half a mile away but when he saw a horse and team, he leaped to the side of the road and remained quiet until the team had passed.

Cling never wore civilized clothing. He made his own suits out of the bags and old gunny sacks he found lying around the salt ships and freight sheds. They were awesome looking clothes but serviceable. On his head he wore nothing except a thick shock of grey hair, which being long, trailed after his head like a veil when he was going full tilt. He always went barefoot until the snow came, then he fashioned pieces of bags into funny-looking footwear. These, and his socks, shirt and suit, he washed out every three or four days, regardless of the weather. There are folks living in New England today who can remember seeing this strange character doing his laundry, on the ledges near Trenton, Me., when the temperature was down below zero. When he had a blanket or bedding with him, he always washed it in salt water and spread it on a bush to dry.

One winter's day, after Cling Clang had been seen in Sullivan, going from house to house with his tin ware, he was suddenly missed. Somebody said, "You don't s'pose he's sick or something? Maybe he's asleep under that overturned boat." Well, they went down and looked and there was poor old Cling Clang, his steel-like fingers, frozen in death to his beloved barrel head. The town of Sullivan buried the queer, pole-jumping character, but I can't say just where, for all the records were burned. □□

[17]

The Victory of the Christmas Keepers

by Katharine Van Etten Lyford

"No one," read the new law, "shall keep Christmas or any saint day, read common prayer, make mince pies, dance, play cards or play any instrument of music except the drum, trumpet and jew's harp." This would be a hard one to enforce . . .

The Puritan battle over the celebration of Christmas was long, vindictive and strangely out of harmony with the gentle spirit of the day. It was a fanatical losing fight, and the way in which religious competitors and trained animals restored Christmas as a church festival and Yuletide as a joyful season is a curious chapter in our New England history.

Christmas was an anathema to the Puritans, who abhorred it. And abhorring was something they did with self-righteous relish and vigorous vocabulary. Not content to condemn the December festival as "one of the earliest apostacies and superstitions of the primitive times," they held their noses when it was mentioned and called it a "stench to Puritan nostrils." With considerably more zeal than logic, they further damned the day as both popish and pagan.

Our pious Yankee ancestors were already on record as against the Prayer Book, wedding rings, long hair for men, funerals, dancing, and the theatre; so it was not difficult to add Christmas to the list of taboos. In 1659, all recognition of the day was banned and anyone found guilty of celebrating on December 25 was excommunicated from the church, had his ears clipped, and/or served time in the public stocks or billboes. Holiday foods were condemned as "superstitious" and official village snoopers were appointed to sleuth private homes for signs or smells of Yuletide fare that had been traditional in Merrie England. Woe and public reproof to the housewife in Plymouth or Providence from whose kitchen drifted the tempting aroma of mince pie, plum pudding or other dishes "dangerous to the soul." In these early, intolerant days there was no quicker way to lose status and alienate fellow Puritans than to be known as a Christmas Keeper. And, as such, a social outcast, legally classed with swindlers and cheats.

It must be admitted that our New England Puritans had understandable reasons for their passionate dislike of Christmas. In old England the *over celebration* of the yearly festival had become such a scandal that it was one of their motives for migrating to America. During the 16th and 17th centuries, Puritans watched the Twelve Days of Christmas degenerate into a series of unbridled orgies, with an extravagant and licentious Court leading the desecration of the Holy Season. Miracle plays and pageants dramatizing scenes from the Bible were turned into vulgar routs in which all spiritual significance was lost.

Moreover, all over Britain it had become the custom for the town rabblerousers to elect a King of Misrule at Christmas, who, according to a Puritan observer, led his followers "into the Devil's own recreation to mock at Holy things." Masquerading in fancy green and yellow costumes, bells tied to their ankles, they would dance through the quiet churchyard and on into the church itself. Ignoring the Mass being read, they pranced on wooden hobby horses up the center aisle. To the accompanying din of skirling pipes and rattling drums, the poor protesting priest was pulled from his place while the shameless King of Misrule took his place and desecrated the altar by drinking and dicing before it. Meanwhile, riotous companions drowned out the measured music of the Mass with coarse shouts of *Yule, Yule, Yule, Three puddings in a pule. Crack nouts and cry Yule.*

When outraged clergy or shocked parishioners tried to halt the irreverent rabble, they were hurried out of church to be publicly ridiculed or ridden on a rail. Those refusing to give money to the King of Misrule were dunked head first into the nearest duck pond. When in 1633 one distinguished Puritan barrister protested in print against such sacrilegious abuse of Christmas, he was fined three thousand pounds, had his ears clipped, and was sentenced to life imprisonment.

Demanding reform, the Puritans began a relentless campaign against masques, plays and dramas. Any and all were proscribed as "contrary to the word of God and sucked out of the Devil's teats." Equally frank and forceful criticism was levelled at Christmas interludes. One of these, reported to have cost the Court eighteen thousand pounds, was branded by Puritans as "a bastard of Babylon, daughter of error and confusion." Just in case they hadn't made their distaste clear, they also blasted it as a "hellish device."

When continued public protests brought no results, the now politically powerful Puritans ordered the abolition of the day itself. Gentle Sir Thomas More tried in vain to convince them that it would be wiser to "take Christians to task for misdemeanors" than to do away with the holiday altogether. Half-way measures had no appeal for the ardent, arbitrary Puritans, however, so out went the baby with the bath! In 1644 Parliament decreed that the celebration of Christmas was a punishable offense.

While pushing Christmas off the calendar, the zealous Puritans also took over the "purification" of the Sabbath. Here they promptly ran into royal opposition that resulted in many of them taking to the New World in a hurry. To the fury and frustration of the Puritans, King James the First publicly defended the right of country folks to enjoy Sunday sports—with preliminary church attendance a requirement for all participants, of course. His Majesty further recommended Maypoles, Whitsun Ales and Morris Dancing and insisted that women be allowed to trim the churches at Christmas with mistletoe. This in the face of the well-known Puritan abhorrence of dancing and their ban on mistletoe as pagan and directly responsible for promiscuous kissing so scandalously fashionable in 17th century England! Smoldering Puritan anger burst into flame when they found the King had ended his decree with a command to the bishop in each diocese to "order all Puritans and Precisians to conforme themselves or leave the country."

Conforming, except to his own rigid ideas, was impossible for any Puritan. The ink was scarcely dry on the Book of Sports (as King James' decree was called) before many had set sail for America. There was discretion as well as pious valor in this voyage, for Puritans who stayed home and defied the King's decree were quickly popped into prison.

Once in the New World, the purist pioneers scotched all potential

Christmas keeping by passing an ordinance that was a collection of prohibitions and musical exceptions. "No one," read the new law, "shall keep Christmas or any saint day, read common prayer, make mince pies, dance, play cards or play any instrument of music except the drum, trumpet and jews harp." This ordinance reflected the current antipathies of all Puritans, while recognizing the importance of the drum to call people to church and the trumpet to rally the military in a crisis such as an Indian raid. But who can guess why our self-denying ancestors officially permitted themselves the pleasure of the jew's-harp's twittering twang?

Plymouth Puritans spent their first Christmas in America consistently ignoring the significance of the day as they wrestled with the construction of a storehouse on the rocky shore. A year later some high-spirited lads dared to protest that it was against their conscience to work on Christmas. A just but disapproving Governor Bradford excused them from labor "until they were better informed." Later in the day, when he found them hard at play with stool ball and pitching bar, he took sardonic satisfaction in telling them that it was against *his* conscience to let them *play* while other colonists *worked*. Such public reproof seems to have discouraged other possible Christmas keeping, for Bradford reported there were no further attempts to celebrate—"at least (not) openly."

A constant thorn in the flesh of the Plymouth pious was Thomas Morton. An Englishman and an Episcopalian, he was well established in nearby Wollaston and famous for his gay Christmas parties. Well aware of the open disapproval of his hilarious holidays, he took revenge in writing witty rhymes about his Puritan critics, who found it frustrating and infuriating for him to have fun at their expense. They were greatly relieved and, no doubt, self-righteously smug, when Miles Standish caught Morton acting as King of Misrule, entertaining his holiday guests with a "Schoole of Athisme," and promptly banished him from the colony.

News of other willful Christmas Keepers travelled so slowly in those days that the Popham Colony in Maine was able to enjoy three Christmases, complete with church service, traditional food and games, before word of it leaked southward to the Bay Colony. Once aware of this heresy, the Plymouth Puritans sent the Pophamites a solemn, severe and retroactive rebuke.

Meanwhile folks in Rhode Island began to fall from grace. Narragansett was discovered to have celebrated Christmas for two whole weeks and compounded this crime by dancing, not only the staid Minuet, but the bouncy Pea Straw, *I'll Be Married in My Old Clothes,* and some fancy new steps ironically christened Boston's Delight.

Their neighbors in Connecticut, however, seemed to be following the strict Puritan pattern. These "sober and considerable people knit together in beautiful order" were as convinced as their Massachusetts kin that the sure route to Salvation lay in restrictive regulations. Their comprehensive Blue Laws covered everything from a ban on long hair for men as contrary to the Word of God to a five-shilling fine for Christmas keeping. Gradually rumors began to reach Boston that the famous Blue Laws were being ignored as Nutmeg Staters gave and attended Christmas "frolicks" and even played cards. Connecticut's reputation reached a new low somewhat later when Congregationalist Puritan Ezra Styles, first President of the newly established Yale College, was found to be a *secret Episcopalian.* And as such an unregenerate Christmas Keeper.

One of the final and hottest battles against Christmas was fought in the sleepy seaport of Marblehead. In 1630 Mr. Pigot, the newly arrived vicar of the struggling little Episcopal church, announced a Christmas service—only to have it denounced sharply by Dr. Barnard, the portly parson of the large-entrenched Puritan church. Parson Barnard then let it be known *he* would give a *lecture* at the same hour as the Episcopal service, during which he bombarded his congregation with arguments against Christmas, marshalling his considerable oratorical and scholarly talents to prove that Christ was really born in October. The December observance, he claimed, was just a pagan hangover from the Saturnalia.

These were fighting words to young Mr. Pigot and his small but courageous flock. His answer to Dr. Barnard was a printed treatise bearing the long-winded title of A *vindication of the practice of the ancient Christian as well as the Church of England, and other reformed churches in the observation of Christmas-Day; in answer to the uncharitable reflections of Thomas de Laune, Mr. Whiston and Mr. John Barnard of Marblehead.*

With the ecclesiastical fur set a-flying, members of the rival churches lined up behind their sparring pastors. For months the town was in a constant uproar of verbal brickbats and frequent fistfights, all of which made lively reading in the local press. It was the feeble-minded (or was he?) sexton of the Episcopal church who finally brought a truce to the dramatic doctrinal war. Facing a belligerent Puritan on the street, he frankly stated what many a shame-faced Marbleheader had been thinking. "Well," said the peacemaker, "Christmas here or Christmas there, I'm not so narrer contracted as to like to see the surplices of two such good men as your Doctor and my Doctor dragged in the dirt."

Not only Episcopalians, but Universalists and Catholics contested the Puritan point of view on Christmas. Growing in size and influence they finally forced the repeal of the law against Christmas in 1681. Four years later, stubborn Judge Sewall expressed the die-hard Puritan point of view by noting that although the law against the observance of the holiday was removed from the statute books ". . . blessed be God! No authority yet to compel them to keep it."

While adjusting to the idea of a legal Christmas and other changes, the Puritans continued to split theological hairs and to read and discuss printed sermons, as popular in those times as whodunits today. Women embroidered Bible texts on their dresses and revelled in the mournful stanzas (all 224 of them) of a best-seller poem grimly entitled "The Day of Doom." Although conventional amusements continued to be suspect as "misspence of time," strangely enough exhibits of trained animals brought about the public acceptance of Christmas as a *joyous season*.

Adamant against the theatre and public entertainments that might lead to the licentious masques and interludes that had so shocked them in England, the Puritans gradually yielded to pressure for some kind of December relaxation before folks faced the rigors of the long, cold winter. Calling it *educational*, the Christmas exhibit of a polar bear was permitted on Boston Common. Believe it or not, young Fight-the-good-fight-for-Faith Brewster was actually allowed to escort his demure Puritan Priscilla to see this marvel. The next year he could squire her to Dock Square where a pair of camels, a sea lion, and a "strongly chaped" leopard drew crowds of admiring spectators.

Not to be outdone by Boston, Salem provided the Yuletide treat of a "sapient dog" that could read, write and fire a gun. Meanwhile Connecticut towns had begun to brighten their holidays with tight-rope walkers, solar microscopes and even Archimedial Phaetons—less glamorously known as balloons. From such entertainments as these, it was no distance at all to "scenical divertisements" (the theatre in educational dress) and eventually the free and legal enjoyment of the holiday season by all Yankee Christmas Keepers.

[23]

She had been hung that day on Gallows Hill and she must be laid to rest in secret before daylight. It would take courage to bring "the witch" home . . .

They Dared Great Things

In the deep dark night the little boat, propelled by muffled oars held in the hands of Samuel Nurse, glided almost silently up the river. In the bottom of the boat lay Samuel's beloved mother Rebecca who, that day, in her seventy-first year, had been hanged as a witch on Gallows Hill in Salem. And now Samuel, in defiance of the law and risking a similar fate if discovered, was bringing his mother home. She must be laid to rest in secret before daylight, so that no one but the family would know.

How quietly Samuel had crept to the crevice in the hill where his mother and the other four had been flung after execution. He was thankful for the darkness that hid from him that distorted face. He had wondered whether or not he would be strong enough for the task, yet the thought of leaving her in such a place was more than he could bear. Quickly he gathered her into his arms and groped his way back to the boat. Then down the North River, up the Danvers and Crane Rivers and up the little river that flowed behind their homestead, he rowed.

At the same time, other members of the family were preparing the grave, slipping out of their houses singly in the darkness and stealing down the lane to the family cemetery. When all was ready they would wait for Samuel, to help him with his precious burden and to give their mother a decent burial.

Once Samuel placed his mother in the boat he felt better, although he was still far from safe. If he were discovered, not only would they all be hanged, but his mother would be returned to the pit, no doubt in some sort of hideous parade. After all, she had been loaded with chains and driven through the streets to the church when she was excommunicated. There was no telling what might not happen to her as an executed witch.

The boat slid down the North River and passed near Skerry Street where they used to live. No wonder people thought his parents "different." Hadn't they both been in their late fifties when they bought the farm? Seven of their eight children were already married; only Sarah was still single and living at home. But Rebecca had been so happy and excited when they heard about the property. There were two hundred acres of good land at the farm, as well as a fine sturdy house. His parents said that those who wanted to could clear land and build there,

by Louise S. Morgan

[25]

Nurse House, Danvers.

too, and they would be near each other. It was an expensive undertaking for the Nurses but with the help of the children they were able to meet the payments on time. They were a loving, generous family, glad to help each other. And, as somebody once said, "They dared great things and they succeeded."

His mother, however, had had faults, just like anybody else. She had a quick temper and could be very impatient. When the Holten's pig repeatedly wandered into her flax, she had finally given Mrs. Holten a good piece of her mind. After all, that flax represented linen which they all needed. How unfortunate that Mr. Holten had died so suddenly, soon after that. Who would imagine that such a coincidence would eventually help put her to death.

Looking back, it was easy to see how some people came to think that his mother had bewitched the Putnam girl. When the child threw a tantrum in church, claiming that there were yellow birds flying about. Rebecca, followed by some of the rest of the family, finally walked out of meeting in disgust. It was easy then for people to say that she must have been the one who bewitched the child. The Devil liked aged churchgoers; they weren't so apt to be suspected.

Both of these incidents, as well as the fact that the payments on the house had been made promptly, were cited in court as evidence against her.

The barking of a dog interrupted Samuel's reverie. In the stillness of the night it seemed that you could hear it for miles. Samuel sat motionless in the boat and finally the dog subsided. He let the boat drift for a while, not daring to risk a sound. He wondered how they were making out at home. It would take them hours to dig so silently that the Parris family, only a quarter mile away, would hear nothing.

The boat was now in more familiar waters. They had often rowed down to Salem town, as did many of their neighbors. He wondered how near dawn it was, as he tried to row rapidly and at the same time silently. Some of the people whose homes he now passed would be friendly to him; after all, forty people had signed papers in her behalf, at risk to themselves. But Samuel did not want to involve them further.

The Porters had been so good. When the talk about Rebecca had started in the village, they came to warn her. They had great difficulty in convincing her that they were serious, the whole thing seemed so preposterous to her.

Rebecca was arrested on March 23, 1692. All through the preliminary examination, her trial, and even to the very moment of her death, she refused to save her life by saying that she was a witch and now repented. What courage she had! He did not stop to think that it had been passed on to her family. Although they could not save her, they risked everything to bring her home again.

As Samuel turned into the little river that runs behind the homestead, he heard the first faint chirping of the birds. It would not be long until sunrise. He prayed that the others would still be waiting; he had not realized that it would take so long. He could barely discern the outline of the house on the top of the knoll as the boat slid past. And then finally, a little way beyond, there they were waiting for him. Gently they laid their mother to rest. And when the first rays of morning light stole across the little Nurse burying ground, there was no sign at all that Rebecca had come home at last.   □□

The Roving Skeleton of Boston Bay

by Edward Rowe Snow

Edgar Allan Poe's greatest work in the short story field is said by many to be The Cask of Amontillado, *the tale of a man's being all walled up alive. Perhaps the most horrible aspect of the story is that it wasn't fiction, after all.*

Edgar Allan Poe's greatest work in the short story field is said by many to be *The Cask of Amontillado*, the tale of a man's being walled up alive.

It is not generally known that Poe was a New England Yankee. Born in Boston on January 19, 1809, this master of mystery and atmosphere became a private in the army in 1827, and was sent out to Fort Independence on Castle Island in Boston Harbor. Actually, were it not for Poe's serving at Castle Island, *The Cask of Amontillado* would never have been written.

While at Fort Independence Poe became fascinated with the inscriptions on a gravestone on a small monument outside the walls of the fort. He decided to return and copy the inscription when he had enough time off.

One Sunday morning he arose early and visited the sloping glacis of the fort, where he sat down and copied with great care the entire wording on the marble monument. The following inscription was recorded from the western side of the monument:

The officers of the U. S. Regiment of Lt. Art'y erected this monument as a testimony of their respect & friendship for an amiable man & gallant officer.

Then he moved to the eastern panel, where he inscribed in his notebook the famous lines from Collins' ode:

"Here honour comes, a Pilgrim gray, To deck the turf, that wraps his clay."

After resting briefly, he attacked the northern side of the edifice, and then copied the fourth panel facing South Boston:

Beneath this stone are deposited the remains of Lieut. ROBERT F. MASSIE, of the U. S. Regt. of Light Artillery.
Near this spot on the 25th, Decr, 1817, fell Lieut. Robert F. Massie, Aged 21 years.

Extremely interested in the wording of the fourth panel, which said "Near this spot fell" Lieutenant Massie, he decided to find out all he could about the duel. Interviewing every officer at the Fort, he soon learned the unusual tale of the two officers and their fatal combat.

During the summer of 1817, Poe learned, twenty-year-old Lieutenant Robert F. Massie of Virginia had arrived at Fort Independence as a newly appointed officer. Most of the men at the post came to enjoy Massie's friendship, but one officer, Captain Green, took a violent dislike to him. Green was known at the fort as a bully and a dangerous swordsman.

When Christmas vacations were alloted, few of the officers were allowed to leave the fort, and Christmas Eve found them up in the old barracks hall, playing cards. Just before midnight, at the height of the card game, Captain Green sprang to his feet, reached across the table and slapped Lieutenant Massie squarely in the face. "You're a cheat," he roared, "and I demand immediate satisfaction!"

Massie quietly accepted the bully's challenge, naming swords as the weapons for the contest. Seconds arranged for the duel to take place the next morning at dawn.

Christmas morning was clear but bitter. The two contestants and their seconds left the inner walls of the fort at daybreak for Dearborn Bastion. Here the seconds made a vain attempt at reconciliation. The duel began. Captain Green, an expert swordsman, soon had Massie at a disadvantage and ran him through. Fatally wounded, the young Virginian was carried back to the fort, where he died that afternoon. His many friends mourned the passing of a gallant officer.

A few weeks later a fine marble monument was erected to Massie's memory. Placed over his grave at the scene of the encounter, the monument reminded all who saw it that an overbearing bully had killed the young Virginian.

Feeling against Captain Green ran high for many weeks, and then suddenly he completely vanished. Years went by without a sign of him, and Green was written off the army records as a deserter.

According to the story which Poe finally gathered together, Captain Green had been so detested by his fellow officers at the fort that they decided to take a terrible revenge on him for Massie's death. They had

Massie at a disadvantage and ran him through

learned that the captain had killed six other men in similarly staged duels and that not one of the victims had been at fault! Gradually their hatred toward the despicable bully grew, until Massie's friends, enraged by Green's continual boasting, determined to take a life for a life.

Visiting Captain Green one moonless night, they pretended to be friendly and plied him with wine until he was helplessly intoxicated. Then, carrying the captain down to one of the ancient dungeons, the officers forced his body through a tiny opening which led into the sub-terranean casemate. Following him into the dungeon, they placed him on the granite floor.

By this time Green had awakened from his drunken stupor and demanded to know what was taking place. Without answering, his captors began to shackle him to the floor, using the heavy iron handcuffs and footcuffs fastened into the stone. Then they all left the dungeon and proceeded to seal the captain up alive inside the windowless casemate, using bricks and mortar which they had hidden close at hand.

Captain Green shrieked in terror and begged for mercy, but his cries fell on deaf ears. The last brick was finally inserted, mortar applied and the room sealed up, the officers believed, forever. Captain Green undoubtedly died a horrible death within a few days.

Realizing the seriousness of their act, Massie's avengers requested quick transfers to other parts of the country, but several of the enlisted men had already learned the true circumstances.

As Edgar Allan Poe heard this story, he took many notes. Several of the other soldiers reported Poe's unusual interest in the affair to the commanding officer of the fort. Poe was soon asked to report to the post commander, and the following conversation is said to have taken place:

"I understand," began the officer, "that you've been asking questions about Massie's monument and the duel which he fought?"

"I have, sir," replied Poe meekly.

"And I understand that you've learned all about the subsequent events connected with the duel?"

"I have, sir."

"Well, you are never to tell that story outside the walls of this fort."

Poe agreed that he would never *tell* the story, but years afterwards

In 1827 Edgar Allan Poe served in the army at Ft. Independence in Boston Harbor (above). There he managed to uncover the gruesome details of the Massie duel.

he did *write* the tale based on this incident, transferring the scene across the ocean to Europe and changing both the characters and the story itself. He named the tale *The Cask of Amontillado.*

In 1905, eighty-eight years after the duel, when the workmen were repairing a part of the old fort, they came across a section of the ancient cellar marked on the plans as a small dungeon. They were surprised to find only a blank wall where the dungeon was supposed to be. One of the engineers, more curious than the rest, spent some time examining the wall. Finally by the light of his torch, he found a small area which had been bricked up. He went to the head engineer and obtained permission to break through the wall. Several lanterns were brought down and a workman was set to chipping out the old mortar. An hour later, when he had removed several tiers of brick, the others held a lantern so that it would shine through the opening.

What the lantern revealed made them all join in demolishing the walled-up entrance into the dungeon. Twenty minutes later it was possible for the smallest man in the group to squeeze through the aperture.

"It's a skeleton!" they heard him cry a moment later, and he rushed for the opening, leaving the lantern behind him.

Several of the others then pulled down the entire brick barrier and went into the dungeon where they saw a skeleton shackled to the floor with a few fragments of an 1812 army uniform clinging to the bones.

The remains could not be identified but they were given a military funeral and placed in the Castle Island cemetery in a grave marked UNKNOWN.

The Massie monument came to achieve a fame which attracted thousands of visitors to old Fort Independence each Sunday, especially after a bridge was built out to the island in 1891. But in 1892 the monument was moved, along with Massie's remains, across to Governor's Island, and set in a new cemetery there. Massie's skeleton was dug up again, however, in 1908, and taken, with the monument, down the bay to Deer Island to be placed in the officers' section of Resthaven Cemetery. Then, in 1939, Massie's bones were removed from the Deer Island grave, and taken, with his tombstone, across the state to Fort Devens, in Ayer, Massachusetts.

Thus, after his death, Massie became the Roving Skeleton of Boston Bay, a man who was buried four times in four different places within a period of 122 years. □□

"Who Can Stand Against His Cold?"

by Louis A. Lamoureux

Barn raisings and husking bees represent the warm, loving side of our New England tradition . . . but this is a story about the other side.

North Star, Danville, Vermont, March 5, 1869:
"It is hardly necessary to say simply as a matter of news that this section has been visited with a great snow storm. The fact is known by all men. But all may not be informed as to the extent of the storm . . . the biggest storm we have had for years."

Most Danville farmers settling down that evening by their kitchen stoves to read the weekly newspaper were informed first hand as to the extent of the storm, having just come into the house on paths cut through head-high snowbanks from evening chores in chilly barns. But they would not be informed until next week's issue of a tragedy of the storm discovered that morning in neighboring Peacham—one of which, the *Vermont Watchman and State Journal* in Montpelier, would end its account with the remark, "we have no heart for a word of comment"; a

[34]

tragedy that would set the citizens of proud and prosperous Peacham to anguished breast beating for a long time.

A sequence of horrible adversities began on the morning of Thursday, March 4, 1869 in the town of Hardwick, or it could have been Stannard or Marshfield—it is unrecorded in diaries, and newspaper accounts give a choice of towns. Whichever the town, Mrs. Esther Emmons, 74 years old, of no settled abode, had been visiting her son there. He had suffered a crippling accident in the woods and, as a consequence, needed to apply to the town for assistance. It is strongly hinted that officers of the town, fearful that the mother would become a town charge, too, had ordered her to leave.

A daughter, 35-year-old Mary Davis, went to fetch her in the company of 8-year-old Willie, a grandson of Mrs. Emmons and a nephew of Mary. They planned to walk that day the 20 miles to Peacham, where Mary had been engaged to work for the season as a servant girl for a former employer, Charles Gates, a wealthy farmer. Mrs. Emmons and Willie would stay with the old lady's sister in the extreme south part of Peacham. They were penniless and homeless transients who lived here and there with one poor relative or another.

Mrs. Emmons made last-minute efforts to make her ailing son comfortable before the three set out on foot at daybreak in cold, clear weather on the long trip. They were thinly clad in shabby hand-me-downs and carried their few personal belongings in a small bundle.

The old lady, for all the frailty of her many years, seems to have set the pace and to have taken command. Mary Davis was passive, a little dull and dispirited—her husband had deserted her. Willie was a lively little fellow; gay company on the grim trek.

Nothing is recorded of their trip until they were a few miles out of Marshfield and approaching Peacham Woods. The uphill route was over the winter road, little traveled in summer because of the rough road bed; but in winter, packed with snow, it made good sledding and the long stretch of woods gave comparative shelter from fierce winter winds. Before they entered the woods, the sun had disappeared and the sky was a tumult of heavy gray clouds, foreboding heavy snows. After six miles, Mrs. Emmons, now beginning to tire, decided that they should not attempt to go all the way through that day. At the next house—and few there were on that lonely road—they would ask for a night's shelter, as it would be a long way before there would be another. But at the little cottage at the foot of the mountain, they were gruffly turned away by a man named Bean. There was no choice but to go on, aching though they were with cold, and little nourished by the cold lunch they had taken with them.

By midafternoon they entered Peacham Woods, taking some comfort, no doubt, in the knowledge that they were now within Peacham town limits, but still with many miles to go. The snow started lightly at first, then heavily, relentlessly—piling up on their heads and shoulders and clinging to the women's skirts and the boy's leggings. And then the wind came, rattling the bare limbs of the trees and stinging their numbed faces with sharp crystals. They clung to each other as they struggled through the deepening snow—toes, ankles, fingers aching, their bodies shivering under thin clothing. But hark! Could it be? The jingling of sleigh bells. A man, heavily bundled to his ears, overtook them in a light, one-horse sleigh. He recognized the old lady and stopped. He would give her a ride to town, but his spent horse could not carry them all in the small sleigh. The old lady thanked him. No, she could not leave the others; they would stay overnight at the next house. He slapped his horse with the reins and drove on into the storm.

The old lady, summoning all her determination, moved forward again; but exhaustion began to overtake her soon after they emerged from the woods into open country. She sat down frequently in the snow. Mary and Willie helped her to her feet and supported her until she had to rest again.

As waning daylight was adding a new dimension to their peril, they reached the farm of a man named Stewart. With what expectation of merciful relief from their excruciating sufferings they must have presented their red, pinched faces to the farmer to request a night's refuge. He was watering his cattle at a hole chopped in the ice of a small brook across the road from his farm buildings. Why he should have been so insensible to their plight will never be known. Perhaps the storms of winter had given him so many problems that he could not measure the extent of theirs. He curtly refused them, saying he was taking no one in. Turning away from them, he shouted angry commands to the cattle and herded them back to the shelter of the barn.

The despairing trio trudged on again through the drifting snow, Mary and Willie supporting the old lady between them. Surely there would be shelter for them at the next place, the Farrows, kindly folks living within a mile down the road.

It was a long mile and the old lady was now so fatigued that no hope could rally her strength. Without the force of her strong will, the

He curtly refused them, saying he was taking no one in . . .

others were thrown into confusion—the simple girl looked to her for direction, and the young boy to both of them. Mrs. Emmons fell again and again. They would pick her up to stagger on for a few more feet through the snow now up to the knee. When she could no longer be raised to her feet, they dragged her until, at last, cold, hunger, fatigue, and panic made that too much exertion for them. The old lady now lay still in the snow, breathing heavily, her words incoherent, and then no words at all. It appears that they stayed by her side for some time in the angry, swirling, total darkness before leaving her to search for help.

In the blackness of the stormy night, Mary and Willie lost the road and stumbled into a field. While resting on a stone wall, a few yards from where the old lady lay, they must have distinguished a light through the veil of snow at the back window of the Farrow house some 120 feet distant. From tracks still visible in the snow the next day, it appeared that Willie crawled on his hands and knees in a path "as straight as an arrow" over a drift toward that window. Perhaps both were hysterically screaming for help at the same time, or calling to each other. The Farrows heard repeated cries but, thinking that they were coming from a demented daughter locked in an upstairs room, paid them no heed. They blew out the lamp and went to bed. Ben Kimball, living some distance leeward, heard a single cry, not repeated, and felt he must have been mistaken as the violent wind caused many noises.

The storm raged all night over the darkened countryside. Dawn broke, gray and dreary, with the thermometer at 24° below zero.

[37]

By midmorning, Ben Kimball and other men were breaking out the drifted road with oxen. They were curious about some bright piece of cloth churned up by the sled—a remnant of the pitiful baggage. Then they made the horrifying discovery of the old lady's frozen body which the sled must have dragged down the road about a half mile beyond the Farrows'. Then they made two more gruesome finds: the frozen corpse of Mary lying face up across the stone wall where she appeared to have died without a struggle, and Willie stiff upright in the snow, having started back towards Mary after being within 30 feet of a warm fire.

Word was sent to the village. The civil authorities arrived in a short time and started inquiries along the route that pieced together the tragic story.

It was small consolation to conjecture that if Mary and Willie had kept to the road they would have reached the Farrows house safely; that if the Farrows had not extinguished the light at the very time, Willie would not have become confused and turned back in his tracks to die.

The bodies were transported to the town hall in the basement of the church, where they were prepared for burial. News of the tragedy spread rapidly through the town—with many embellishments. The townspeople were in shock; how could it be that in their midst, in that enlightened community noted for its humanity and compassion, some of their own could have violated the most elemental tradition?

Nearly everyone in town filed silently into the large church for the funeral service where the big box stoves gave only a crackling promise of heat, and the March wind shuddered the building and pelted the long windows with sleet. They sat miserably in their cold pews in a transport of spiritual confusion to hear a powerful sermon; a true apologia. The sermon was afterward published in full in the *Caledonian-Record* of St. Johnsbury at the request of town officials and several citizens.

Rev. P. B. Fisk chose as his text: "Who Can Stand Against His Cold?" These words are found in Psalm 147, a song of praise to Jehovah:

"He giveth snow like wool; scattereth the hoar frost like ashes. He sendeth forth His crystals like morsels; who can stand against His cold?"

He wove the text into a narrative of the tragedy.

"He giveth snow like wool to clothe the earth for winter. *He scattereth the hoar frost like ashes,* as easy for Him as for one to sprinkle ashes. *He casteth forth His ice crystals like morsels,* as a housewife casts

[38]

away crumbs from the table with little thought of their importance. Cold comes like a stealthy enemy, takes possession, stays during its own pleasure, and leaves us no choice but to fly for shelter to our own firesides or perish in its ruthless embrace. There is no coldness of heart in our God, never indifferent to one of His needy. This tragedy is an exception for which He is not responsible; *mankind tempts the elements*."

He reviewed the events as they were known to him. How Mrs. Davis had gone to Stannard and South Hardwick with the purpose of bringing her mother back, saying that she would take care of her as long as she lived. "When she goes, I want to go, too." No one else would help.

The three or four roughly dressed relatives in the mourners' pew sobbed piteously.

It would do no good to curse the cold. "There is a design in cold. Cold has a beneficial influence on character. The tone and vigor of our winters are ingredients to our success. Animals are all clothed anew as winter closes in. There is material for dwellings and wood to keep warm."

But "there is blame somewhere." The congregation leaned forward for the judgment. "None who lay this side of the fatal spot is guilty." They relaxed against the back of their seats. "If they had been thrust out, those who thrust them out bear the guilt." A hundred eyes looked hard at Stewart's empty pew.

He touched upon the irony of the trio's last unhappy moments with a quotation from the Scriptures: "Oh, how hard, how impossible it is sometimes to reach the light."

The sermon ended with a strong exhortation. "Against these three no evil word is spoken though they were extremely poor. It is man's fault, not God's, if there are inequalities. In permitting inequality, God has left the way open for the cultivation and exercise of one grace. An individual can aid his fellow. Remember he that giveth to the poor, lendeth to the Lord and He will repay him. Remember the poor!"

The bodies were committed to the frozen earth in Peacham cemetery where they lie under a monument erected by the citizens of the town.

Some elderly Peacham natives, who heard the story directly from those who knew the principals, uphold a curious legend. Stewart, they say, suffered thereafter from an intense feeling of guilt. While on his deathbed many years later he seemed, in his delirium, to be reliving the awful tragedy. His body tremors and his cries were of one who was freezing. Though it was mid-July, his corpse was cold as ice. □□

The *Funny* Bank Robbery

by Cal Cameron

When you rob a bank and your horse walks off with the money and you're caught cold, there's only one thing to do—pay the reward for your capture and then threaten the president and cashier of the bank with a suit unless they return your safecracking tools.

Tuesday, June 11, 1859 had dawned a lovely, early-summer day in Charlestown, New Hampshire. The Connecticut River swept placidly by on its way to the great falls a few miles below. As George Olcott walked to the bank, he enjoyed the brisk cool morning air. It was one of those days that made him feel that all was well with the world.

Promptly at eight o'clock he inserted the heavy brass, cumbersome key in the lock of the massive door, and experienced his first surprise of a day destined to be long remembered. The lock appeared to be stuck. It took him some little time before he was able to open it.

When he finally did get inside, he was shocked to see that the door to the banking room had been forced. Thoroughly alarmed, he hurried into the room and drew a breath of relief to find the great safe, in which the money was kept, closed and locked. His relief was short lived, however, when, for the second time that morning, another key which had always worked smoothly stuck when he tried to turn it.

After what seemed an eternity, he swung the heavy door back, only to find the inner iron door had been blown open. The safe was empty. Not a single one of the bags of gold and silver coin or bundles of paper money he had so carefully locked away the previous afternoon was there.

He hurried a messenger to ex-Governor Hubbard, president of the bank, with the calamitous news. By the time Hubbard arrived, Olcott had ascertained that not a dollar had been overlooked by the robbers. Not only had they left no money, they had not left a single clue. It was a perfect crime. In a short time, men on horseback had left the village by every road, scattering in all directions, carrying the news and also telling of the bank's offer of a reward of $500 for the return of the money and an equal sum for the apprehension of the culprits.

The robbers had come almost 100 miles from Oxford, Massachusetts with horse and buggy. Such a trip must have taken them at least five days, for one didn't drive much over twenty miles a day using the same horse day after day.

As it turned out, there were two robbers, and to allay any possible suspicion when they reached Charlestown at nine o'clock that Tuesday night, one of them was dressed as a woman. No time was lost after they arrived. Skeleton keys got them into the bank without delay. By midnight their work was completed. The loot was in the buggy and they were on their way home after a highly profitable three hours' work.

About eleven miles southeast of Charlestown they came to the foot of Hatch Hill, long, steep and winding. Desiring to get as far as possible before morning, they both got out of the buggy to lighten the load. One walked in the road ahead of the horse, the other followed behind. The one who walked ahead was a fast walker. He outdistanced the horse. The one who walked behind found it a mighty tiresome climb. He took it slowly; so slowly in fact that soon even the sound of the plodding horse and buggy was lost to him.

Imagine the consternation of the two when the second reached the top and found neither horse nor buggy there. The first one was sure that the rig had not passed him, and the second one was just as positive that he had not passed the rig! In those days there was no such thing as a flashlight to search with. They both started down the dark, long, winding hill; but search as they would, they could find no trace of the horse.

In desperation, they awakened a farmer and borrowed a lantern, but even with this they were unable to find where the horse had gone. It seemed to have vanished into thin air, taking the rich loot with it. They continued to search up and down the mountainside till dawn. Realizing that the entire countryside would soon be on the lookout for them, they were forced to abandon any hope of finding the proceeds of their work. Exhausted from their hours of search up and down the mountain, they decided to look after their own safety.

To better effect their escape, they separated. One hired a farmer to drive him about in search of the lost horse and buggy. Finally he dared tarry no longer, and asked that he be driven to Walpole. In the village he hired another farmer to drive him to Keene, where his trail was lost. No trace of the other robber was found.

At this time Marlow was a small farming community twenty miles east of Charlestown. Mr. Horace Gee, a young, well-to-do farmer who lived there, had a neighbor who was seriously ill. As was the custom in those times, Gee had gone to sit with the sick man through the night. By five o'clock on the morning of June 12, it was daylight, and Gee left to go home.

On the way he found a horse and buggy without a driver. The reins were dragging and Gee could see that the horse had come a considerable distance. He figured that sooner or later the owner would come along, so he took the rig home and, after giving the horse a drink, tied him in his door yard where he could be easily seen from the road. Then he went to bed.

Later in the morning, one of the riders bearing news of the robbery stopped at the Gee farm, leaving word of both the crime and the rewards the bank had offered. When Gee awoke later and heard of this, he decided to take another look at the horse and buggy he had found. In the wagon were bags of both gold and silver coins, bundles of bank bills, and burglars' tools. What he was most surprised to find, however, were woman's clothing and a buffalo robe marked "S. Barton, Jr."

The disappearance of the horse and buggy on Hatch Hill was easily explained by those familiar with that section. Part way up the hill, a crude sort of road had been cut into the woods for purposes of bringing out logs. As the logging continued, the road was lengthened. Finally it was extended to a point where it met another road that led east into Marlow. The horse, sensing that the grade on the logging road was less than on the hill he was ascending, and in the darkness seeing what no human could, had turned off to ease his climb.

Gee drove the rig to the bank in Charlestown and claimed the $500 reward for the return of the money. The money was checked and found to be the exact amount stolen. By this time Gee had told his story and the bank felt that, having found the loot so quickly and easily, perhaps they had been a little hasty in offering such a large reward.

They explained to Gee that they had been put to considerable expense, which of course would have to be deducted from the reward money, so he would only get $400. This he accepted under protest. Apparently the fact that the bank had won a fine, fast horse and a good serviceable buggy was conveniently overlooked.

In reporting the matter, the *Keene Sentinel*, a weekly newspaper, regarding the "expenses" Governor Hubbard had deducted, commented: "It was rather a small business, and should hardly, we think, have been countenanced by the Directors." However, the bank felt the matter was closed, regardless of what others thought.

The name on the buffalo robe turned out to be a valuable clue. Police officials recalled that Barton, a well-known bank robber, lived in Oxford, Massachusetts. Fortunately for him, he had an unbreakable alibi. However, the Larned brothers, who are referred to in news dispatches of the day as "notorious burglars and bank robbers," were not so lucky. Neither were they at home to discuss the matter.

For some reason not revealed, a warrant was sworn out for only one of them, Abijah. It was not until December that a New Hampshire deputy sheriff named Baker, acting on a tip, caught up with Abijah in the vicinity of Utica, New York. Apparently Larned wanted no publicity there (possibly because of a very recent successful job he had done) for he agreed to accompany Baker to Charlestown without any court appearance or formality in New York State. They were back in the Connecticut River town by the middle of the month.

Abijah asked to be taken to the bank officials, where he made a complete confession of his part in the robbery, professed great regret for the trouble he had caused, and made some astounding proposals.

He admitted that he had had an accomplice, but he did not name him nor does he seem to have been pressed in the matter. The most unusual thing was that, although he had not got a cent of the money he stole, he insisted on paying every expense to which the bank had been put.

[44]

He reimbursed them for all expenses incurred in repairing the blown safe and forced doors which he could not open with the skeleton keys. He also paid them the $1,000 reward money and was adamant that Gee be paid the $100 which the bank had withheld! He even made good the cost of his own capture! All of this was sworn to by the president of the bank when Larned was arraigned. Apparently no one inquired as to where the money came from!

It is said that his willingness to make good all the bank's losses and his insistence that Gee receive his full reward created a "favorable impression." In any event, when arraigned, although known to be a habitual criminal, he was released on bail of only $2,500. The provision that some local man furnish part of his bond presented no problem. Larned, finding a man whose bond would be acceptable to the court, offered to give him the full amount of the bond, plus $250! The offer was promptly accepted and Larned was back in circulation.

He must have been affluent at the time, for he still had money to buy a horse and sleigh. Now comes the most ridiculous part of the whole story. In its issue of December 19, 1850, the *Keene Sentinel* reported that he "then demanded of the officers of the bank the tools with which he had forced it. This the president and cashier refused to do but on being threatened with a suit, they concluded to have no misunderstanding with the gentleman, after so agreeable an intercourse, and they accordingly delivered them up. Larned touched his beaver (hat) and left in good spirits, congratulating himself, very likely, on his fortunate escape, with the means at hand of replenishing, by professional skill, his purse, which had proved to be a friend in need."

Abijah Larned did not appear when his case was called. His bail forfeited and the gentlemen who had gone his bond was $250 richer. He was never rearrested for this crime, but he did have the misfortune to be caught after robbing a bank in Cooperstown, New York. The authorities there were neither so favorably impressed nor understanding. He was sent to jail and died before the expiration of his sentence.   □□

The Legend of Handkerchief Moody

by Gail M. Potter

Was he demented? Had he been scarred by an accident? Were his eyes overly sensitive? One of these, his parishioners reasoned, must be why the Rev. Mr. Joseph Moody of York, Maine always appeared with a face covering. Finally, the secret was revealed . . .

In the 18th century, most Yankee congregations had inured themselves to the awesome sight of the ponderous powdered wigs that framed the stern Sabbath visages of their clerics. But the good folk of the Second Church of York, Maine, possessed a parson whose weird headgear caused him to go reverberating down in the annals of New England history, folklore, and legend as "Handkerchief Moody."

Joseph Moody had not always worn the black crepe veil knotted above his forehead and hanging down below his chin. For fourteen years after his graduation at Harvard, he was quite content with and competent in successive positions as Clerk of the Town of York, Registrar of Deeds for the county, and Judge of the County Court.

However, his father thought he ought to preach, and *he* thought his father knew best. Chiefly through his father's influence, a second parish was incorporated in 1730. In 1732, Joseph hesitantly accepted the charge and was ordained its pastor.

For six years he got along tolerably well with the saving of souls, while his wife took charge of temporal things. But when she died, the care of two worlds proved too much for him, and he fell into a state of deep melancholy. In this clouded condition, his once brilliant mind developed a pronounced phobia: no one must see his face.

And so he presented himself to his congregation with his features masked in a black silk handkerchief. For weeks, wonder, speculation, and rumor churned with whirlwind intensity through the village. *Was he demented?* His sermons were too logical for that. *Had he been scarred by an accident?* If so, no chirurgeon knew of it. *Had his eyes been weakened by working far into the night on his sermons?* With no other plausible explanation, his parishioners convinced themselves that this was the true one.

While he was as often besought for funerals as he had previously been, the veiled parson's services became less in demand for weddings, christenings, and socials. The timid people turned out of their way to avoid him; the bolder were often flippant or impertinent on the road.

So Joseph Moody curtailed his day-time walks, limiting his strolls to the protecting anonymity of night. Then, without the fear of embarrassing encounters, he prowled peacefully through the seclusion of the churchyard or wandered unchallenged along the deserted shore.

Little by little he abandoned his public labors, refusing to officiate at public gatherings except in cases of unusual urgency. More and more often he sought the sheltering safety of his own chamber. Only on rare occasion, when bounden duty demanded it, did he leave his sanctuary and partake of a meal with others. He was soon relieved of even this obligation. For nothing cast a quicker and more efficient pall over the gayest of village affairs than the sight of a black-clad figure, crouched alone at a small side table with its face turned to the wall.

The confused, equivocal, and tortuous groping of his unsteady mind at this time may be inferred by an extract from his diary: "This day, while engaged in prayer, I thought of a way to fasten my study door, and afterwards found a better."

Before long, the Reverend Mr. Moody abandoned entirely his feeble attempts at preaching, parceled his children out among relatives, and, relieved of all responsibility, went to live with the family of Deacon Bragdon.

By 1745, he had so well recovered from his mental depression that his 70-year-old father, old Sam Moody, tore off with the younger lads of York to the siege of Louisburg. Into the hands of his son, Samuel committed the care of his congregation and the delivery of the Sabbath sermon.

Joseph supplied his father's pulpit in his own peculiar way. Turning his back to the people, he lifted his veil and read distinctly and audibly a written sermon. But when he faced the congregation for prayer and the benediction, the black handkerchief, fluttering with the rhythm of his breath, muffled and obscured his words.

Along with the genes of eccentricity, the Reverend Joseph inherited his father's remarkable gift of oral supplication. His memorable "long prayer" from the pulpit of York's First Church during the Louisburg campaign has been cited as more than mere coincidence.

Frequent communications from Cape Breton conveyed the disheartening news that the fortress was still untaken. Therefore, June 17 was appointed as a day of fasting and prayer in York, and the neighboring ministers invited to attend. In the course of the service, Joseph Moody offered the prayer, and a very lengthy one it was.

He first used all manner of arguments, suggested several compromises, and uttered fervent pleas that the Lord would give the place into the hands of the English Protestants, thereby cutting off "this limb of Anti-Christ." Suddenly he ceased his entreaties. Then, scarcely pausing for breath, he began to give thanks that the citadel was at last ours and to praise God at great length for His unmerited mercy. He closed his devotions with the words: "Lord, we are no better than those that possessed the land before us; and it would be righteous if the land should spew out its inhabitants a second time."

When the forces returned from the expedition, and compared dates, it was found that the capitulation was closed on the very day of the fast and, as near as could be ascertained, at the very hour when Mr. Moody was presenting his petitions to heaven. Two years later, when peace was settled between the two countries, Louisburg was restored to France, and its inhabitants spewed out a second time when the English troops withdrew from the garrison.

Death called unexpectedly for Mr. Moody in 1753. Joseph had pushed back from the deacon's dinner table and repaired to his room in exceptionally good spirits. In his exuberance, he began to hum, and then to sing aloud one of Watts' hymns in which occurs the lines:

Oh for an overcoming faith
To cheer my dying hours.

All afternoon long he caroled lustily, refusing to take time from his song-fest to join the family at supper. The next morning he was found dead in his bed.

Years later, an old friend said in retrospect, "It is my opinion that, if he had been let alone to follow his own course in society, without preaching, he would have done more good in the world. He could have brought up his children himself, instead of leaving them to the care of others, would have had more real enjoyment, and perhaps saved himself the trouble of wearing his handkerchief so long."

But by then, legend had taken over and ascribed another reason for the minister's idiosyncrasies and his doleful departure from the realities of this life.

Feeling that his hour had come, Mr. Moody sent for a fellow clergyman to soothe his dying moments, commend his soul to mercy, and hear his confession. "Brother," he said, "the veil of eternal darkness is falling over my eyes. Men have asked me why I wear this piece of crepe about my face, and I have borne the reason so long within me that only now have I resolved to tell it."

Long ago, Joseph revealed, he had inadvertently killed his best friend while on a hunting trip. Dreading the blame of his townsmen, the anguish of the dead youth's parents, and the scorn of his betrothed, the minister concealed his guilt. The town believed that the killing was a murder, the act of some roving Indian.

But for years the face of his dead friend rose accusingly before him. In desperation, and determined to pay a penalty for concealing his sin, Joseph finally resolved that never again would he look his fellowmen openly in the face. "Then it was," he whispered, "that I put a veil between myself and the world."

As he had requested, "Handkerchief Moody's" black crepe hid his face in the coffin. But the clergyman who had raised it for a moment to compose his features found there a serenity and a beauty that were majestic.   □□

"Capitall Laws": 1645

by E. Robert Stevenson

Our stern forefathers would not have doubted the justice of
Caryl Chessman's execution—
he'd have met the same fate for swearing!

Connecticut and California, 3000 miles apart, in common hold laws
calling for capital punishment. They also have in common men
and women who have made horrified protests against putting to death
Caryl Chessman or any other under these laws. Recently this horrified
shudder even crossed the Atlantic, bringing protests from England and
France.

Over 100 years before white men settled in California and over 200
years before California became part of the United States the founders
of the first colony in Connecticut enacted capital punishment laws.
These "Capitall Laws," as they called them, were formulated in 1645,
thirteen years after the first settlement at Hartford. Not murder alone
but several other offenses were set down by these Puritans, in strong religious conviction, calling for the death penalty.

Among these was what we today term "juvenile delinquency." Our
colonial founders did not call it by this fancy name, but the wording of
the law leaves not the slightest doubt of what they were endeavoring to
control. They may not have been plagued to the extent we find ourselves
plagued today, but their harsh law shows that teen-age delinquency existed. They kept no record of executions so we do not know whether or
not their rigid code nourished a more contrite spirit in the youth of those
early days.

Condemnation to death these colonial lawmakers recognized as a
most serious proceeding. There undoubtedly were sensitive souls among
them, even as today, who found it difficult to accept the idea of a death
penalty. These lawmakers, therefore, carefully fortified and justified
their actions by attaching to each law Bible quotations sustaining them.
They found plenty in the Good Book. Puritans took their Bible most
seriously and literally.

JUVENILE DELINQUENCY

Two laws were made pertaining to juvenile delinquency. The first
reads as follows:

"If any Childe or Children above sixteen yeares old and of suf-
ficient understanding, shall curse or smite their natural father or

[51]

*mother, hee shall bee put to death, unless it shall bee sufficiently
testified that the parents have been very unchristianly negligent in
the education of such Children or so provoke them by extreme and
cruell correction that they have been forced thereunto to preserve
themselves from death or maiming."*

In Bible support of this, the law referred to the book of Exodus,
Chapter 21, Verse 17:

"And he that curseth his father, or his mother, shall surely be
put to death."

MURDER NOT FIRST

Murder was not put first in this code for "Capitall" punishment.
God-fearing Puritans saw other offenses as more shocking and set them
first in order before murder. Their very first listed law reads:

*"If any man after legal conviction shall have or worship any
god but the Lord God, hee shall bee put to death."*

Coupled with this was reference to Exodus 22, Verse 20:

"He that sacrificeth unto any god, save unto the Lord only, he
shall be utterly destroyed."

[52]

Above: "If any Childe or Children above sixteen yeares old and of sufficient understanding, shall curse or smite their natural father or mother, hee or she shall bee put to death."

"The Ducking Stool" (opposite page) was used for punishing women whose "tongues wagged" too much or, in other words, to curtail town gossip. Exhibiting criminals in the market place (top left) and whipping them (bottom left) were also considered au fait.

WITCHES CAME NEXT

Witch practices came next. Connecticut has no record of anyone being hanged, burned or otherwise destroyed as a witch, but its earliest law makers were taking no chances. They provided for the destruction of witches. Puzzled by this strange and inexplicable witchcraft stuff, they left it to the Bible to define it. The law reads briefly:

"If any man or woman bee a witch, that is hath consulteth with a familiar spiritt, they shall bee put to death."

This was most thoroughly backed up by Bible references as follows:

Exodus 22, Verse 18:

"Thou shalt not suffer a witch to live."

Leviticus 20, Verse 27:

"A man also or woman that hath a familiar spirit, or that is a wizard, they shall surely be put to death."

BLASPHEMY WITH QUALIFICATIONS

Still holding firmly to religious matters as of first importance, the next law set down by these Puritans dealt with blasphemy:

[53]

"*If any person shall blaspheme the name of God, Sonne or Holy Ghost with direct, express, presumptuous, or high-handed blasphemy, or shall curse in the like manner, hee shall bee put to death.*"

The qualifications, "with direct, express, presumptuous or high-handed blasphemy," are sure indications that men drew up this code. Women in those days had no hand in governmental affairs. Men were the law makers. Men, therefore, left a loophole for the man who might utter a sudden swear word when he hit his finger with a hammer or who let loose when some other troublesome thing suddenly fell upon him.

Justification for this law was indicated in the Bible quotation from Leviticus 24, Verse 16:

"And he that blasphemeth the name of the Lord, he shall surely be put to death."

WILFUL "MURTHER"

At this point and not before, these early law makers came to consideration of murder. They drew up a law in which they again set qualifications:

"*If any person shall commit any willful murther, which is manslaughter committed upon malice, hatred or cruelty, not in a man's necessary and just defense, nor by mere casualty against his will, hee shall bee put to death.*"

The Bible quotation with this is from Exodus:

"He that smiteth a man so that he die shall be surely put to death."

KIDNAPPING AND SLAVERY

The next law of this Connecticut list might almost seem a parallel of our present-day kidnapping laws except that it is impossible to conceive that any holding for ransom could have existed in the primitive days of our colonies. It should be remembered, however, that the colonists had experienced cases of seizure of whites by Indians who had carried them off to their tribal teepees to be held in serfdom. Slavery had not yet made its appearance in the Connecticut colony, though it had made its beginning in Virginia. The law reads:

"*If any man stealeth a man or mankinde, hee shall bee put to death.*"

The term "mankinde" may have been made to cover Negroes who were then being brought from Africa to Virginia. First instigators of this slavery sought justification by speciously arguing that these blacks were not really to be considered as men and women in the same sense that whites were. Hence the "man or mankinde."

Nevertheless, in its later history the Connecticut colony also had slaves, a very limited number, but slaves just the same, and no one paid a death penalty for thus holding "man" or "mankinde" against his will. To support this law, reference was to Exodus 21, Verse 16:

"And he that stealeth a man, and selleth him, or if he be fonud in his hand, he shall surely be put to death."

FALSE WITNESSES

In their "Capitall" laws the colonists also set the following:

"If any man rise up by false witness, wittingly and of purpose to take away any man's life, hee shall bee put to death."

In support of this the reference was to a verse in Deuteronomy:

"If the witness be a false witness and hath testified falsely against his brother, then shall ye do unto him as he had thought to have done to his brother."

Finally came a law for which they could find no Bible quotation and for which they undoubtedly firmly believed they needed none. It reads:

"If any man shall conspire, or attempt any invasion, insurrection or rebellion against the commonwealth, hee shall bee put to death."

THE FIRST MURDER

Opponents of capital punishment may wonder why these Puritans with all their turning to the Bible in support of their death penalty laws closed their eyes to what the book of Genesis relates concerning the penalty put upon the very first murderer. Cain was not put to death. In punishment, the Bible tells us, God made him "a fugitive and a vagabond." When he complained to God fearfully that, "Every one that findeth me shall slay me," the Lord replied, "Whosoever slayeth Cain, vengeance shall be taken on him sevenfold." And, "He set his mark upon him lest any one finding him should kill him."

But enactors of these early colonial laws found plenty in the Bible to support their rigid "Capitall Laws." □□

The Unfathomable Borden Riddle

by John U. Ayotte

Top left: Andrew Borden. Top right: Abby Borden. Bottom left: Lizzie Borden.

*Whether Lizzie Borden took an ax and gave her
mother 40 whacks has intrigued the most exacting of
murder connoisseurs ever since it happened.
Recently, some of the "accepted theories" have
come under searching attack . . .*

Much has been said of the individuality of New England, expressed in its scenery, its food, and in the character of its people, but little is ever mentioned when that same individuality appears in another aspect, the practice of the grisly art of murder.

Every murder is a major tragedy for the persons immediately concerned, but most homicides arouse no lasting interest outside the small, intimate circle affected, and their history is soon buried in the limbo of official records and newspaper files. On occasion, however, there is a murder, one out of thousands perhaps, with qualities that keep memory of it alive. These may reflect the personalities involved, the setting of the crime, the technique of its commission, the mystery shrouding important details, and, sometimes, the identity of the murderer. Of such cases, the archives of the New England States have more than their fair share.

Practitioners of the scarlet art, active in New England for over three centuries, have produced enough grim masterpieces to satisfy the most exacting connoisseur of murder, even though he were a second Thomas DeQuincey or William Roughead. And Edmund Pearson, no mean judge of what constitutes an outstanding homicide, believed that one needed to look no farther than Fall River, Massachusetts, to find not only the premier murder case of New England, but of the United States as well.

The Bordens were a moderately wealthy, rather stodgy family, socially acceptable and church affiliated, who received much literary attention in the 1920s and 30s, especially from crime historian Edmund Pearson. After considerable writing on the subject, he seemed finally to have said the last word on the stark tragedy that beset the family; but recently he and his theories came under searching attack, and the Fall River murders—always a fascinating study—were opened again to examination and reappraisal.

Shortly after nine o'clock on the sweltering morning of August 4, 1892, elderly, tight-fisted Andrew Borden left his house at 92 Second Street for a walk to the business section of Fall River. By his first wife—-

then dead nearly 30 years—Mr. Borden had two daughters, both unmarried and living at home: Emma, 41, and visiting that day in 15-mile distant Fairhaven; and Lizzie, an active church worker, 32 years old, and in the house when her father left. With her was her stepmother, Abby Borden—married to Andrew when Lizzie was a small child—and the maid of all work, Bridget (Maggie) Sullivan. An overnight guest, John Vinnicum Morse, brother of the first Mrs. Borden, had gone earlier in the day to call on other relatives.

(There is no reason to believe that either Emma or her uncle, Mr. Morse, was anywhere near the Second Street house during the crucial two hours, which began very soon after Mr. Borden walked out through the front gate.)

The Bordens were particularly careful about keys and bolts. Their house, with its near neighbors and locked doors, was virtually impregnable to access by a stranger, and barren of hiding places in the very unlikely event of clandestine entry.

Andrew Borden returned sometime between ten-thirty and eleven o'clock and was admitted by Bridget, who opened the bolted and double-locked front door. Lizzie Borden stood at some point on the front stairs, which led to the guest bedroom and the bedrooms of the two sisters, and laughed as Bridget struggled with the door. In the light of our afterknowledge, the laugh was a macabre sound. Whether it had any sinister significance, no one now can tell.

Miss Borden joined her father and Bridget in the downstairs sittingroom and remarked that Mrs. Borden had received a note and had gone out. To the servant, who asked who was sick, Lizzie replied that she did not know, but "it must be someone in town." (Whether a note actually came to Mrs. Borden and, if so, who sent it, was never determined, in spite of wide publicity and the offer of a $500.00 reward for information.)

Very soon thereafter, perhaps ten minutes before eleven, Mr. Borden lay down for a nap—a not unusual act for him—on the sittingroom couch, which stood against the inner wall, which placed the sleeper's head very near the dining room doorway. Bridget, who had been washing windows most of the morning, went to her attic room for a short rest, while Lizzie, by her own story, walked to the barn at the rear of the Borden yard, in search of lead for fishing-line sinkers to be used on holiday the following week.

Andrew Borden's last earthly sleep was brief. Reaching, it may be, around the side of the dining room doorway, an arm poised a hatchet, or a similar narrow-bladed weapon, over the slumberer's head and cleft his

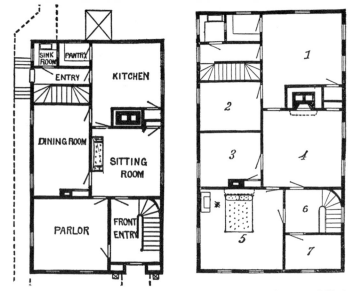

Left: Ground plan of the Borden house. Mr. Borden was killed on the couch in the sitting room.
Right: Second floor of the Borden house. 1. Mr. and Mrs. Borden's bedroom. 3. Miss Emma Borden's room. 4. Miss Lizzie Borden's room. 5. Guest room, where Mrs. Borden was murdered. 6. Hall or landing at head of stairs.
From Porter's *The Fall River Tragedy*

skull with a rain of blows that spattered victim, floor, and wall in a flying shower of blood.

As Lizzie Borden later told it, she was out of the house only a few minutes and returned to find her father weltering in blood on the couch where she had left him asleep. She hurried to the back stairs and called:

"Maggie, come down!"

"What's the matter?" Bridget responded from the attic.

"Come down quick. Father's dead. Somebody came in and killed him."

When Bridget hurried down, Lizzie sent her across the street for the family physician, Doctor Bowen. In the next few minutes, several persons reached the house: Doctor Bowen, who verified the fact of Mr. Borden's death; Mrs. Churchill, a next-door neighbor; Miss Alice Russell, close friend of the Borden sisters; and a police officer, George W. Allen.

Lizzie Borden presently expressed concern for her stepmother, saying she "thought she had heard her come in." Mrs. Churchill and Bridget had already been in the rear bedrooms on the second floor to find a sheet to cover Mr. Borden. As the only direct access from the rooms of the elder Bordens to the three bedrooms in the front of the house was by a door habitually kept locked, the two women now ascended the front

Possibly the murder weapon.

stairs and Bridget, who was in the lead, entered the guest bedroom. On the far side of the bed lay the corpse of Mrs. Borden. Five feet tall and weighing 200 pounds, she sprawled on her face on the bloodstained floor. The same weapon and the same hand had apparently slaughtered both husband and wife, but medical evidence later proved that Mrs. Borden had preceded her husband in death by at least an hour. Unlike him, she had received the first of 19 vicious blows while facing her assailant and must have known a heart's beat of terror before the first slash of the hatchet blade.

The police made several detailed searches of the house, barn, and grounds in the next few days, but found neither bloodstained clothing nor the murder weapon, unless it may have been the "handleless" hatchet found in the Borden cellar and subject of much argument and discussion later on.

Lizzie Borden admittedly had been close in time and space to each murder, and had possible motives in alleged hatred of her stepmother, dislike of her father's penuriousness, and in the fact that with Andrew Borden's death and the pre-decease of his wife, his daughters inherited an estate of some $300,000. After an inquest, at which Lizzie testified, she was placed under arrest. Next came a hearing before the district court, succeeded by a grand jury indictment. Finally, ten months after the murders—a period she spent in jail—she stood trial before the superior court at New Bedford.

Interest in the case was nationwide and the many correspondents present furnished extensive and detailed news coverage. Testimony and arguments by counsel consumed 13 days, and both Commonwealth and defense brought distinguished legal talent in action. After little more than an hour's deliberation, the jury returned a verdict of "Not Guilty," which was hailed with elation by Miss Borden's many supporters and acclaimed by a considerable section of the press. There were exceptions, however, to the general belief that an unfairly accused woman had been properly vindicated.

Thereafter the Borden case gradually grew dim in public memory until 1924, when Edmund Pearson published his graphic and fascinating "Studies In Murder." The first long chapter brought the Fall River murders to the attention of enthralled readers, many of whom now heard of the slayings for the first time. Four more books on celebrated murders followed the "Studies;" in each Pearson gave space to the Borden mystery. In 1937, the year of his death, he edited "The Trial of Lizzie Borden," prefaced by a long and detailed foreword. Acknowledged as the foremost expert on the Borden tragedy, both before and after the two sisters' almost simultaneous deaths in 1927, Pearson made no secret of his firm belief in Lizzie's guilt, a judgment probably accepted by most of his readers.

Then, in 1961, Edward D. Radin attacked Pearson and his theories in the book "Lizzie Borden, The Untold Story." After thoroughly combing the research field, Radin became very critical of Pearson's investigative methods and, backing up his argument by numerous citations from official and other sources, accused his predecessor of deliberate omissions and distortions in discussing and reporting testimony and evidence. In addition, Radin set out to demolish the case against Miss Borden and to build a new one against the servant, Bridget Sullivan.

The gist of Radin's reconstruction can be stated briefly. Bridget killed Mrs. Borden in a burst of anger triggered by a reprimand. (In support of this hypothesis, he cited two cases where trivial correction of an employee led directly to murder.) The murder in the guest bedroom took place while Lizzie was in the cellar. As the slain woman lay on the far side of the bed, there was only one step on the stairs from which the corpse could be seen through the open door; hence Miss Borden could go up to her room and back to the ground floor without being aware that her stepmother was huddled in death only a few feet away. The killing of Mrs. Borden made necessary the silencing of her husband before he became curious over the absence of his wife. This was done while Bridget was ostensibly in her attic room and Lizzie absent on her errand to the barn.

The evening after the murders, Bridget was permitted to leave the house to spend the night with a friend. Departing unsearched and unwatched, she had opportunity to dispose of the hatchet and any blood-marked clothing, which in the meantime could have been hidden in her room in a disused water tank, not searched by the police until next day. By contrast, had Miss Borden been the one to tomahawk her father, she would have had only a few minutes for the disposal of the death weapon and any other incriminating material.

Around these basic assumptions as to motive, opportunity to kill, and ability to hide bloodstained hatchet and garments, Mr. Radin wove in various incidents, which tended to strengthen his theory of the murderer's identity. Taken as a whole, his book is a formidable indictment

[61]

of Bridget Sullivan, and one which some reviewers of the work and other "crime experts" accepted as a belated but true solution of the Fall River enigma. Bridget, like Lizzie Borden before her, had passed beyond the jurisdiction of the Commonwealth of Massachusetts; she had died in Montana in 1948 at the age of 82. However, in the opinion of this writer, while Mr. Radin made a notable contribution to the literature of the tragedy and corrected a number of errors made by Pearson, the author of "The Untold Story" failed to clear two formidable hurdles in the path of any believer in Miss Borden's innocence. These are the note allegedly received by Mrs. Borden on the morning of her death, and the conduct of Lizzie after the murders were discovered.

The story of the note originated with Lizzie; no one saw it delivered; no one found it afterwards; no one appeared to claim authorship. If the note actually existed, it came from a person well enough acquainted with the Bordens to know how vital proof of its existence was to the daughter under accusation of murder. In view of the substantial reward offered by a newspaper—plus further benefits to be expected from the grateful and now wealthy Borden sisters—it is almost impossible to believe that this tale of a scrap of paper was anything else than a fabrication to lull the suspicions of Andrew Borden as to the whereabouts of his wife.

Of the reactions of Miss Borden after the crimes, it should be noted that when she came upon the gory corpse of her father, she did not immediately rush outside for help, but chose to stay in the house which, for all she knew, probably still harbored a lurking assassin who had just hacked her father to death. She called Bridget down from the attic, but sent her for Doctor Bowen, and then remained for long minutes close to the bloodstained slaughter room, a vulnerable target should the unknown murderer decide to strike again.

As the full horror of the morning unfolded with discovery of the second hatchet victim, it surely became apparent to the mature, educated, and intelligent Lizzie Borden (if we assume her innocence) that the most likely person to have committed the murders was the only other living individual known to have been on the premises between half past nine and eleven o'clock. Suspicion of Bridget would then quickly grow into a logical dread that the Borden maid was a homicidal maniac who might at any moment choose to add another notch to her hatchet handle.

But Lizzie evinced no concern that the probable perpetrator of a double murder was in attendance upon her. Neither she nor her sister Emma, nor Doctor Bowen, nor the friends and neighbors showed any mistrust of Bridget or insisted to the police that the servant girl's person and her room be immediately and thoroughly searched. Afterward, Lizzie underwent the humiliation of arrest, the strain of ten months' imprisonment, and the torture of a public trial; endured, if the Radin theory be correct, because she, her sister, her friends, her lawyers, the district attorney, and the police turned blind eyes on the probability that Bridget Sullivan and not Miss Borden—the active church member and charity worker—had engineered the ghastly butchery in the Borden home.

Edmund Pearson and Edward Radin have championed the respective claims of the two most likely candidates for the title of Number One murderer (or murderess) of New England. Others have proposed different solutions to the Borden riddle, most of them nearly or quite preposterous. But whomever one selects as the Fall River slayer, there remain questions difficult to answer. If the choice is Lizzie, her whole life before and after the fatal 4th of August is inconsistent with the savage butchery of her parents; and if she were the hatchet wielder, how did she avoid bloodstains, and where in a brief space of time could she hide her weapon? (The weight of evidence seems to rule out the "handleless" hatchet.) As the assassin, Bridget appears to lack adequate motive, showed no signs of insanity during her long life, and seems never to have been considered suspect by the police or by Lizzie Borden, her lawyers, and her friends. If a faceless killer from outside—homicidal maniac or otherwise—slew the Bordens, how could he have entered the house, how could he hide there undetected for over an hour, how could he leave unseen, and where did he go?

Seventy-four years afterward, it is no longer possible to offer an argument-proof solution of the Borden murders. They remain an unfathomable mystery, one of the most fascinating and puzzling deeds in the history of crime. □□

Editor's Note: Yankee Magazine originally published this story in August 1966. Soon after the magazine appeared on the newsstands, we received a flood of mail related to the article. Certain letters offered surprising testimony—some of it firsthand, most of it hearsay, all of it interesting. Here's one that reads something like an epilogue.

November 16, 1966

• When I was a young woman, I heard the story of a man who perhaps at one time held the key to unlock the mystery of the Borden tragedy.

One day many years after Lizzie Borden of Fall River, Massachusetts, was tried for murder of her parents, I happened to meet a man who unexpectedly brought the whole gruesome tragedy into focus again.

I had stopped at a farm in the adjoining county to ask the

owner if a new kind of squash he had grown that season would be satisfactory for me to plant in my own small vegetable garden, another year.

He answered my query and then as his wife was still busy, clearing up after dinner, he showed me over his place. We finally came to a standstill beside a fenced orchard where contented hens were pecking around beneath the trees. As we did so a little oldish man hurried past us with a pan of table scraps and called the biddies to a feast. I watched him casually. I never dreamed he could possibly have any connection with the unsolved Borden murder mystery, nor that, as long as I lived, I would never forget him.

You could see that he understood hens for they circled about him clucking companionably. "That fellow belongs on a chicken farm," observed my host. "But," he added, "It wouldn't work. He could feed the biddies and collect the eggs, but he couldn't kill a chicken for market, if his life depended on it."

The man had turned now and I could see his somewhat vacant but gentle face topped by straggly gray hair. There was a nervous twitch to his mouth, however, and an anxious look in his faded blue eyes that made me ask, "He's a bit nervous over something, isn't he?"

"Yeah, and I guess I'll let you hear what he told me about that last night. You aren't a blabbermouth, and it won't hurt to repeat it to you. He's been worse than he is today, for over a week, but he says he'll be better now and I sure hope so."

Just then the wife came out and we three went around to the front piazza. There the farmer nodded in my direction and said "I'm a-telling her about Joe, Molly." Then he turned to our conversation, and went on.

"I've always called my men 'Joe' no matter what their real names are. Well, this Joe, every night when we'd finish supper and sit at the table to talk about what had happened during the day, would get up and go into the sitting room to glance over the paper. Then he'd start up to bed for he was tired early since he got up at four o'clock every morning along with me.

"One night he seemed terribly jittery and upset after he'd read the news, and when he left I looked to see what it was that made him feel that way. All that I could come across that was unusual was a piece about the Lizzie Borden case.

" 'Course that was a terrible affair, but it happened so long ago it didn't seem as if anyone ought to be upset about it now. Well Joe, he got more jittery every day. His hands shook, his legs wobbled and he seemed in a daze. "What's the matter Joe?" I asked finally. "You sick?

"He said he'd tell me about everything sometime, and then he'd feel better and last night he did just that, and it's quite a yarn. Now I'm the jittery one. He feels better because he's got it off his chest but my wife and I, we don't know what we ought to do about him."

"Tell me and let me share the responsibility," I said.

The farmer looked relieved and in a few moments began again.

[64]

"Joe was the runt of a big family that had a good old New England name. They lived on a farm and his brothers and sisters made fun of him because he was too spleeny to do heavy work. He didn't go far in school either. He grew up a loner, for the others were so much stronger and smarter than he was.

"When he was twenty-one his father gave him a little money for a start and he walked to the nearest city. That city was Fall River and here he looked about for a job. He was lucky too. You wouldn't expect jobs to be plentiful in a mill city for someone that could only do light farm labor.

"But there were a good many people there who didn't want a man all day every day, to look after their places, but would like a handy man to do jobs now and then as needed—clean a stable, curry and harness a horse, cut grass, weed a flower bed—you know what I mean.

"Joe was just right for such things and he always kept busy. One man let him sleep in a room over a stable. Cooks were always giving him leftovers to eat, so his living expenses were small and though he didn't charge much for what he did, he got along fine.

"One of the places he worked at, he told me, was the Borden's, and here a curious thing happened. He sort of fell in love with the daughter Lizzie. She was older than he was, but she was so domineering and strong, where he was shy and weak, he thought her wonderful. Said she was a good looker too, and her not being a favorite in her family, just as he hadn't been in his family, made her seem closer to him. He never told her how he felt but he was so glad to run errands for her, I guess she knew she had him wound round her finger, and figured he'd do anything she wanted him to and not ask questions.

"One day, as he was putting litter he'd raked up into a barrel to cart away, Lizzie came to the kitchen door and beckoned him over. She was wiping off a hatchet with a piece of rag. She handed the hatchet to him and told him to put it in the barn. He saw nothing strange about the request or about her wiping it off. Everyone wiped off used tools in those days to keep them in good condition. Tools cost money and money was scarce.

"She tossed the rag into the midst of the litter in the barrel and then said, 'Wait, I've got something else to throw away.' She went into the house and in a few minutes came out and handed him a bundle wrapped in paper and tied around with a string.

"He put the hatchet in the barn and the bundle in the barrel and the barrel in a wheelbarrow, and soon was trundling his load down the street to a lot where fill was needed. He felt proud he could show Miss Lizzie he could handle a man-sized load even though he knew it was light weight.

"After he'd dumped the stuff, he had to rest awhile, and then finding he was not only hot and tired but faint, as it was noon, he felt in his pocket for the quarter Mr. Borden had given him that morning for what he'd done. He'd spend ten cents of it for two fresh crullers and a glass of milk at a little shop he knew about.

"When he'd eaten he took the barrel and the wheelbarrow back to the Borden barn and put them where they belonged. He noticed people going in and out of the house more than usual. 'What's going on,' he asked a woman he'd worked for as she went along the walk.

" 'Abby and Andrew Borden have been murdered,' and added, 'with a hatchet,' though she could hardly speak for she was crying.

"Joe said he felt sick all at once, and as if he'd slump down right there. He couldn't believe Mr. and Mrs. Borden could have been murdered. And with a hatchet! Why such things hadn't happened since Indian times. If anyone was around killing with hatchets, he'd better hide the Borden hatchet out of sight. He didn't want any more murders. He went in the barn, took the hatchet and put it behind the horse stall. As he did so he remembered Miss Lizzie. She'd handed it to him that morning. What had she been using it for? Not to kill her father and mother. Oh no, he was sure of that, though he knew she hated them at times and she did have a terrible temper.

"He stumbled out into the yard. A policeman passed by and greeted him with a sober nod. Would the police question him later as to what he'd done every minute that morning? Suddenly he recalled Miss Lizzie cleaning off the hatchet with the rag. Was there blood on the rag? He recalled the bundle. Were there bloody things in the bundle? He must go down to the rubbish lot and find out. If there were bloody things he would have to take them to the police and tell how they

got there. He couldn't believe Miss Lizzie had done the killings but if she had she must pay for doing them. Would they hang her? He shuddered. All the same he must find out before the police asked him questions. He hurried away to where he had dumped the litter.

"When he reached there he found he was too late. During the noon hour one or two cartloads of cultch had been dumped right on top of his little pile. His was buried so deep he could not possibly unearth the rag or the bundle.

" 'Guess it's a sign I'd better mind my own business,' he thought. In a way he felt better. He wouldn't have to be the one to find out for sure if Miss Lizzie was the killer or not. The police would come up with the murderer. He sure hoped they would. He liked Mr. and Mrs. Borden. He couldn't bear to think they hadn't been let to live out their lives peacefully.

"He went to his room after that and flung himself, spent and shaken, on his cot. For a long time afterward he did his usual work but he felt half-sick and stunned.

"When the Superior Court trial took place a feeling of guilt developed in his mind and he worried. He should have told the police at the beginning. They would have known how to get at the rag and bundle. Now rain and snow and still more cultch had fallen on his rubbish pile. It would do no good to tell about it now. Blood stains would be washed away and everything be a sodden mass. Miss Lizzie's acquittal and the fact that nobody at all had been convicted of the murders bothered him no end. He could not bear to stay in Fall River any longer and made up his mind to leave it for all time. He especially did not want to chance meeting Miss Lizzie.

Of his life after that, the hired man told the farmer little. He never stayed long in one place and became a pathetic drifter. He'd never gone hungry however; there was always a meal for an odd-jobs man. In summer he often slept on haymows or in the lee of a haystack in a field. In cold weather he looked for work where he could stay in a house nights, though a barn with cows in it was always warm. So the hired man, after he got started, had talked on and on. He never mentioned names of people or places though. Folks were always good to him, he said.

"And now," concluded the farmer, "what shall I do with him? Turn him over to the authorities? Their questions and reporters would drive him crazy or kill him; I don't know which. He couldn't be called guilty of doing any wrong but concealing possible evidence even if they believed what he said. There'd be no way today to disprove or prove his story either. The wife and I thought we might tell an old judge that comes here summers, all about it. What do you think?" It seemed a good idea. They could abide by the judge's wisdom.

But there was no need to tell anyone. Some extrasensory perception must have made the hired man sure that the stranger who saw him feed the hens was hearing his story, and he didn't know what the consequences would be. That night he quietly assembled his few belongings, then stole down stairs and out into the night, completely vanishing. The farmer never saw him again.

We all wondered what had become of him. Could he have got to a box car on the tracks not far away, and slipping within its safety, later been whisked out to the midwest? Could he have reached the waterfront and boarded a packet that had a soft-hearted skipper? Could he have tramped along woods roads to the cranberry bogs and joined the pickers there? No one ever knew. Joe just couldn't be located.

Do you believe his story? It was plausible.

Do you believe he was a crackpot? Perhaps. He had been through a great deal.

Whatever you believe, I am sure you feel, as we did, that wherever he was, someone would look out for him and care for him to the very end.

It's half a century since I was told I was not a blabbermouth but I feel I am not betraying a confidence now in telling the story of this pitiable, bewildered man, who tried so hard to be independent and make his own living and do what was right. I can never forget him.

Sincerely,
Marion Hicks Campbell

"The Old Leather Man"

The Old Leather Man

by Richard Morgan

One misty, moisty morning,
When cloudy was the weather,
I chanced to meet an old man
Clothed all in leather.

> *Old nursery rhyme—*
> *Anonymous*

New England has had its share of eccentrics, and legends, but none has been so mysterious as "The Old Leather Man." *

In the early 1860's there appeared in Connecticut a singular figure, dressed in leather garments made from discarded boot tops held together by leather thongs. He soon established a definite route for his travels, and adhered to his schedule so accurately that townsfolk could almost set their clocks by his appearance. From town to town he trudged, through eastern Connecticut and into New York State. He appeared to be in no great hurry, neither was he slack, for he continued his travels at a constant

---

* YANKEE *wishes to thank many readers, including Mrs. Ellen A. Danaher, Thomaston, Conn., for their help in preparing this article.*

Jules Bourglay (right) survived the
blizzard of 1888 but was found dead
the following year in a cave (below)
near Mount Pleasant, N.Y.

PHOTO BY GIRARD.
NOHCG.

speed. All accounts state that he spoke little or nothing, indicating his need for food or tobacco with gestures. Unlike most tramps of the time, The Old Leather Man was never seen to take a drink. As a matter of fact, he once resisted the attempts of some pranksters who tried to force liquor down his throat. When he could not eat all that was offered him, he stuffed the balance into a large leather bag. This contained all his worldly goods. He never slept in a building. Instead, he preferred to sleep in caves or in lean-tos he constructed along his route. If one of his sleeping places was discovered by curious children, he would abandon it immediately and find another spot. Although uncommunicative, The Old Leather Man left certain clues as to his identity, most of which were construed to the point of fiction by enthusiastic writers. Generally speaking, the mystery of this strange character was as follows.

Jules Bourglay was a young Frenchman who fell in love with the daughter of a prosperous leather merchant. The father opposed the match and, as was the custom of that country, could have forbade any further meetings. However, he said Jules might serve a probation of one year and accordingly gave him a position of importance in his firm, where, incidentally, he could keep an eye on him. Jules made a success of business life and was allowed, in time, to make important decisions. At one point the leather market seemed about to rise quickly, and Jules invested most of the firm's and his employer's money. Instead of rising, the market fell, 40% in one day, thereby ruining the firm, and Jules' chances for marriage. He soon lost his senses and eventually was placed in an institution, from which he escaped in a short time, never to be seen in France again. He emigrated to America, there to serve his penance by trudging away his life, dressed in the leather that was his financial and mental undoing. This he did until he was found dead in his cave near Mount Pleasant, New York on March 24, 1889.

After his death he was mourned, not as a friend, but as one mourns the passing of a way of life. People pasted clippings about him in their scrapbooks; they told their children about him and they in turn told their children. Memory fades quickly, however, and today few remember The Old Leather Man and his story is not frequently told. He is long gone and with him the answer to one of NewEngland's most peculiar mysteries.□□

BOOBYTOWN

Text and photographs by L. F. Willard

*Legend had it that, about 1850, Lewiston, Me.,
solved its "welfare" problem by rounding up
all its "free loaders" and shipping them to
Rangeley where they lived in caves. So in 1964,
YANKEE decided to investigate . . .*

Did you ever hear of Boobytown? Well, we hadn't heard of it either until we received a letter from one of those loyal YANKEE readers who occasionally tip us off to a good story. Mr. E. S. Norris wrote earlier this year from Great Neck, New York, to tell us about something he thought we ought to look into.

"More than thirty years ago," said Mr. Norris, "our next door neighbor in Portland (Maine) took us to his camp at Rangeley. While there, we visited a place called 'Booby Town.' His story was that about 1850 the town of Lewiston rounded up all its free loaders and shipped them off to Rangeley. There, the new inhabitants literally went underground. They lived in earth caves and mounds which they constructed. I went in some of these caves and know they existed. A couple of houses were constructed and pigs lived inside with the people. When I saw Boobytown in 1927 it was uninhabited and in ruins. It was a novel way to take care of a serious problem and may be successful."

It sounded like an interesting story, but the part about Lewiston shipping her poor up to Rangeley to get rid of them sounded like a Maine yarn to us. And since it happened over a hundred years ago, it would be pretty hard to find anybody who would know much about it. It also seemed doubtful that the city of Lewiston would keep any written records of that kind of solution to civic problems. Still, it was an intriguing story, the kind that sticks in one's mind. So we decided that somebody (me!) should drive up to Rangeley and look into it.

If I'd had any fears about finding the place, they were gone after I got to Rangeley. Everybody in town knew about Boobytown, and most people had stories to relate about its inhabitants. I was shunted from one to another of Rangeley's oldest citizens, one or two of whom had once lived in Boobytown. Leland Nile was one of these. At 85, he raises vegetables for a living and has one of the sharpest memories in Rangeley.

"Well," said Mr. Nile, "Boobytown—that was an interesting place. Actual name was Lower Dallas. I lived in Upper Dallas and I can tell you the name of every person in Upper Dallas in those days. There was—"

There certainly were a lot of people in Upper Dallas. Finally, however, we got back to Boobytown, and Nile admitted that he didn't know too many people down there, but he did know the Bubier family.

"That's where the town got it's name—Boobytown—from the Bubiers. Ike Bubier had six kids," said Mr. Nile, "Riley, Elwell and Ira

[73]

were the boys, and Calista, Lura and Rosella were the girls. They lived in a small cabin and they were always hungry. Riley once told me he got so hungry when spring came around that he used to go into the field and dig up dandelions and eat 'em raw."

Riley Bubier must have been a memorable character, because he popped up early in a conversation I had with Vance Oakes, proprietor of a grocery store and meat market in Rangeley.

"My father hired Riley to work for him when he was alive," said Oakes, "and I hired him afterward. Riley was a big man—six foot two and weighed 220 pounds. He cut three cords of wood for me the day he died. He was 88. He told me he never had any milk or any white bread until he was grown up. He never had any shoes, even in winter. He used to heat up a couple of shingles and stand on them to chop wood. When he'd walk over the mountain into Rangeley, he'd borrow his old man's shoes."

Oakes proved to be a natural raconteur, and willingly told a number of stories about the Boobytowners.

"They often brought produce in here to trade—raspberries, blueberries. They lived off the land, hunted, fished, and rarely had any money. Once in a while one of them would pick up a dollar or two as a guide. Riley used to tell me how he took deer and the warden never could catch him with the evidence. Riley would put the meat out the window of his cabin and the snow would cover it up and there wouldn't be any tracks."

"Rangeley people thought a lot of the Boobytowners," said Oakes. "They were sharp traders, maybe, but they were honest in their dealings. We've always enjoyed swapping yarns about them. They used to hold church services in the schoolhouse, and when the minister didn't come out from Rangeley to preach, which was more often than not, one of the Boobytowners would fill in. On one of these occasions the substitute said: 'We're going to plant corn tomorrow, and I want everybody to plant a prayer in each hill.' A man in the rear stood up and said in a loud voice: 'I'd a damn sight rather have some good hog manure.' Another time the minister came out from Rangeley to do some baptizing. One young Boobytowner thought the minister was trying to drown him and put the minister down in the stream."

field and dig up dandelions and eat 'em raw."

Oakes said that, as far as he knew, the story about the original Boobytown settlers coming from Lewiston was true.

"They had a depression some time after the Civil War and the story is that a lot of people on Lewiston relief rolls were given seed potatoes and brought up here. They settled in what is now Lower Dallas and when the narrow gauge railroad came through they went into lumbering. At one time there were several sawmills there and a sizeable settlement."

Following directions I had been given in Rangeley, I drove along the road toward Stratton and turned right on a gravel road leading along the Dead River. I stopped beside a small building where a man was sharpening an ax on an old grindstone.

"Where is Boobytown?" I asked.

"This is it," he said.

He identified himself as being Sherwood Merrill and said that if I would drive back along the road to the old schoolhouse, leave the car, and walk down the remains of an old road, I would find what was left of the old Boobytown.

"I remember when I was a boy," he told me, "I used to come up here with my uncle who traded hens. I remember one family was living in a cave dug into the side of a hill and they had chickens and pigs living in there with them."

I parked the car near the schoolhouse (in good repair and with a sign on it saying "Sportsmen's Paradise") and walked a short distance downhill to find a group of old buildings still standing, though some were tilted at crazy angles. One had apparently been a small sawmill—machinery was still inside. Two small one-room cabins still had beds and furniture inside, and one of these had a pile of newspapers in it dated 1942 and 1943 with big black World War II headlines. I didn't see any caves or cellar holes here, but crossing a stone fence grown up with bushes I found an adjacent clearing with the remains of a number of crude shacks, and some depressions and mounds of what had been cellar holes or underground shelters. One was still partly roofed over and had the rusted remains of a stove inside. Undeniably, somebody had once lived here. After taking a number of photographs, I went back to the car and drove to the nearest farmhouse to see if I could get any more

[75]

Above: Interior of one of the one-room cabins still has remains of a bed, a stove, and furniture used by squatters long after Boobytown was deserted. Newspapers are dated 1942 and 1943. Opposite page: Some of the shacks that were still standing in Boobytown in 1964.

formation about Boobytown.

I was welcomed by Ken Bachelder, who said that his father and his grandfather had lived in Boobytown and that the old building I had seen with the machinery inside had been a shingle mill built by his grandfather.

"Grandfather ran that mill for many years, and my dad after him," said Bachelder. "I used to work in that mill as a boy. One of those old houses over there was my father's house and we shingled it partly with shingles from the mill. One of those small shacks you saw was lived in by my father and mother before they built the larger house, and I lived in it with my wife for two years when we were first married."

I told him about the newspapers dated as late as 1943, and he said that squatters had come and gone periodically after the old inhabitants all moved away. Bachelder remembers Boobytown when there were about 200 people there.

"There were thirty-six kids in that school at one time," he said, "but it's been closed for more than thirty years and a group of sportsmen from New Jersey owns it now."

Bachelder said that he recalled only one family that lived in a cellar hole, but he did remember that chickens and pigs lived in there too. However, Bachelder's memories are of a Boobytown as it was maybe fifty years after its early beginnings, and he could not throw any light on the possible Lewiston origin of the first settlers.

The early families included the Bubiers—the Bachelders apparently married into that family—the Thomases and Campbells, and the Flaggs, among others. Bachelder offered to go back to Boobytown with me and show me the cellar hole to the Bubier cabin. It was grown up with trees and hidden in underbrush.

"The Bubiers had seven children," Bachelder said, "and they all lived in a cabin that couldn't have been more than fourteen feet on a side."

I'd heard earlier that Bubier had only six children. I didn't argue the point. Bachelder posed for me in front of the old shingle mill, and I left Boobytown, still without any evidence to support the story that these people had been paupers from Lewiston. But I had wandered through a real ghost town, and with fall sunshine filtering through the pine trees I had the uneasy feeling that the ghosts of these hardy people hadn't been gone long, and might be back.

If there was any further information to be found, it would be in Lewiston—and to Lewiston I went. I went through some of the records in Lewiston's City Hall, but they were incomplete; an earlier City Hall had been destroyed by fire along with many of the records. In the Lewiston Library I had better luck. I found a small, paperbound pamphlet, "Farrar's Guide Book to Rangeley, Richardson, Kennebago, Umbagog, and Parmachenee Lakes, Dixville Notch, and Andover, Me., and Vicinity," published in 1876. In it was an engraving of the "Log Hut inhabited by Bubier Family, Rangeley, Me." There was no explanation of the picture anywhere in the book, and no mention of Bubier and family. But it proved one thing: Bubier came to Rangeley sometime before 1876, and this narrowed my search of the Lewiston City records which the library had.

At last I found what I was looking for. In the annual report of 1865

[78]

is this entry: "Paid town of Rangeley for supplies for the poor: $168.79."
And in the overseer of the poor's report were these figures:

> Daniel Bubier, Rangeley, $75
> Bubier Family, Rangeley, $ 7.05
> Lowell Family, Rangeley, $80.50
> Andrew Bubier, Rangeley, $36.79

And in the annual report of 1856 the overseer of the poor reports:
"Paid on account of persons off the farm as follows:

> *The Bubiers at Rangeley, $176.14*"

So there is at least some truth in what sounded like a Maine yarn. The first settlers of Boobytown were from Lewiston, and they were on the relief rolls. But were they "dumped off" to fend for themselves? One can only make an educated guess, but the answer seems to be: probably not. From the early town records it is easy to get the picture of a town where jobs were few and money scarce. There are constant references to crowding at the poor farm and the need to practice economy in dealing with the poor "consistent with Christian Charity." The Bubiers were apparently French Canadians who had settled in Lewiston, and there are references to the large number of foreign-born in Lewiston at that time. Certainly Lewiston didn't just dump these people off in Rangeley, since relief payments were still being made to them. Whether the Bubiers and other energetic but destitute families refused to live at Lewiston's poor farm and volunteered to start a new life at Rangeley, or whether the city fathers suggested the idea to them may never be known; but there certainly seems to have been some kind of gentleman's agreement.

Lewiston certainly did extend financial help to them at the start, and should stand exonerated from charges of having cruelly carted its indigent citizens off into the woods—at least until somebody turns up some solid evidence to the contrary.

Today the old Boobytown is deserted, the sawmills and narrow gauge railroad are long gone. But Ken Bachelder and one or two other farmers in the vicinity still consider that they live in Boobytown, rather than Lower Dallas. And Boobytown will live a long time yet in the yarns told in Rangeley, particularly to summer visitors. □□

Section II

Great Yankee Ghosts

GHOSTS
Are Where You Find Them

by Donald Purcell

The next time you hear a person ask, "Why doesn't someone study these queer things?" apropos of a local ghost, you might refer the questioner to Curt J. Ducasse, retired chairman of the Department of Philosophy at Brown University.

The existence of psychic phenomena, Ducasse says, is as well attested as a great many historical facts that we accept unquestioningly. That the field reeks with charlatanism scarcely invalidates such a case as that of Mrs. Piper of Boston who, after having been investigated and pronounced genuine by William James, was continuously studied over the next eighteen years by a learned man who even employed detectives to keep track of her in her spare time, and who subjected her seances to rigid scientific control. Mrs. Piper convinced a Columbia professor, Dr. James H. Hyslop, that through her "control" she communicated with Dr. Hyslop's dead father. The father identified himself to his son by referring to long-forgotten private conversations, bodily marks, and even some personal details that the son didn't recognize but which, on checking with relatives, he found to be true.

But even among professional philosophers, Dr. Ducasse believes, prejudice seriously obstructs the progress of psychic research. Last summer (1955) he took part in an international parapsychological conference in Cambridge, England on the subject, "What Sort of Evidence of Survival after Death Would be Regarded as Conclusive?"

The phenomena studied by the American Society of Psychical Research, of which Dr. Ducasse is an active member, are classified in three categories: Controlled, Spontaneous, and Phenomena involving mediums. Though Dr. Ducasse specializes in the two latter types, he does keep on his desk a plastic-enclosed nonmagnetic strip of metal balanced on a pivot. In odd moments he stares at the metal to see if he can move it by psychokinesis—thought-energy. So far, he confesses laughingly, it has never stirred.

Dr. Ducasse is of a theoretical temperament, preferring to read the accounts of others, check on the reliability of writers, and ponder on the meaning of phenomena rather than to cultivate psychic experiences directly. He is not, however, entirely devoid of sporting blood. He has assisted at at least one "successful" seance.

The semi-obscurity of this successful seance—by "successful," Dr. Ducasse says (not writes) that he means "that the guy produced some spook-like things, though not this time a spook. I've never yet seen a spook"—was shattered every five or ten minutes by the popping of Dr. Ducasse's flash camera. His dozen photos show a rather good-looking well-dressed youngish man slumped stupefied in an easy chair. From the man's mouth floats a trail of what may have been ectoplasm, the famous ideoplastic substance that often establishes contact between a medium and a "control," or ghost. The ectoplasm in these photos curls about in the air like a rope of cotton batting and terminates at an aluminum megaphone standing on the floor a dozen feet away from the medium.

Between photos Dr. Ducasse got up and felt of the ectoplasm. His report, written soon afterwards, describes the sensation: "It was coldish, causing in my hand a temperature sensation about the same as would be caused by touching a piece of steel—say desk scissors—indoors. The consistency of the string seemed about the same as that of a string of fairly firm dough. It felt dry, and its surface . . . a little flaky. In weight, it felt perhaps slightly lighter than dough. . . . The string then

[83]

glided forward over my fingers and out of my hand towards the center of the room."

Dr. Ducasse shrugs his shoulders over this experience. "This medium is worthy of more investigation, that's all. The other persons present are all old trustworthy friends. I went over the room carefully before and after, and I found nothing phony; but I wouldn't dream of publishing my pictures or even beginning to have any opinion without a lot more study and some trained witnesses with whom I could check."

Ducasse has currently come across what can be a case of precognition. He asked a western acquaintance who always receives unexpected money after the recurrence of a certain dream, to send a post card the next time the dream occurred. A day or so later Ducasse, before embarking for that year's international parapsychological conference at Le Piol, France, put a dollar in an envelope and sent it to his friend. When he arrived in Europe, there was a card announcing the recurrence of the dream. The card had been air-mailed the day after Ducasse had mailed the dollar.

This example, similar to several others involving the same person, also evokes a shrug of Ducasse's shoulders. He adds that if it could be unmistakably proved to be a paranormal talent on the part of the dreamer, one would still have to try to determine whether it were a case of precognition, telepathy, or clairvoyance, distinctions of weighty philosophic import.

Controlled psychic phenomena, which Dr. Ducasse finds dull, have become widely known through the now controversial, some say, work of Dr. J. B. Rhine of Duke University.

Last year when Ducasse and Rhine presented papers at a meeting in Baltimore of the American Philosophical Association, Ducasse disagreed strongly with Rhine's opinion that the proved existence of extrasensory perception holds optimistic "implications for human freedom, responsibility, and values."

As to survival after death,* the evidence indicates that there is,

---

* The now admitted failure of Sir Oliver Lodge to communicate successfully with this world has been quite a setback to any immediate hopes of this kind of communication. He is said to have left seven envelopes one within the other—a message on each leading to the other—to help him remember, others to receive.

indeed, such a survival, but the evidence is insufficient for us to form a detailed picture of what that survival is like. From the standpoint of justice, Ducasse might agree, survival is a necessary condition "if the life of humanity is to be more than a rather second-rate farce;" but such an opinion does not affect the poverty of the evidence. Spooks themselves, Ducasse says, have usually been rather stupid and often downright nonsensical.

"Of course there are exceptions," Ducasse says. "There was Patience Worth, the Yankee Puritan girl murdered by red Indians who about thirty years ago spelled out a book on the ouija board of a Mrs. Curran in the midwest. Patience's book has an extraordinary literary quality; she must have had an interesting mind. But most spooks make dull company."

Actually, Ducasse muses, when you consider all the evidence, it is amazing how little attention is paid to paranormal phenomena. In view of the evidence, if these phenomena *have* occurred, they are important from the standpoint of human *in*-credulity and *in*-credibility. If they *have not* occurred, we have an immense body of material that we'd have to study "from the standpoint of the psychology of perception, of delusion, illusion or hallucination, of credulity and credibility, and of testimony." Yet, unless it is sensationalized, people show little concern for psychics. □□

*The author has taken great pains to ascribe to natural –
phenomena the "incidents" which have occurred in his
Hingham, Mass., house—but with little success.*

The "Ghosts" of Eastgate Lane

by Lawrence D. Copeland

Illustration by Margo Letourneau

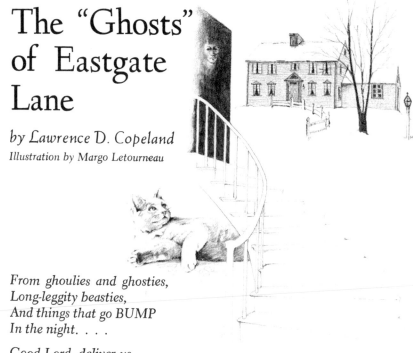

From ghoulies and ghosties,
Long-leggity beasties,
And things that go BUMP
In the night. . . .

Good Lord, deliver us.

This ancient Scotch litany, handworked in crewel, and presented to us by a compassionate friend, hangs on our living room wall.

Over the years, however, it must have lost its power. It doesn't seem to work for us. In the months since we displayed this warning to the "presence" the noises have been more frequent than ever. In fact, the most uncanny experience of all took place *since* we were given this "sure fire" protection.

In order to be of much help to us it ought to read: . . . "things that go BUMP in the day. . . ."

Take one recent Saturday morning. A clear cold day with last night's snowfall on the lawns and walks. My wife, Marian, is alone in the house and busily writing a letter. She hears a series of knocks. Not unusual, certainly; people frequently come to the house on a Saturday

[86]

morning. She goes to the door . . . no one there. "Must have been the children playing," she tells herself. She returns to writing her letter. Ten minutes later, more knocking . . . louder this time and from somewhere *inside* the house. She looks through all the rooms. She goes outside; walks around the house. Nothing. "Kids," she thinks.

A longer period passes. This time the knocks are sharp and "demanding." And now they are on an inside wall, next to the room where she is sitting! My wife is not a scary woman, but she does get concerned about things that cannot be explained. She goes outside and sits on the doorstep. She gets thoroughly chilled, but she is not willing to go back in that house alone.

No dramatic background accounts for what has happened at our house on Eastgate Lane.

It is not a gloomy old manse but a lovely colonial reproduction built in 1966. Aside from the portraits there is not one single authentic ghost-producing item in or near our house . . . no nearby cemetery, no dismal swamp, no cave of bats.

For my part, I cannot concede that what we have heard and seen is of supernatural origin. It is difficult to reconcile ghostly footsteps with a crisp Saturday morning or a pleasant Easter afternoon. Or more, to imagine ghosts who turn on water, lights, and automatic appliances, and who drive automobiles!

Nonetheless, we have heard the footsteps, we have heard the knockings, beds squeaking, doors creaking, and invisible vehicles driven into our garage. We have found lights and water and appliances turned on. We have heard and found these things not once, but over and over. They have been heard by many people.

One eerie incident took place on an autumn afternoon. Marian was dusting in the dining room. A shadow—clear and distinct—falls on the wall. It moves slowly along the wall and the sideboard. Marian turns to see what is causing the shadow. There is nothing.

That evening I tell her, "It must have been a child outside the house passing by the window." To prove my theory I go out and, calculating the sun's position and using all sorts of props, I try to establish what could have caused the shadow. It is impossible.

Marian told me later that she *felt* the shadow before she saw it.

About eleven o'clock one evening, my wife sat bolt upright in bed. In the guest room—two doors from our room—someone has gotten up out of bed to stand on the floor. The springs of the bed creak as the weight of the body is removed; there is a thud as feet hit the floor. Marian thinks she must have been dreaming. Then, in the dark, she is aware that I have been awakened by the noises and am straining to hear further.

We do not dwell on the ghostly noises. They do not seem malevolent and there are long periods of time when we hear or see nothing.

Then it happens again.

My daughter, Meredith, stayed with us for a time with her two babies. Hers was one of the most inexplicable experiences.

She was sitting in the kitchen with baby Peter in her lap. She heard a car drive into the garage which is under the kitchen. The motor was turned off, the door slammed. Someone got out of the car, walked across the garage, through the cellar, and up the cellar stairs. "It" paused at the top of the stairs, then opened the door. "It" walked through the den, causing the dozing cat to stir and follow "it" with her eyes. "It" walked into the kitchen and behind the rocking chair where Meredith was sitting. Baby Peter stirred, looked up, and watched the stranger pass.

There was no one.

One recent Easter there were seven of us for dinner. Only Jonathan, our youngest boy, and Peter, Senior, who was in Vietnam, were absent. But Jonathan must have come home unbeknownst to any of us. We heard him come down the stairs. There is no mistaking Jonny's bouncy walk! Sitting at the table we all looked expectantly at the hall door. We called to Jonathan. But Jonathan was not there. In fact, he did not return home for several hours.

I mentioned the portraits. These are heavy gilt-framed oil paintings of Marian's great-great-great-grandparents. They were painted in the 1840s. For fifty years the portraits had been hidden away in a closet at Marian's mother's house. When our house was built we asked to have the paintings. They were perfect for the decor of our colonial. We cleaned them up and hung them on the living room walls. That's when the strange noises began.

Or, so it seems. And we may be stretching things to ascribe a connection between the portraits and the "happenings"; but we find ourselves searching for reasons, however implausible.

I wish, for example, that I could think of some relation between Saturdays and the noises. There is no earthly reason why there should be any. But, again, a peculiar incident happened on a Saturday.

It happened to me.

I remember the time; about ten in the morning. I was standing at the foot of the stairs when I heard five footsteps in the attic two floors above. I say "footsteps" because they had the measured sound of a person walking . . . and they could be heard through the house.

I confess that I did not investigate . . . not even in broad daylight. Instead, like Marian, I went outside and waited until someone else came home.

One of our friends had always been amused at our stories. Then, one wintry evening, it happened to him.

We were standing in the dining room. Rich said, "It's mighty cold outside. Why don't you let that poor cat in? Can't you hear her clawing at the screen?"

"I hear her," I replied, "but Rich, are you *sure* that that's what *you* hear?"

"Positive," he replied, "we have cats; I know the sound of one crawling up a screen."

"Well," I said, "I'm sure glad that *you* heard it, Rich, because now you know what we've been talking about."

Not only were all the cats safely inside . . . there wasn't even a screen!

Our visitors are apparently undaunted by modern devices. Repeatedly, we have found the water turned on, the washer and the radios going. It is not always a case of *finding* them on; radios have been known to suddenly blare out for no apparent reason . . . rock music, yet!

But the business with the lights does get scary.

Like most housewives, Marian automatically scans the house as she drives in and out . . . sort of a dress inspection.

Last Christmas she was driving in, just at dusk. She noted that all the Christmas lights in the windows were off . . . a sign that none of her family was home. She came in and set about turning on the candles. There was one that she didn't have to touch: when she got to the attic, she found that the candle in that window—which had been off when she drove in—was now on.

None of the things that I have mentioned are particularly eerie (unless you happen to be alone in the house at the time) and any single one of them can be easily explained. We—who have heard the sounds and who know the surroundings intimately—have been at great pains to ascribe them to natural phenomena. But we cannot yet explain why they happen over and over and over.

We did not intend to live in a haunted house (and we don't really think that we do now)—but we are very puzzled. □□

The Legend of Peter Rugg

by Lewis A. Taft

Illustration by Margo Letourneau

When lightning splits the night and rumbling thunder rolls across the valley, you'll see them in their carriage on the back roads. Peter Rugg and his daughter, gaining fast—she, clutching her father's arm—he, pulling on the reins of his great bay whose eyes, it's said, glow like fire coals of hell . . .

———————◆•◆•◼———————

Tom Cutter of Menotomy (now West Cambridge) was the last person to see Peter Rugg alive. There is no doubt that Tom saw and spoke to Rugg that evening, and that Peter was very much alive at the time. Ghosts or apparitions are not noted for striking people on the nose and that evening Peter Rugg, in one of his frequent fits of temper, struck Cutter on his proboscis hard enough to draw blood.

The story begins a few years before the Revolution. At that time, Peter Rugg lived in a large, comfortable house on Middle Street, Boston. He was a horse and cattle dealer, had a diligent wife, a lovely young daughter and was considered to be a good citizen by most of his neighbors. However, he possessed a fiendish temper that overruled his judgment whenever he became angry.

One day late in the Fall, Rugg harnessed his horse, a large Roman-nosed bay, and hitched it up to a light carriage for a business trip to Concord. It was a fine day so he took his little daughter along for company. When they were returning to Boston that afternoon, a violent thunderstorm overtook them. Peter stopped at Tom Cutter's place in Menotomy for a dram of hot, spiced rum and his host urged him to spend the night there. In fact, Mr. Cutter, who had already had a few drams of rum, became very insistent,—so insistent that Peter's hot temper began to boil.

"Don't be a fool, Rugg," Tom Cutter said. "Night will soon be here and this pelting rain could be the death of your daughter. Can you not see that the storm is increasing in violence?"

"Let the storm increase," roared Rugg, "I will see home tonight in spite of storm or the Devil or may I never see home."

Peter raised the whip to his horse but his host grabbed his arm. That was when Tom Cutter received a punch in the nose from his irascible friend. Peter Rugg, his daughter, carriage, horse and all disappeared that night.

A week went by before the authorities, goaded into action by the frantic insistence of Mrs. Rugg, instituted a sharp search but not a trace of the missing cattle dealer or his daughter was found.

Time went on, however, and the snows of winter came and then gave way to the warm breezes of Spring. Then Peter Rugg was seen on Middle Street.

It was late one night in May when the householders of Middle Street were awakened by the clatter and rattling of a conveyance, traveling rapidly over the uneven cobbles. Thomas Felt, the gunsmith, leaned out of his window to see who could be traveling at such an unseemly hour. Looking up the street, Felt saw a carriage rapidly approaching, and seated in the rig were Peter Rugg and his daughter. The lateness of the hour, the effects of a dampening rain and the sight of a phosphorescent glow that appeared to envelop the conveyance and its occupants, gave the gunsmith such a turn that a chill shook his lean frame and his teeth began to chatter.

The next day Felt told his neighbors of the appearance of Peter Rugg and his account quickly became the leading topic of conversation on the street. They were careful, however, to say nothing to Mrs. Rugg.

The good neighbors again initiated a search for the missing man and his daughter and this time several people were found who claimed to have seen them, but always under strange circumstances.

The toll-gatherer at the Charleston Bridge claimed that several times (always in a rainstorm) he had seen Peter Rugg driving his carriage over the bridge at a furious clip, his daughter holding onto his arm while the bay horse seemed to enjoy the racing pace. Every time, the toll-gatherer had been unable to collect his fee. Once, as the rig rolled by, the angry tender threw his stool at the horse. To his horror and amazement, he saw the stool go through the animal and bounce off the guard rail on the other side of the bridge.

A sea captain, who had arrived from Providence on the stage, claimed that a man resembling Rugg stopped the coach and asked the direction to Boston. The man, his carriage and a little girl seated beside him were dripping wet even though it was a cloudless day. After receiving directions, the man thanked the stage driver and took off at a swift pace toward Boston. Shortly afterwards, a fast-traveling thunderstorm overtook the coach and everyone was soaked.

After these testimonials, the search for the missing cattle dealer was abandoned. But the stories of the appearances of Peter Rugg in various localities of New England still continued.

At the turn of the century, the publisher of a Boston newspaper became interested in the many stories of Peter Rugg and asked an itinerant tin pedlar if he had ever seen the man.

"Aye! That I have!" the pedlar answered sourly. "I was unfortunate enough to see the man and his carriage within a fortnight, in four different states and each time I was shortly afterwards visited by heavy thunderstorms. If I meet them once more, I shall be forced to take out marine insurance on my wares."

The newspaperman next interviewed Adonariah Adams, the veteran driver of the Portland Mail. He was a fat genial man who usually beamed upon the world with a friendly smile but he looked disturbed when the question was put to him.

"Yes! I have seen Peter Rugg," he admitted reluctantly. "One day after we drove through Newburyport, I noticed thunderheads in the southern sky and whipped the horses into a trot. Ahead of us, heavy streaks of lightning flashed across the horizon and I realized that we were in for a nasty tempest. We ascended Witch-Hang Hill at a fast clip and as we reached the top, something compelled me to look back. There I saw Peter Rugg's carriage tearing after us and gaining fast. My horses took fright and began to run at a desperate and dangerous pace but Rugg's great beast steadily gained until he was racing neck and neck with my wheel-horses. Suddenly, a bolt of lightning struck the Rugg conveyance. In the instantaneous flash, I saw Peter and his daughter glowing with fire like a horseshoe as it is taken from the blacksmith's hearth. At the same time, flames and sparks cascaded from the mouth and ears of the huge bay horse and I was almost stifled by the odor of brimstone, yet the bolt seemed to have no effect on the creature for the carriage continued on. My horses were so frightened that they leaped from the road, wrecking the coach against a boulder." The driver of the Portland Mail shook his head slowly.

"It is my opinion," he vouchsafed, "that what I saw was the Devil's shade of Peter Rugg."

The last story concerning the appearance of Peter Rugg came from Rhode Island several years later.

An itinerant preacher, the Rev. Samuel Nickles, after a fortnight spent in the village of Wickford, packed his meager belongings, with the exception of his Bible, in the saddlebag, mounted his aged, near-sighted horse and departed for Providence. His worthy steed was blessed with the name of Romeo, a misnomer if there ever was one.

According to the story, this aged Pegasus and his master were caught in a fierce thunderstorm as they neared Quonset. There was no shelter so the Pastor hunched his shoulders under his dripping coat, bowed his head and let his horse set the pace. The road skirted a large sloping rock and narrowed as it passed between two sandy hillocks. As Romeo plodded into the narrows, the Rev. Mr. Nickles heard the sound of a fast approaching carriage. When the startled man looked up, he saw a rig racing toward him at a terrific pace. On the seat, a pale frightened man pulled on the reins while a girl held to his coat with

both hands. The horse drawing the carriage was a huge, Roman-nosed bay whose eyes, in the misty half-light, shone like live coals.

In the narrows, there was not enough room to avoid a collision. The frantic Romeo lunged up on his hind legs, flinging his rider through the air where he described a complete somersault and landed astride the huge bay.

"Stop! Stop!" the Pastor shouted in terror.

Instantly, a great bolt of lightning struck the ground nearby. The bay let out a neighing that was not of this world and dashed up the sloping sides of the rock outcropping, tossing the Rev. Mr. Nickles unconscious, to the ground.

When the unfortunate man regained consciousness, he was lying at the base of the rock, Romeo was nibbling grass nearby, the storm was over and the sun was again shining brightly. Staggering to his feet, he saw a set of cloven hoof tracks burned into the hard surface of the rock. Hastily mounting Romeo, the Pastor left the vicinity as fast as his steed would travel.

Later, the Rev. Mr. Nickles told of his encounter to several congregations in New England and many curious folks traveled to Quonset to see the cloven hoof tracks in the solid rock. To this day, the phenomenon beside Route #1 near Quonset, is called "Devil's Foot Rock."

Although the stories of Peter Rugg were told and retold for many years after the Quonset affair, it is a strange fact that never again was he or his carriage reported to have been seen in New England. □□

[95]

The True Nature of New Milford's Talking Stove

by Dale Hartford

Illustrations by Mel Crawford

In September of 1930, New Milford, Conn., experienced the presence of what appeared to be a <u>bona fide</u> ghost. The phenomenon attracted writers, spiritualists, clergy, and simply the curious from all over the country. It was described in newspapers around the world! After ten days, the ghostly voice ceased and since then no explanation of it has ever come forth
—until now.

"Hawk left a trail of yelps and onions behind him as he headed into Young's Field."

It was after midnight when Hawk Palardy trudged up the alleyway in back of the New Milford Restaurant, entered the rickety storage shed and began collecting an armful of onions.

Suddenly an eerie voice broke the stillness of the night:

"Hawk, can you hear me? Hey, Hawk, can you hear me?"

For brief seconds Hawk stood transfixed, blinking his eyes against the darkness, vainly attempting to locate the voice.

"Hey, Hawk, come on down!" repeated the voice, in a hollow, inhuman inflection.

Gangling Hawk Palardy bolted through the door, sending onions scurrying on their separate paths as he raced down the alleyway and across the railroad tracks into nearby Young's Field.

It was September, 1930, and the famous New Milford Ghost had made its first appearance.

Perhaps it was the Crash of '29 that created the strange mixture of skepticism and spiritualism which enveloped New Milford, Connecticut, a year later. Whatever the cause, the mood was hospitable to a band of wandering spirits—or was there only one?

Old Charlie Hoffman was surely a believer. For years on end he sat in the dilapidated train depot, sending and receiving the telegraph messages which called and sent lumbering freight trains through the town.

But late into each night, long after sign-off time, Charlie continued his work, painstakingly recording a detailed Life of George Washington which came to him on a second, disconnected receiver. A fairy tale? Obviously . . . except to those living witnesses who today recall with clarity the unexplainable clickety-clicks of that wireless machine, which Charlie often slipped into his pocket like a pack of cigarettes.

And Charlie's friend, Luke, was another believer.

Late at night he would be admitted, one of a chosen few, into the ill-lit center of the depot. Often his face was bloodless, his eyes enlarged, his voice and body shaking.

Charlie would softly ask, "What's the matter, Luke—did you see your father tonight?"

"I . . . I was coming down to the depot," came the hesitant reply, "and he walked right by me. But he wouldn't speak to me." No wonder he was shaken. His father had been dead for 10 years.

Hawk Palardy's rapid exit from the old wooden storage shed was not unnoticed, despite the hour. The New Milford Restaurant was operated in those days by Gus the Greek (Gus Jones to some, but really Gus Ghiones), and it sat on the north end of Railroad Street, which unlike today was alive with workers and drifters and railroad men in need of coffee and camaraderie. Gus rarely closed his doors before 3 a.m. The tailor, Mario Garcia, only three doors away, often was cutting his carefully made suits until the same hour. The town and the street were alive; what better pastime than conversing with the dead?

Hawk left a trail of yelps and onions behind him as he headed into Young's Field. His close friend, Jack Comstock, savoring a cup of Gus's fine coffee, heard the commotion and hurried to the door in time to witness his friend's odd performance.

Quieted finally, Hawk was led into Gus's, where he told his tale of the strange voice calling to him. Hawk was a fun-loving, emotional man. Now he was frightened. But his story fell on disbelieving ears.

Still the tale spread throughout the village, causing a few chuckles over the dinner table the following night and a good deal of scoffing among Hawk's many friends.

But the following night, when Gus told his young helper and fellow immigrant, Tommy, to go up to the shed and peel potatoes for the following day, he was met by sullen reluctance. Caught up by the fanciful tale of the odd voice in the night, more men than usual were crowded into Gus's small eatery. It took their collective prodding before young Tom grabbed his shiny bowl and with a display of indifference went out into the black night.

"Gabriel Heatter broadcast to millions [and] suddenly New Milford's ghost was being discussed by Russians and Englishmen, as well as Californians and New Yorkers."

A half-hour after beginning his task, Tom was relaxing. One potato after another plopped into his bowl; his work was nearly done. Then came a plaintive plea:

"Help, help!" intoned the hollow voice. "I'm buried 40 feet underground. Help! Help!"

Tommy didn't hear that last call for help. Younger by a dozen years than Hawk Palardy, he set an all-time record for getting down that alleyway.

The men in Gus's buzzed and murmured into the morning hours. Many were sure the voice was a prank. They wanted to be in on it. Others were skeptical but unknowing. A few felt a ghostly presence, including Tom, who swore in his heavy accent that never again would he set foot in the old shed.

Next day New Milford sizzled with the story, and it was enriched as it passed from mouth to mouth. By two in the afternoon, Gus counted 120 people—men, women, and children—in front of his restaurant and jammed into the narrow, 30-yard-long alley. He viewed their presence with both nervousness and pleasure. So many people—they might cause trouble. But they got hungry milling about and business had never been so good. That was for sure.

Many in the crowd ventured into the tiny wooden shed, and in daylight inspected its wares. An old pot-bellied stove. Shelves filled with tomatoes and preserves. Sacks of potatoes and onions. And that was all.

Late in the afternoon the voice spoke again, and a wave of apprehension swept through the crowd. A lady bending by the stove heard what appeared to be an infant's cry. Promptly she swooned and had to be carried through the throng. But others took her place.

The cry became a discernible voice. The infant, between gasps, reported it was buried in the cellar of a Kent home, some 14 miles away. And then it became silent.

The message was charged like an electric bolt. Derisive cries were heard: "Tear down the shed! It's a hoax!" But many more stood in wonder and awe, and the few did not move against the many.

Fearful that it would become party to a prank, the local *New Milford Times* treated the story gingerly in its first report. Some "radio-minded men," it said, felt the voice was being heard "because of some electrical phenomena. They were all of the opinion that the stove served as an antenna and receiver, it being of metallic composition with properties similar to radio tubes."

The *Times* admitted that a "great majority felt the infant's appeal was genuine."

While the newspaper refused to heat up the story with detailed reporting, an enterprising employee (and son of the owner) tossed considerable fuel on the flame.

Diminutive Harry Worley, as enterprising today as he was nearly 40 years ago, fulfilled his responsibilities as a "stringer" for the three major wire services by letting them in on the story. They were skeptical, he remembers, but nonetheless they flashed the yarn across the country, and later, around the world.

Harry Worley did not stop there. He placed calls to all the New York City newspapers and had lengthy talks with their reporters. He repeated the tale for Gabriel Heatter and heard the substance of his remarks broadcast to millions the following night.

Suddenly New Milford's ghost was being discussed by Russians and Englishmen as well as Californians and New Yorkers. Harry Worley—collector of clippings extraordinary—had done his work well.

At the end of his first week in town, the ghostly voice was attracting science fiction and mystery writers from throughout the country, reaching the village of 5,000 by plane, train, and car. Charlie Hoffman sent off urgent dispatches to eminent spiritualists in Chicago and New Orleans, and was informed that they were on their way.

Nuns came two-by-two and four-by-four, followed by priests and the clergy of all faiths. "I thought it was going to become another Lourdes," says Harry Worley, pronouncing it "Lord-ees." Obviously he had not been dismayed by the prospect.

Law enforcement officers of every rank and reputation came to town, intent on solving the mystery. In the tenth day of the voice, a long black Packard limousine pulled into Railroad Street, discharging six uniformed New York City policemen. They studied, probed, investigated, then left at day's end still unknowing.

Gus the Greek agonized in his dilemma. Now when he looked out from his tiny restaurant he saw a throng of a thousand people packed into Railroad Street, all intent on visiting his woodshed. The crowd included rowdies and troublemakers and fist-fights between believers and non-believers became common. The lame and the halt prayed for recovery in front of his old time-worn stove, the women fainted with increasing regularity, and still the crowds came. Should he demand of the army of police on the scene that they close the alley to the public, and

"*For several days Gus and his crew had been making $1000 a day feeding the hungry mob.*"

return order to the street?

But for several days Gus and his hard-working crew had been making the fabulous sum of $1,000 a day, feeding the hungry mob. One does not turn off such a bountiful faucet with a simple twist. The agony, Gus decided, was worth it.

The ghostly voice, meanwhile, did its work well. It could, by the tenth day, be heard at all hours, and few visitors to the shed left without hearing its intonations. Generally it had now been dubbed "the talking stove," and its messages varied.

Most often it continued to be the infant entombed in the cellar of a Kent home. Harassed Kent officials refused to order a cellar-by-cellar search, but they reported that "all infants in this community are accounted for." No check on the cellars was made.

Then the voice became George Thatcher, a Negro worker murdered in that very alley 25 years before. Mournful pleas for retribution issued from the old stove, as the ghost of Thatcher called upon the listeners to find his murderer.

Another time the voice became a famous Indian chief; still again it was an unnamed man buried deep in a nearby well. To hundreds and even thousands of people the stove became a medium for communication with the world beyond, and they flocked to it with their urgent requests and pleas for salvation.

As the voices began their second week, worry lines on the faces of officials grew deeper, New Milford's Railroad Street mob threatened to get out of control. State police were assigned to the area around the clock, and all special constables in the town were actively employed along with the local police.

Monday night of the second week, over 40 men were huddled together in the tiny woodshed, when all lights in the area suddenly went out just as a tortured voice issued from the stove. There was a mad scramble for the door, and in the melee men fell and were cut and bruised, clothing was ripped, and a ripple of panic shivered through those hundreds in the alleyway and on the street.

Still the carnival of uncertainty went on. By the middle of the second week, an estimated 3,000 people were in town to hear the fabled voice. Included were an array of hucksters and promoters, intent on making quick gain from the turmoil.

New York City reporters and others from throughout the East were intent on solving the riddle. One, from the *New York Daily News*, walked into Garcia's tailor shop and laid a fat roll of bills on the counter.

"Tell me what's going on, and it's yours," said the newsman.

"I don't know a thing," said Mario, pushing the bills away.

Another promoter offered Gus a "fabulous sum" for his restaurant, and when that offer was refused, he begged the Greek to sell him the concession to the famous woodshed. Gus shook his head.

A reporter for the *Bridgeport Herald* finally got Gus to agree, for $100, to let him dig a three-foot ditch around the shed, but when the work was three-quarters done, Gus made him stop.

"Thatsa nough of these. You bringa too many people. Get off my property." And he handed back the $100 to the reporter.

Two days later, the population of New Milford had doubled and still the ghostly voice talked on. Sleepless Gus Ghiones was besieged by crackpots and law officials. The bizarre situation, he agreed, was finally getting out of hand.

In marched a cordon of police officers. The alleyway was cleared. Even as the voice continued to lament its state, the doors to the shed were nailed shut and barricaded. Another barricade was placed at the foot of the alley, and stern signs warned that trespassers would be severely prosecuted.

"The ghost has gone away," officials told the mob. "It will never be heard again. Go back to your homes."

It took several days for the mob to disperse, but slowly a semblance of normalcy returned to Railroad Street. The curious still plied Gus the Greek with questions, but to no avail. Months later, most minds had turned to other thoughts. The ghost was gone, without explanation, just as it had come. With the passing of time, as the story went from old-timers to newcomers, from parents to children, it was often suggested it had all been a marvelous hoax.

But was it really? And, if so, how had it been done? Nobody could really say for sure.

Now, nearly 40 years after the fact, the nature of New Milford's ghost—beautiful in its simplicity—can publicly be reported for the first time.

Most of those responsible for creating the spirit are still living. Some, if asked, may vigorously deny the following account. But too many intimately involved in the affair have agreed to the facts to deny its credibility.

New Milford's ghostly voice was, first of all, an accident.

At one time the little woodshed behind the restaurant had housed a refrigerator. Electricians had run a wire cable underground from the shed into the restaurant.

Purchase of a new, larger refrigerator, placed in the restaurant itself, caused Gus the Greek to sell the old unit, and at the time it was disconnected the electricians removed the wire from the cable—but not the cable itself. Purely by happenstance, the old stove was placed over the tiny opening in the shed leading to the marvelously conductive cable, providing amazingly effective camouflage.

Hawk Palardy was not an employee of the restaurant, but like many others he often, late at night, offered a helping hand when needed. He was performing such a favor on the night when he went to the shed to gather onions.

Soon after Hawk left the restaurant, the night chef—oldtimers believe his name was Nick, but no one is quite sure—remembered that he also needed more hamburger meat, as well as onions. He suddenly remembered the small cable opening which entered his kitchen just behind his stove. He wondered, half aloud, whether the cable would carry his voice.

So he bent over the stove and shouted:

"Hawk, can you hear me? Hey, Hawk, can you hear me?"

And the New Milford ghost was born.

Fun-loving Hawk Palardy was a principal in perpetuating the stunt. He knew first-hand how eerie the voice sounded. Gus the Greek, after that first experience, shortly told Hawk where the voice had come from —and Palardy instantly recognized the potential for deviltry.

It was Palardy and several others—in all, perhaps a dozen men were finally in on the ruse—who discreetly kept the ghost alive during the first days. But the mobs drawn to the scene, poking about, made it impossible to communicate through the cable without being discovered. The kitchen was simply too accessible.

At three o'clock in the morning on the fourth day, a half-dozen men met secretly to consider their creation. One was a night watchman whose keychain proved vital to the plot that was finally hatched. Another was a plumber and another a telephone man. All talents were needed.

Working in the quietest hours of night, they extended the cable through three adjacent stores, ending in the small men's room in Garcia's Tailor Shop. Six keys were distributed, and six voices played on the nerves of thousands for another 10 days. Of the six, only Hawk Palardy is no longer living. The others have never been named. It would be pointless to do so now. □□

Block Island's Fiery Ghost

by Noel Powell

For still, on many a moonless night,
From Kingston Head and from Montauk Light
The spectre kindles and burns in sight.

Now low and dim, now clear and higher,
Leaps up the terrible ghost of fire,
Then, slowly sinking, the flames expire.

J.G.W.

John Greenleaf Whittier, in 1865, wrote his long narrative poem, "The Palatine," in which he revived a tale long buried in the lore of Colonial New England and set aflame a controversy which still rages on the Island which he immortalized. For the legend of the Palatine Light is a strange and eerie one and was once so widely credited that historians recorded it, and scientists still seek to explain it.

Eleven miles off the deeply indented coast of Rhode Island, Block Island stands, rugged and rolling, guarding the entrance to Long Island Sound. With its towering bluffs, its soft green hills, its many lakes and broad white beaches, the Island (which the Indians called by the "gently flowing" name, Manisees) was settled in 1661 by sixteen families from the Massachusetts Colony. They came to farm the lush fields and to fish for the tuna, the blues and the swordfish in the surrounding waters. It was a plentiful life and, once an accord had been reached with the Indians, a pleasant one. But beyond the beaches stretched dangerous shoals which caused so many wrecks that the Island came to be known ominously as the "Graveyard of the Atlantic." And the Islanders, "God-fearing Christians and Baptists all," soon learned to set signal fires in some quiet cove or on a sandy beach and many distressed ships were brought safely ashore and many lives saved by their bravery.

But in the middle years of the 18th Century a strange rumour, widely believed by sea-faring men, swept the southern coast of New England. A "great irradiance" was said to arise from the open sea north of Block Island and, gaining in brilliance, take the form of a "flaming ship." After several minutes, the ship sank slowly into the sea. The sight was first noted officially by the Captain of the Somerset, an English trading vessel, who wrote in the ship's log that, "I was so distressed by the sight that we followed the burning ship to its watery grave but failed to find survivors or flotsam."

In the years that followed, the irradiance was seen by so many people that, so one rumour goes, the Colonial Governor of Rhode Island decided to send an emissary to the Island to discover, if possible, the truth. This gentleman is said to have become enthralled with the bland climate and so intrigued with the friendliness and hospitality of the Block Islanders, that he lingered overlong. It is, of course, quite possible that, in his desire to justify his absence, he repaid that friendliness and hospitality with a tale so weird and frightening that from it grew the beginning of the Legend. For this was his story:

One stormy December night, several years before, a ship was seen to be in trouble in the waters north of the Island. The usual alarm was sent out to the farms and, while some set about making preparations for the rescue, another group were sent to light the traditional signal fires. But the latter, "overcome by greed and avarice," set the fires, not in a safe and sandy cove, but on a rocky point and led the ship to its doom. After all but one of the passengers, "a mad woman who had hidden herself away," had been brought to shore and the valuable cargo removed, the Islanders are said to have set the ship afire and afloat. As it sailed westward into the night, the screams and pleas of the lone passenger could be plainly heard while, the tale continues, "the guilty stood in terror."

The story lost nothing in the retelling; many accounts were set down in early history and fiction. But it was Whittier's poem, written a century later, which gave it the widest renown and which has lived ever since to plague and annoy the good people of the maligned Island.

Through the years Island historians, the best known of whom was the Reverend S. T. Livermore, tried to establish the true story of the wrecking of a ship called the *Palatine*. Dr. Livermore wrote that a ship of that name was swept ashore on the "Hummock," at the north end of the Island, sometime in the middle of the Eighteenth Century. It was a Dutch ship which had sailed from the German Palatinate "bearing wealthy Dutch and German merchants to their new home in Philadelphia." For many weeks the *Palatine* was delayed by storms and, as food grew scarce and no happy end of the voyage seemed in sight, great unrest arose among the crew. Then, as "a sudden calm came upon the sea," land appeared and the crew mutinied, killed the Captain, robbed the ill and starving passengers, took to the long boats and left the hapless ship to drift for many days. Then, Dr. Livermore continues, "the kind and God-fearing Block Islanders rescued the passengers, some twenty in number, and bore them with great gentleness to the farm of Mr. Simon Ray." There they were "tenderly nursed and a few survived." Those that died were buried on the Ray farm and the "Palatine graves," carefully marked on the Island's maps, are still to be seen.

Dr. Livermore makes no mention of the fate of the ship but, in his *18th Century History of Rhode Island*, Samuel Greene Arnold, after recounting the tale in great detail, says that "the *Palatine* floated off the Island and away, never to be heard from again." He concludes by mentioning "a curious illumination which rose from the waters to the north of the Island" and says "the appearance of this light was considered supernatural and, from its supposed connection with the mysterious crime that

[108]

involved the ill-fated ship, came to be known as the Palatine Light."

For all its contradictions and "supernatural" connotations the story of the Palatine Light has continued down through the years and even scientists have sought some reasonable explanation. Mr. Edward Snow, in his book on Atlantic Island lore, attributed the phenomena to the presence of a "school of menhaden" and Mr. Walter Johnson, of the U.S. Geological Bureau, suggests that the light might be caused by gas escaping from vast deposits below the ocean floor; gas which, on reaching the surface, would ignite.

So many explanations, historical and scientific! But what is one to think when one has met, as this writer has, the only living Islander who has seen the Palatine Light? In a snug, comfortable home tucked away on the Island's dramatically towering Mohegan Bluffs, lives, with her sea-captain husband, an intelligent, soft-spoken woman in late middle life. Quietly and seriously she tells of how, when a young girl living on the north shore of the Island, she was awakened one night by her parents and saw, for several awe-struck moments, a flaming ship which "rounded the point" and disappeared beneath the waves.

The Legend of the Palatine Light!

Legend? □□

Newburyport's Haunted Schoolhouse

by Ned Brown

—After an old Illustration—by Effie Berry

*It doesn't take much to distract a young student from his lessons
—certainly not the best efforts of Newburyport's most
bell-ringing, stool-rattling, door-knocking, wind-blowing
ghost on record . . .*

No one ever knew the real story of Newburyport's famous haunted schoolhouse of the early 1870's.

Amos Currier was said to have boasted in later years that he was responsible for all of the eerie doings which terrified teacher and pupils in the little one-room building on Charles Street; but no schoolboy could have been responsible for the more baffling phenomena recalled.

The school board held inquisitions and columns of reports were printed about them; but some things which happened would have baffled even the most astute of today's sophisticated scientists.

You can read exhaustively about the haunted school in the yellowing files of local newspapers in the public library; but a compact account is preserved in a "tract" published by Loring of Boston and selling for twenty cents a copy. Unusual news stories of the time were frequently given this journalistic treatment and pamphlets could be bought at book shops and newsdealers.

The little pitched-roof building, locale of soul-shuddering incidents, was described as drab in color, with green blinds, "and not in the best condition outwardly."

The door posts were soiled, the weather boards were scratched, characteristic of many school buildings, and a broken fence bordered the bare yard.

The entryway and classroom were described as close and stuffy, with the familiar scent of southern pine that haunts the nostrils of those who attended the humbler schools of the era.

There was said to have been nothing peculiar about the rude classroom; no niches to give echoes, no mirrors to refract the light; no closets where one could be secreted; and no objects outside the windows near enough to cast shadows within.

It was a primary school for boys, with seats for about sixty pupils, a raised platform for the teacher's desk, and chairs for a few visitors.

As far back as 1870, people became cognizant of disturbances in the Charles Street School. It was reported that certain unaccountable sounds had taken place from time to time, but the incidents attained no prominence in the community because of their rather common character.

While the children were murmuring their morning prayers, a thundering knock would sound on the floor; then it would come upon the wall, then near the teacher's desk. On one occasion the sounds were so rapid and powerful that the teacher could not hear the children recite their lessons.

One child was spelling the word "cannot." He pronounced the letters c-a-n, but the noise which had been going on for such a long time suddenly increased, and the voice was completely drowned. The teacher could see the boy's lips moving, but could hear nothing.

A day or two later a series of raps was heard on the outer door. The teacher went to admit the expected visitor. She found no one; closed the door and locked it. The raps were instantly repeated. The teacher returned to the door, but found no one.

Then the phenomena became all the more inexplicable.

In an open space, in front of the pupils' desks was a tubular stove. It had a cover which could be raised by a wire handle. The handle was at times seized, as though by invisible fingers, and raised upright, and the cover was lifted bodily several inches above the burning coals; and after keeping its position in mid-air for some minutes, it was lowered again and restored to its place. The janitor of the building, an ordinarily courageous man, finally refused to enter the building in the morning, unaccompanied, saying "the noises and disturbances were too much for him."

He often found the stove moved from its position, the utensils scattered in various places, and the fuel disarranged.

Upon the teacher's desk there were two bells, one smaller than the other. Frequently the lighter was seized by the unseen power, raised from its ledge, and rung violently before the eyes of the pupils. The schoolroom was ventilated by means of a circular hole in the ceiling, closed by a wooden valve, which could be raised or lowered by means of a cord descending from the garret. It was a trick of the rogue to shut the valve when it was supposed to be open—and open it when it was supposed to be shut.

Surely not the prank of any schoolboy or adult was the phenomenon of the strange light. At times the whole schoolroom was illuminated, while the school was in session, by a strong yellow glow, which on dark days had proceeded from the entry and entered through a partition window.

In the midst of storms, when the sky was heavily overcast and the school was almost lost in gloom and obscurity, "a soft and equal radiance" stole over the scene and lighted up the farthest corner of the apartment.

This is nothing that can be ignored and treated with brave indifference. Over the faces of the pupils, who had put aside their books because of the darkness, there suddenly began to creep this terrible light. There was no burning focus; the appearance was described as an "illuminated exhalation."

Further, the schoolhouse was often attacked by powerful currents of air that arose, suddenly at times, when the atmosphere was entirely at rest.

At times there appeared to arise a great storm outside, as billows of air appeared to rush upon the building and to sweep about it with all the vigor of a tempest. The joists creaked, the eaves moaned, and the chimney became an organ pipe.

The teacher, Miss Lucy Perkins, who endured all of this, was, fortunately, not a sensitive soul. Twenty-three years old, angular, with a strong frame, she was not easily frightened.

Sometimes she bid the children sing. To drive away their disturbing fancies, they would break out, in their high-pitched, unmusical voices, with: "Here we stand, hand in hand."

Miss Perkins underwent a firm and rigid examination on the part of school authorities. The schoolboys were bribed and threatened. It was said that Oliver Wendell Holmes had tried his hand at teasing a confession of trickery from the Currier boy by means of a dollar bill. But he failed.

The school committee was initially reluctant to give color to the case by taking notice of it. There was agitation to close the school, even to remove the building. Some pupils were withdrawn. Others threatened to leave. By 1875 the disturbances had ceased and the school was used for some time after that.

The school was long ago remodeled as a house, and the family of Joseph F. Garand lives at 32 Charles Street today.

Joe says everything is serene. ☐☐

Boston's Lady in Black

by Edward Rowe Snow

Edward Rowe Snow, who successfully led the campaign to preserve Fort Warren, tells about the real Lady in Black —whose ghost has appeared to visitors of the Fort on 28 occasions!

Part of the garrison at Ft. Warren in 1862. The author feels that the woman in the upper right is very possibly the Lady in Black, herself!

Possibly the greatest unsolved mystery in New England history which includes ghosts and mystic connotations involves a girl who arrived in Boston Harbor from Crawfordville, Georgia, during the Civil War. Her name was Mrs. Andrew Lanier.

Andrew Lanier was a young Southern soldier. When called away to fight for the South in the Civil War, he hurried to the home of his intended. He asked that a quick war-time marriage be arranged, as he would soon leave for what might prove to be the duration of the conflict. After a moment of reflection, she agreed and the ceremony took place on June 28, 1861. Within forty-eight hours he departed for battle.

A few months later, Lanier was captured and sent with many other Southern soldiers to the Northern Bastille in the middle of Boston Harbor known as Fort Warren.

The fortification, located on George's Island, seven miles out to sea from the City of Boston, had a prison which was known as the Corridor of Dungeons. After a week in the Corridor of Dungeons, Andrew decided to write a letter to his bride. He told her of his capture, the location of his incarceration, and ended the letter with endearing words of his deep love and terrible loneliness.

Passed through the battle lines, the letter was eventually received by the girl. On learning of her husband's fate, she determined to leave her pleasant home, travel to Massachusetts, get to Fort Warren and, in some way, free her husband.

Mrs. Lanier got in touch with a blockade runner who agreed to take her up the coast. She then obtained a suit of men's clothes and an old pepper box pistol, after which Mrs. Lanier had her hair cut short. Two-and-a-half months later, the blockade runner set the "young man" ashore at Cape Cod. There she stayed in the home of a Southerner, and a week later she had established herself in Hull, Massachusetts, at the house of another Southern sympathizer. Now less than a mile away from George's Island, for the next few days she studied the fort through a telescope until she had entirely familiarized herself with the section of the bastion which held the famous Corridor of Dungeons.

On the first stormy night, January 15, 1862, when the rain was coming down with such driving force that it obscured all vision, Mrs. Lanier's Southern host rowed her across to the island and left her on the beach.

Crouching on the shore, she watched the two nearest sentries, soaked to the skin, methodically patrolling their posts. They strode slowly and automatically toward each other, and then, turning on their heels, walked slowly away. She estimated that there was almost a minute and a half after they turned when she could run between them.

Watching alertly, Mrs. Lanier grasped the bundle which held her pistol and a short-handled pick. At the exact moment when the two men began to walk in opposite directions, she stole toward the spot where they had met. A minute later she had reached a hiding place in a tangle of shrubbery a short distance from them. She lay there in the rain until they came back. They met and walked off again, back to back. Then she rose quickly and scrambled over the cover-face outside the bastion where her husband was imprisoned. Except for the sentries some distance away, the entire fort seemed asleep.

Standing there alone, she recalled a tune which she and her husband had used to signal to each other. She began to whistle it, softly at first and gradually louder. There was no answer. Could it be that her husband had been transferred to another Yankee prison since she had received his letter? A score of possibilities flashed through her mind.

She decided to risk everything by giving a final, shrill, piercing whistle. When she had finished she threw herself down on the banking. There was complete silence for several minutes, but finally an answering whistle came from within the fort. Looking up cautiously at the walls of the bastion, she noticed that there were narrow slits in the stone some distance above her. From one of these slits a rope of cloth emerged and dropped lower and lower until she could grasp the end.

"Hang on," cried a voice, and a moment later she had been pulled up, bundle and all, to the seven-inch slit in the granite wall. Several hands lifted her up so that she could squeeze through the tiny aperture. Soon she was in the arms of her husband.

A short time later, hurried conferences were held among the six hundred Confederate prisoners inside the Corridor of Dungeons. With the arrival of the girl and the short-handled pick, they saw the chance they had been waiting for. Instead of digging a tunnel out of the fort and escaping aboard the schooner which Southern sympathizers would provide, they decided upon a bolder idea.

They would tunnel from one of the dungeons located at an outer corner of the bastion and dig toward the inner part of the fort. They planned to come up under the parade ground, where they could break into the arsenal, arm themselves, capture the small garrison of eighty Union soldiers, and take over the fort. Then they would climb up on the parapets, turn the 248 guns of Fort Warren against Boston and besiege the city. This plan, they believed in their enthusiasm, would change the entire course of the Civil War, and victory for the South would be assured.

Beginning work on the tunnel before the guards arrived for the morning check-up, the prisoners piled earth in front of the tunnel's mouth in the dungeon. Whenever the guards appeared a group of prisoners sat down on the fresh earth, completely concealing the tunnel from view.

As the weeks went by, the tunnel was lengthened and its direction was plotted and replotted. The earth they dug was laboriously carried back into the Corridor of Dungeons by the prisoners, who used their shirts and jackets as containers. Each windy night they threw the dirt out of the narrow slits in the walls of the bastion. Finally, those who were engineering the project believed that the tunnel had reached a point between the granite wall of the fort and the center of the parade ground.

The next night the prisoners were to make the final upward thrust toward the surface of the parade ground. At one o'clock in the morning, a young lieutenant swung the pick vigorously against the top of the tunnel. The pick went through the earth and smashed against the granite wall of the keep which is inside the parade ground. The plotters had miscalculated.

Unfortunately, one of the sentries guarding the area heard the sharp sound of the pick below and suspected what had happened. He shouted a warning to the next sentry, who passed the word down the line to the guardhouse. The sergeant in charge visited the scene and heard the sentry's story. Immediately the entire fort was on the alert.

At that time, the commanding officer of Fort Warren was Colonel Justin E. Dimmock of Marblehead, veteran artillery expert, who was formerly in charge of Fortress Monroe. Ten minutes after the sentry

[117]

Above: Just seven nautical miles from downtown Boston, George's Island and its historic fort (arrow points to the spot where Mrs. Lanier joined her imprisoned husband) have become a popular summer tourist attraction. Opposite page: Caretaker Andrew J. Sweeney and "Lady" walk into dungeon which once held the Lady in Black.

heard the suspicious noise on the parade ground, Colonel Dimmock made a surprise visit to the Corridor of Dungeons. There he caught several of the prisoners scattering dirt outside the walls.

One by one the Southerners were taken out into the dry moat, until the Corridor of Dungeons appeared completely empty. But eleven prisoners were missing when roll call was taken. A careful examination of the corner dungeon revealed the opening of the tunnel.

Colonel Dimmock shouted down to those in the shaft. "You have failed, so you might as well come out and surrender."

The unhappy Southerners crawled out of the tunnel, all except Lanier and his wife. After a few words with her husband, the girl decided to make a final attempt for freedom. Her plan was for her young soldier husband to crawl out and quietly surrender. Afterwards, they hoped, the guards would count the prisoners. Finding them all accounted for, the guards might relax their vigilance. The wife would then appear behind the Union soldiers, cock her pistol, and order them to surrender. It was a radical plan, born of desperation.

The young husband emerged from the tunnel. The guards counted the prisoners, found that they were all present, and began moving the last of the Southern prisoners to a new place of confinement. Colonel Dimmock announced that in the morning the tunnel would be filled up and sealed off with cement. Then, just as the prisoners were leaving the dungeons, the girl sprang out of the tunnel and ordered the guards to surrender.

"I've a pistol and I know how to use it," she shouted.

Colonel Dimmock thought quickly. He advanced slowly towards

[118]

the girl, his hands raised in surrender. Slowly his men followed him, forming a circle around her. Then, with a rapid motion, the Colonel hit against the barrel of the gun, knocking it to one side as the girl fired. The pistol was old and rusty, and it exploded, a fragment of the metal passed through the brain of the young husband.

Two days later the soldier's lifeless body was buried in the lonely cemetery of the fort. The following week his desolated widow was sentenced to be executed as a spy.

On the morning of February 2, 1862, the girl's guards asked if she had a final request. "Why, yes," she replied. "I'm tired of wearing this suit of men's clothes. I'd like to put on a gown once more before I die."

A search of the entire fort revealed only some black robes which had been worn during a theatrical performance given by the First Corps of Cadets the summer before. It was in this costume that the lady was hanged an hour later. That afternoon her body was cut down and placed in the Fort Warren cemetery by the side of her husband.

As time passed, the guards at the fort were shipped away, and recruits arrived to take their places. But the key men, eight in number, stayed on. One of them, a private named Richard Cassidy, had witnessed the execution of the Southern girl and it was his duty night after night to patrol the cover-face where she had been hanged. The other men joked with him, warning him to watch out for the "Lady in Black." He laughed with them, but actually he was not too pleased with his duty.

One night, seven weeks after the execution, Private Cassidy came running toward the guardhouse, screaming at the top of his voice. Finally, he was calm enough to tell his story. He had been patrolling his post and was thinking about the execution when suddenly two hands came out of the night and fastened around his throat. He squirmed and twisted until he faced the being who was trying to choke him and saw to his amazement that it was none other than the Lady in Black. Then he summoned all his strength, broke free from her grasp and ran for help.

The guardhouse rocked with laughter as Cassidy finished his story, but it was no laughing matter to Cassidy either then or the following morning when they sentenced him to thirty days in that same guardhouse for deserting his assigned and official post.

Ever since that night, it is said, the Lady in Black appears from time to time. In the winter of 1891 four officers walking out through the massive sally port looked ahead into the fresh snow and saw several footprints made by a woman's slipper. As no woman was then living at the fort, they held the Lady in Black responsible.

During World War II, one unfortunate sentry went stark, raving mad when ordered to patrol the area where the execution had occurred. He was placed in the island hospital to recover, but his condition went from bad to worse, and he was finally taken to an institution, where he is to this very day.

A few years after World War II ended, non-commissioned officers were allowed to have their wives and families living at the fort. One woman, known for her practical jokes, heard about the Lady in Black and decided to play a prank on her next-door neighbor. She removed her false teeth, smudged her face with charcoal and let her long, black hair down over her shoulders. Completely dressed in black, she threw a huge black shawl over her head and started for her neighbor's back door.

Not realizing what a terrible sight she presented, the prankster knocked on the door and, as it was opened, she bared her toothless gums and screamed. Her neighbor gave a single horrified glance and slumped to the floor in a dead faint. It was fully half an hour before the poor woman recovered her senses. During that time this modern Lady in Black vowed that if her friend recovered she would swear off practical jokes forever.

A more recent story involving the Lady in Black occurred in 1947. It was told to me by Captain Charles I. Norris of Towson, Maryland. Captain Norris was alone on the island one night, reading in the first-floor library of his house on the post, when something tapped him on the right shoulder. He turned, but there was no one in the room. As he began reading again, he felt another definite tap on his left shoulder.

Again there was no one to be seen. Then the upstairs phone rang. Leisurely putting down his magazine, he climbed the stairs and picked up the telephone. A man's voice said, "Operator speaking. Number, please."

Captain Norris asked the operator who it was that had been calling him. "Why," answered the operator, "your wife answered and took the message, sir!"

"My wife!" cried the startled captain. "My wife is not on the island."

Captain Norris was completely bewildered and went downstairs to sink exhausted into a chair. There were no more manifestations, but he decided that only the Lady in Black could account for the tapping and the mysterious telephone call.

Since 1946 thousands and thousands of interested visitors have gone ashore at Fort Warren and walked through the Corridor of Dungeons. Although the graves of the Lady in Black and her husband have long since been moved from the island, one of the commanding officers had a spurious tomb built into the floor of one of the casemates at the Corridor of Dungeons. Originally planned as a surprise to the lady guests at an officers' dance, the casket, which is merely a great wooden box set flush in the dirt of the casemate, proved such an overwhelming success that it has been allowed to stay there ever since.

Whenever newcomers enter the Corridor of Dungeons, the ritual first performed at the officers' dance is repeated. A small soldier, or perhaps a girl, is dressed in black and taken up to the casemate ahead of the others. The "Lady" of the particular occasion is placed in the coffin and the lid is closed over her. The unsuspecting guests enter the casemate and gather around the story-teller, who, with proper embellishments, tells the tragic history of the Lady in Black. At the end of the story, and usually with a flourish, the narrator swings open wide the cover of the casket, whereupon, with a blood-curdling scream, the Lady in Black leaps to her feet. Visitors who have been fortunate enough to see this performance are never likely to forget it.　□□

Spirit Capital of the Universe

by John Mason

COURTESY OF
THE ALTON H. BLACKINGTON COLLECTION

It's been nearly a century since the tiny Vermont town of Chittenden was the scene of an unbelievably bizarre and baffling phenomenon. To this day, no one has been able to provide a plausible explanation . . .

W hen Col. Henry S. Olcott, special correspondent for the *New York Sun*, arrived in Chittenden, Vermont, in the latter part of August, 1874, he found it a "plain, dull, and uninteresting town" whose inhabitants "trouble themselves about nothing except to get the usual modicum of food and sleep." To be sure, people were well aware of the strange "goings-on" in the old two-and-a-half storey farm house of William and Horatio Eddy. In fact, one person told Colonel Olcott soon after his arrival in town that the "devil, himself" had taken up his abode at the Eddy farm—and had the whole Eddy family under its influence!

It was Colonel Olcott's task to visit this "abode of the devil," talk to the Eddy brothers, observe the strange supernatural phenomena allegedly occurring there, and report everything back to the *Sun*. His subsequent dispatches caused a sensation. People from as far away as California—and even from Europe—made pilgrimages to the Eddy house and to "Honto's Cave," located in the woods nearby. For a few short years, Chittenden was truly the "spirit capital of the universe."

Before describing the actual supernatural happenings themselves, as well as Colonel Olcott's exhaustive attempts to disprove them (all described in his book PEOPLE FROM THE OTHER WORLD, privately published a year after his visit to Chittenden and now somewhat of a collector's item), it would be well to strictly examine the background of William and Horatio Eddy.

The brothers' father, Zephaniah Eddy, was a plain dirt farmer of

The Eddy homestead, to which people from all over the country once pilgrimaged, is shown above as it was in 1874 and, at top of page, in 1969. Horatio and William Eddy died in 1922 and 1932 respectively. It was some time later that the house was moved to face away from the road.

Spirit writing—in Latin—done at the Eddy farm in 1874.

"The medium was in a deep sleep, his features relaxed, his breathing almost imperceptible, his skin free from moisture . . . I have seen three or four hundred different materialized spirits and in every imaginable variety of costume (while William Eddy was in this state). True, the light has been dim . . . though I had no trouble, for instance, in recognizing the aged from the young . . ." (Henry S. Olcott in a report to the New York Sun *which had assigned him to investigate the Eddy brothers—and in his subsequent book* "People from the Other World.")

Weston, Vermont, who married Julie Ann MacCoombs, a girl of Scottish descent, also of Weston.

About 1846 they sold their farm in Weston and moved to Chittenden where Mrs. Eddy startled the natives with her amazing predictions and visions. She had inherited this gift from her mother, who was said to have "second sight"; that is, she would allegedly go into a trance and carry on conversations with wholly invisible people.

The Eddy brothers' great-great-great-grandmother had been tried and sentenced to death at Salem during the dark witchcraft days. However, she had escaped from jail and made her way back to Scotland.

Zephaniah Eddy was a narrow-minded, bigoted, uneducated man who took little interest in the peculiar gifts of his wife. In fact, it was said she kept from him most of the early "visions" that came to her.

But after their first child was born, it was impossible to hide the strange happenings from him. Mysterious sounds were heard around the baby's cradle, voices whispered through the barren rooms, and, according to the scanty records which exist, the first child and those that followed were frequently removed from their beds and transported to distant places by unseen hands.

As the children grew up, the "influences" increased to a point where the spirit "visitors" actually materialized. Zephaniah would be looking at William and Horatio playing in the field when suddenly there would be other boys playing with them. When he advanced threateningly, the "spirit" children would vanish like dew upon the meadow.

(When the late Alton Blackington interviewed a number of people in Rutland and Chittenden back in 1944, in preparation for his radio broadcast about the Eddy brothers, there was a man who well remembered the time he had called on the Eddys, then young men, and found the brothers working alone in a cornfield. He hadn't been there but a few moments when "two other figures appeared out of nowhere and followed the Eddys wherever they went.")

Probably no two kids ever had a more horrible boyhood than William and Horatio Eddy. They couldn't stay in school because of the loud raps that came on their desks; the unseen hands that yanked books and slates away from them. And so at a very early age they seemed to be marked with the power of witchcraft over which they seemed not to have the slightest control.

There were trances, too. The first time William had one of his strange spells, his enraged father pinched and pummelled him until he was black and blue all over. When that didn't bring him to, he poured hot water down the boy's back and dropped red hot embers from the hearth into the sleeping boy's hands.

But William slept on and, to his dying day, he carried the scars of his father's intolerant punishment!

One day it dawned on old Zephaniah that he might make some money out of his strange children by putting them on exhibition. He secured an agent, and the four Eddy children—two boys and two girls— were hustled around the country to perform before sceptics who tied them up, and nailed them down, and poured hot wax over their mouths so they couldn't talk. Their little bodies were pinched and squeezed out of shape by the contrivances into which they were pressed during their

pulses, a figure would emerge. . . ."

sensational seances in Boston, Philadelphia, and New York.

They were mobbed in Lynn, Massachusetts, and stoned at South Danvers. On a second visit to Danvers they were shot at. William Eddy carried the marks of the bullets that grazed his legs for the rest of his life. William was ridden on a rail in Cleveland and barely escaped a coat of tar and feathers.

But as long as the money poured in, Zephaniah didn't seem to care what mobs of sceptics and religious zealots did to his children.

It is not surprising, then, to learn that when Colonel Olcott presented himself to the Eddy brothers on that August day in 1874 that he found them cold, suspicious, and unfriendly. They have "dark complexions, black hair and eyes, stiff joints, a dumpy carriage, shrink from advances," he reported. "And they make newcomers feel ill at ease and unwelcome."

However, arrangements were made whereby the "Investigator" could board and room at the Eddy homestead and take part in the seances that were held every night but Sunday on the second floor of the farmhouse.

Colonel Olcott wasn't the only interested spectator. There were, as he says, "long-haired men and short-haired women." There were professors and scientists and "cranks of every cult," mental healers and bump-rubbing phrenologists. Night after night, they all sat in a semicircle on hard wooden chairs while the Eddys performed on a small raised platform with a so-called spirit "cabinet" in its middle.

The room was always dimly lighted by placing a kerosene lamp in a headless drum that rested on the floor in a distant corner. William Eddy would enter the cabinet, draw the curtains, and slump into his chair. There would be a few moments of silence—then the tinkling sound of far-off voices and music. Tambourines would fly around the stage and mysterious ectoplasmic hands of all sizes and shapes appeared out of the darkness to wave at or touch the breathless spectators.

Then, as everyone strained forward with pounding pulses, the curtain would lift and a figure would emerge onto the darkened stage. It might be that of an Indian girl, with beads and moccasins, or a well-dressed gentleman with top hat and gold-headed cane.

Frequently an old woman with a bunch of fagots would appear.

[127]

Deep in the forest not far from the Eddy farmhouse is "Honto's Cave," where spiritual seances once were held. The photo (left) taken in June 1969, and the drawing from Colonel Olcott's book, were made from the same spot— only 95 years apart.

More than once a young mother with a babe in each arm would emerge from that mysterious cabinet where William Eddy sat sprawled in sweat and psychic sleep.

All of these "spirits" walked, talked, and in some cases sang and danced as they floated back and forth only a few scant feet from the audience. Then, one by one, they would fade into the nothingness from which they came. Some vanished immediately; others would start "melting" at the head and slowly dissolve until only their feet were visible. Sometimes all except the hands would disappear.

After 20, or even 30 moving, breathing figures, in all sorts of costumes, had "materialized" out of a cabinet not big enough to hold two men, it was not surprising that people came all the way from California and Europe to view the fantastic occurrences. They were only too eager to pay $10 a week for board and room and a chance to ransack the house from top to bottom in search of hidden springs, wires, or mirrors. (As far

The following is a partial description of a seance held at Honto's Cave in May of 1874: "The night was warm and a full moon rode high. The company assembled at an early hour and seated themselves on benches . . . The spectators sat silent for awhile . . . Suddenly someone exclaimed, 'See!—up there on the rock!', and high overhead appeared the giant form of Santum in bold relief against the moonlit sky . . . Then successively appeared several other red squaws and chiefs, each dressed with plumes and beads and other braveries . . . William Eddy, meanwhile, kept talking within the cave so as to be heard by all . . ."

as can be determined, none of these things was ever found.)

Colonel Olcott, himself, left no stone or board unturned in his attempt to fathom the mystery. He examined the floors, the ceilings, and the walls to make sure no hidden trap doors made possible the entrance and departure of the spirit visitors.

When local sceptics suggested that these characters were either Horatio or William dressed in handy, hidden costumes, Colonel Olcott had a carpenter paint a huge yardstick or scale on the wall (marked off in feet and inches with plain black figures). It was obvious at a glance that no hulk of a man like William Eddy could shrink to the size of the little "spirit" girl who appeared so often.

After "Honto," the Indian woman, had appeared more than 30 times, it was evident that she was no male person. In one materialization, "Honto" allowed one of the women in the audience (a Mrs. Cleveland) to place her hand on her bare flesh. It was cold and clammy, but there was, according to the witness, "a very weak pulse."

Probably the most startling "materialization" occurred during the visit of Madam Blavatsky, later the founder of the famed Theosophical Society, and often described as the "female Karl Marx of spiritualism."

Madam Blavatsky, a massive, chain-smoking Russian lady with piercing blue eyes and intimate spirit connections with India and Egypt, had spent a previous summer at an Armenian resort near the Mount of Ararat. Her husband, vice-governor of Erivan, had a bodyguard of 50 warriors. Among them was one Ali Bek—a tall, dark man with flowing moustache, usually armed with a brace of pistols and a long, pointed spear, that he always carried when accompanying Madam Blavatsky.

On this particular evening at the Eddy farm, Madam Blavatsky was playing some soft music on an old-fashioned country organ that had been introduced into the Eddy seance room. Suddenly the curtains parted and before the astonished gathering there stood a most unusually attired man. He wore a high, braided, pointed hat, heavy embroidered coat, and trousers of purple velvet (with the tops tucked into his high leather boots). On the boots were curious tassels and long, shining spurs.

WILLIAM H. EDDY.   HORATIO G. EDDY.

As this unusual spirit form advanced, smiling and bowing, he was empty handed. But, seemingly to prove that the dead can do anything, he reached down as if to gather a handful of soil and then pressed his hand to his heart (a gesture familiar to the tribes of Kurdistan). Then there appeared in his hand a most curious looking weapon. It was a spear with a staff at least 10 feet long ending in a steel head of peculiar shape around which was a ring of brightly colored ostrich plumes.

After a few paces back and forth upon the stage (where already more than 400 other apparitions had appeared) the Kurdistan soldier, as surely that's what he seemed to be, waved a salute and slowly faded into a cloud of mist.

Was this an "illusion" that took place solely in the minds of every person in the audience? If so, what did the Eddy brothers do to create it?

In later years, long after the Eddy brothers ceased to hold public demonstrations and had settled down to the rustic life of farmers (with a few private seances now and then), there were many from all walks of life who demeaned them as imposters and fakers.

There are few people in Rutland or Chittenden today who know anything about the Eddy brothers. However, a few can remember their fathers and mothers saying that all these materializations were cleverly organized stage tricks, rivaled only by the exhibitions of Daniel Dunglas Home, who had his strange career about the same time.

There is just one stumbling block to such an explanation. How can anyone account for the fact that it would take 10 or 20 trunkfuls of costumes and theatrical equipment to provide such an evening's entertainment as the Eddy's gave night after night?

If the measurements and drawings and affidavits of respectable carpenters and tradesmen of Rutland and Chittenden are to be believed, the cabinet from which all these "spirit" forms emerged was hardly big enough for one man—let alone the 30 or 40 spirit figures that floated from it.

Where would the illiterate Eddy brothers, with no knowledge of foreign languages, customs and costumes, ever procure the necessary properties to stage such a carnival?

The Vermont of 95 years ago was a wild, isolated country. There were no express men to bring gadgets and costumes from magicians' laboratories in New York, no parcel post, no telephone, no trap doors, or sliding panels.

Do you have a theory as to how it was done?   □□

*And then into the stillness of the
room someone came . . . silently as fox fire comes"*

He Was There

by Jean Mitchell Boyd

Mr. Gideon Welles

The rain danced on the roof and its silver fingers tapped on the windows. The wind haunted the corners of the house and seemed to cry to come in—to come into the library of Mr. Gideon Welles, Secretary of the Navy during the Civil War. The "Old Man of the Sea" he was sometimes called. We sat there in the library on that rainy afternoon, Mr. Welles' grandson and I. It was a wonderful place for children to read. The library was not on the first floor. Opposite the front door was a broad stairway with a polished bannister. It was the best bannister on the street for "sliding down." The stair carpet was thick, so that as you climbed to the landing it was like walking on oysters. If you were going to the second floor, you turned to the right and climbed more stairs, but the library was one high step from the landing. It may have been an ell, added after the old brick house was built. The roof was flat and made a nice dancing floor for the rain. There were windows on three sides, making the light good for reading. The book cases went up to the ceiling. Many of the books were bound in canvas and were worn as if someone loved them and read them.

Mr. Welles had come to Hartford in 1869, after he finished his second term as Secretary of the Navy. He lived there until he died in 1878. Those of us who were children at the turn of the century never knew him, but we always had heard so much about him that he still seemed to be a neighbor. The house was on Charter Oak Place, so named because the oak had stood there which had been the hiding place in 1687 of the Connecticut Charter. Sir Edmund Andros, the royal governor, had come to take it to England to the King, which he couldn't do. We sat there in the library on that long ago afternoon. We each had a book by Joel Chandler Harris—"Aaron in the Wildwoods" and "Aaron the Runaway." Aaron was a slave, an Arab, who knew the language of animals. He understood the mysteries of the swamps—the will-o'-the-wisp and the sound of wind in the loblolly pine. Now and then when I turned a page I looked around the room. Some of the low shelves held neatly folded newspapers, a complete file of Civil War newspapers. I think it was *The Hartford Times* because Mr. Welles had been an editor until Mr. Lincoln asked him to be a member of his cabinet. He needed someone from New England. Once when we were in the library there was a wooden box in the corner. It was one of the boxes from the attic which held all the correspondence concerning the Navy during the Civil War. There were notes signed A. Lincoln and Seward and Porter and Farragut. We were interested in Farragut because his flagship had been the *Hartford* and her flags were in the State Capitol, but you had the feeling that Mr. Welles wouldn't want his papers disturbed. There was a portrait of him over the white marble mantle in the "best parlor." He looked like Mr. Lowell, only fiercer. It would be well for children to leave his papers alone. I wonder now if Mr. Welles' diary was on one of the shelves. It was called "The Deadly Diary" because it was such a frank document. Years after his death, when it was published and I read it, I wished that I might have sat in his library and held the original in my hands. I would have liked to have read in the stillness of that book-lined room about the gray day in 1864 when Mr. Welles "witnessed the wasting life of the good and great man who was expiring before me."

So we sat in the peace of the late afternoon, lost in stories of other years, shuddering pleasantly when bloodhounds bayed and "patterollers" rode after runaway slaves. The little feet of the rain ran more lightly. The wind went away to ruffle the Connecticut River. The door of the room was open, and from downstairs came the sound of the piano in the "best parlor" being played softly, as people often play when twilight glides through the windows in her gray velvet shoes.

And then into the stillness of the room someone came, someone came silently as fox fire comes, unseen as wind in the tree tops, but beyond all shadow of doubting, someone came.

We looked up, both of us. There was no one we could see. We listened, but we heard nothing, no mice running in the wall, no creaking board in the floor. Nothing touched us, no breath of air, no invisible garment. But someone seemed to be there.

I said softly, "Did you think—just now—someone came in?"

"Yes, I did, but I don't see him."

"Do you s'pose it could be your grandfather?"

"It prob'ly is."

"If it is your grandfather, wouldn't it be polite for us to stand up?"

"Yes, it would."

We laid down our books and stood respectfully, as children who lived before the Atomic Age were taught to do when an older person came into a room. You stood because it showed your respect for a person's years, and the wisdom which the years had brought. A disrespectful child came to no good end.

For a short time we stood there, neither frightened nor amazed. A grandfather is a pleasant person. My grandfather had been a captain in the Civil War, marched in his blue uniform in parades, and usually had button peppermints in his pocket. The fact that we could not see this grandfather did not seem particularly strange. After all, it was his library.

And then we heard the heavy steps of Henry Green on the stairs, making a clump-thump sound. He was coming with a taper to light the lamps. Whoever had been with us went away. We sat down.

Henry Green had been a slave in Virginia who had escaped to Washington and attached himself to the Welles family. He had squeezed whole groves of lemons into lemonade for very best people— Mrs. Lincoln, a special friend of Mrs. Welles; the Stantons; the Sewards; Mr. Chase and his daughter, Miss Kate—everybody. He said there was a cannonball in his back which made him lame.

He came into the library and said that night and the bats were coming early. He lighted the lamp on the big round table with the marble top. He drew the plain dark-red curtains and shut out the darkness. As he left, he turned in the doorway. The taper made strange shadows on his dark face.

He said, "Ah 'clare to goodness, sometimes it seem lak he was here."

We nodded solemnly. His fingers went into the pocket where he kept the rabbit's foot. He believed in spirits and witches.

We listened as he went upstairs to light the lamps in the upper hall. Then he started downstairs—thump-clump. Henry Green had been the body servant of Colonel Thomas Welles, son of Mr. Secretary Welles. Once, before a battle, Henry became frightened and fled. But he came to a bridge on which Mrs. Gideon Welles seemed to appear. She cried, "Go back, Henry, go back." She was more awesome than the whole Rebel Army, so he went back. And that was the battle that won the war, so that Mr. President Lincoln took a gold tack hammer and knocked the chains off the hands and feet of every slave in America.

Thump-clump. And after the war Colonel Welles and Henry sailed around the world with Admiral Farragut. The Devil walked beside the boat and ruffled the water just to be mean.

We heard Henry reach the lower hall. We held our books, but we did not read. The lamplight touched the old books gently. Here and there a book was missing from a shelf.

At length I said, "Do you think your grandfather was really here?"

"He was here."

"Why did he come, do you s'pose?"

"I s'pose he came down for a book he wanted. Prob'ly one they don't have in the library in Heaven."

"Do—do—they read Up There?"

"Yes. What else could you do forever and ever, amen?"

And lo, the old New England Heaven of golden harps, a great White Throne and Cherubim and Seraphim passed away. And the new Heaven was a vast Celestial Library beyond the foothills of the Pleiades. The books were bound in solid gold. The reading lamps were of alabaster and the lights were stars. And those who had been good on earth sat in purple velvet chairs and read forevermore. But those who had been disrespectful and had not gone to church on Sunday spent all eternity merely dusting books with dusters of gray cat-stitched clouds.

And so, when the fingers of the rain are on the north windows, and the wind cries like a lost lamb, I look back across the years which make up more than half a century, and see two children standing in the twilight, standing quietly, respectfully, because they thought Mr. Gideon Welles had come back to his library. □□

Mystery House
on Elm Street

by Rufus Jarman

*Here's a ghost story with origins dating back 120
years—a haunt that beguiled psychic investigators
of two continents—a record that offers evidence
that ghosts can be creative too . . .*

Disembodied spirits from the Great Beyond may still sigh and moan
there on wintry nights, but you couldn't have heard them lately
above the creaking of aged timbers and the wind blowing through the
broken windows of the old Phelps Home in Stratford, Connecticut—one
of New England's most remarkable haunted houses.

Human vandals, however, rather than denizens of the Spirit World,
have despoiled the Phelps Place. It was, until comparatively recently, one
of the proudest mansions in Stratford, which was settled in 1639, and is
now a suburb of Bridgeport with 50,000 population. For 145 years the
sprawling, Greek Revival-style house has stood on Elm Street, tradition-
ally Stratford's most aristocratic residential section, and it now adjoins
the famed Shakespeare Theater, one of New England's principal centers
of culture.

Despite such affluent surroundings, the Phelps House stares at the
world nowadays through shattered windows and holes in its walls. One
of the four great Doric columns adorning its facade is missing. "No
Trespassing" signs glare from its exterior, and the once-manicured, five-
acre grounds are a tangle of vines, broken trellises and untended trees.

A drawing of the Phelps House as it probably looked at the time of the famous haunt, in 1850. This picture was originally published by Lippincott's Magazine, of London, England, July, 1879.

The haunt that beguiled psychic investigators of two continents occurred 121 years ago—from March 10 to October 1, 1850. Over those nearly seven months a mysterious something—many observers believed it was a group of highly imaginative and violently disposed spirits—upset the home life of the Rev. Eliakim Phelps, the local Presbyterian minister, and his family by throwing objects about the house, beating on walls and furniture, breaking windows and constructing dramatic tableaus with figures made from old clothing.

For a century following the haunt several families dwelt there, apparently without further molestation from "spirits." But people who lived and worked in it during the last 20 years of the house's occupancy tell of unexplained goings-on, which indicated to them that perhaps a spirit or two might still occasionally wander along the rambling hallways or disport in the ancient stone cellar.

After the last human resident departed, in the winter of 1968, the old house was overrun by vandals, hippies and so-called "psychic groups" wanting to hold seances there. These interlopers so abused it that the owners decided to tear down the Phelps Place, despite anguished cries from the Stratford Historical Society membership. But at this point the old house got a break. Certain unexpected developments caused the owners to decide they would spend a great deal of money refurbishing the old mansion throughout, and restoring its exterior to look as it did when brand new.

The great, three-story frame house was completed in 1826 by General Mattas Nicoll, of a prominent Stratford family, for his son-in-law, Captain George R. Dowell, master of a clipper ship. Mrs. Dowell planned the house and oversaw its construction while her husband was on his final voyage to China before retiring from the sea. She had the main hallway built 70 feet long by 12 feet wide, the dimensions of a clipper ship's deck, so that her husband might have within the house a familiar area to walk and exercise, as he did on shipboard. From either end of the hallway rose twin staircases, meeting at a joint landing on the second-floor level. This would allow the captain to imagine himself going up to his hurricane deck from one side and down to the main deck on the other.

In May, 1849 the property was purchased by the Rev. Mr. Phelps, a native of Belchertown, Massachusetts, and a graduate of Union and Andover Seminaries. The minister had served pastorates at Geneva and Huntington, N. Y., and was secretary to the American Society of Philadelphia before moving to Stratford. He was 59 years old at the time, and soon became well liked and respected by his congregation, despite his enthusiastic interest in clairvoyance and other occult subjects. The Rev. Mr. Phelps had recently married a widow, considerably younger than he, with four children—two girls, aged sixteen and six; and two boys, aged eleven and three, at the time the phenomena began.

That was on a Sunday morning, when the family returned from church to find the furniture at home in disarray. In one of the main downstairs rooms a tableau was arranged to depict a scene of worship. Eleven figures, or dummies, had been fashioned from old clothing and posed in attitudes of devotion, some with foreheads nearly touching the floor, others apparently studying Bibles spread out before them. All of the figures were made to resemble women, except that suspended on a cord in the center of the room, as though flying, was a hideous-looking dwarf.

The New Haven Journal published this account by a Dr. Webster: "From this time on the rooms were closely watched, and figures (dummies) appeared every few days when no human being could have entered

[138]

the room. They were constructed and arranged, I am convinced, by no visible power. The clothing from which the figures were made was somehow gathered from all parts of the house, in spite of a strict watch. In all, about 30 figures were constructed during the haunt. Some were so life-like that a small child, being shown the room, thought his mother was kneeling in prayer with the rest."

Aside from the "old clothes tableaus," which are unique, most of the strange antics in the Phelps House were typical antics of a poltergeist —a compound German word meaning "noisy spirit." Poltergeists love to throw things, make noises and create havoc in general. As H. B. Taylor wrote in the *Bridgeport Standard*: "In my presence, the elder boy was carried across the room by invisible hands and gently deposited on the floor. A supper table was raised and tipped over when the room was empty of people. In one case, the boy's clothing was cut to ribbons . . . On March 13th, in the presence of several persons, articles flew through the air and a brass candlestick fell from the mantelpiece and continued to dash itself against the floor until broken. A shovel and tongs set moved out from the fireplace and proceeded to hop about in a dance in the middle of the floor. A heavy dining room table was raised in the air and a lamp moved across the room and set fire to some papers . . ."

Mrs. Ellen Olney Kirk, a local historian, wrote: "One is tempted to believe that the spirit of Goody Bassett, hanged in 1651 for divers witch-like acts, was never fairly laid and now, after an unquiet term of 199 years, has returned to walk the earth.

"Great crowds came hither by every train," Mrs. Kirk continued. "Editors, reporters, spiritualists, skeptics explored, watched, investigated and interrogated and gave an unwelcome publicity to the scandalous details. During the early period of this unearthly possession the entire village was convulsed with excitement, and lost its character for sobriety. The village hackman bought a larger omnibus, installed on it a large, yellow sign reading, 'Mysterious Stratford Knockings,' and he prospered mightily."

Among the visiting investigators was the internationally famous psychic, Andrew Jackson Davis, "the Seer of Poughkeepsie," who explained that the phenomena in the Phelps House was caused by "vital radiations" coming from the elder boy's organism. The psychic said that when magnetism predominated in the boy's body, objects were attracted to him and to the elder girl. When 'electricity' was stronger, objects were repelled by them. Davis added that he saw five spirits present also, who

. . . *the rooms were carefully watched* . .

The main first floor hallway of the Phelps House was planned to fit the dimensions of a clipper ship deck so that its first resident, Clipper Ship Captain George R. Dowell, would feel more normal after his retirement. Note the double staircase.

were moving the objects and generally directing operations.

(Most psychic students, who believe in the reality of poltergeists, hold that the phenomena is caused by the release of great quantities of vital energy, produced by glandular changes within the bodies of children who are reaching the age of puberty. It is theorized that mischievously inclined, earth-bound spirits are able to collect this energy and use it physically to mystify and amaze humans. Skeptics hold that youngsters create the mischief directly, deliberately and somehow secretly, although poltergeist haunts, with amazingly similar phenomena, are re-

[140]

corded as far back as the Fourth Century, and have been reported from practically every country.)

Professor Austin Phelps, a son of the Rev. Mr. Phelps by a former marriage and for years head of the Department of Theological Science at Andover, recalled that "On one occasion when Dr. Phelps was walking across a room, with nobody else in the room, a key and a nail flew over his head and landed at his feet. That same evening, in the presence of the whole family, a turnip fell from the ceiling. Spoons and forks flew from the dinner table into the air, and one day six or eight spoons were taken up at once, bent double by no physical agency, and thrown at those in the room."

One investigator suggested that the minister attempt to communicate with the spirits by code, with a specified number of knocks indicating each letter of the alphabet. The spirits cooperated all right, but the Rev. Mr. Phelps later wrote: "I have become fully satisfied that no reliance whatever is to be placed in these communications. If it is the work of spirits, they are wicked spirits. Their communications are often proven false, frequently proven trifling and nonsensical. They sound like loafers on a spree."

Not all of those who investigated the Phelps House believed the manifestations were supernatural. An editor of the *Bridgeport Standard* wrote: "The house in question is so constructed that mischievous inmates or neighbors can easily play a variety of tricks with the least risk of detection. We suggested this to Dr. Phelps, who said such was his own opinion until he was compelled to believe otherwise."

The view of some local skeptics, according to one local historian, was that "The young wife, accustomed to the gaieties of the city and dissatisfied with the solemn stillness of Stratford, sought to effect a change to a more congenial atmosphere, aided by a scheming daughter and a precocious son."

In an article written for *The New York Observer*, however, the Rev. Mr. Phelps said: "I have witnessed these manifestations hundreds of times, and I know that in hundreds of instances they took place when there was no visible power by which these motions could have been produced. Scores of persons of standing in the community whose education, general intelligence, candor, veracity and sound judgment were without question were requested to witness the phenomena and, if possible, help in the solution of the mystery. But as yet, no such solution has been obtained. The idea that it is all a trick of the children—which some of the papers have been endeavoring with great zeal to promulgate—is to everyone acquainted with the facts as false as it is injurious."

Charles W. Elliott, author of a book, *Mysteries, or Glimpses of The Supernatural*, quotes Dr. Phelps as follows: "The phenomena have been completely inexplicable to me. I have followed the *slow movements* of objects through the air, observing carefully their direction, their slow movement and their *curving flight*, and I am convinced that they were not moved by any human agency."

(Students of psychic phenomena emphasize two peculiar characteristics of objects supposedly thrown by poltergeists: One, these objects often travel *more slowly* than if thrown by a person; two, in many instances the objects seem to take a *curved path*, often turning in flight at right angles.

The Rev. Mr. Phelps continued: "The noises were most violent when all of the family was present, especially when seated at the table. Our pecuniary loss was between one- and two-hundred dollars. The childrens' health was never affected in any way, except by fright. Twenty-six window panes were broken. The knocker on the front door often resounded with a loud clanging sound, but the door, on being opened instantly, disclosed no one about. Heavy marble-topped tables would rise on two legs and crash to the floor with no one within six feet of them.

"The phenomena continued until the children and their mother finally went to Pennsylvania (October 1, 1850) and the phenomena did not follow them there. When they returned in the spring, the phenomena did not reappear. I myself was in Stratford for six weeks after they left, without any phenomena occurring . . ."

Apparently, nothing further was heard from the "spirits" in the old Phelps House for the next hundred years. The property was sold by the Rev. Mr. Phelps in 1859 to Moses Y. Beach, founder of *The New York Sun* and father of Alfred E. Beach, for years editor of *The Scientific American*, who also lived in the Phelps House with his family for several decades. For a number of years, Alfred Beach operated in the house the exclusive Stratford Institute, which he started as a private school for his own children but later admitted children of gentlefolk of the town. In 1907, Alfred Beach had the old house extensively renovated and modernized.

After visiting the Phelps House in 1939, William Howard Wilcoxson reported in his *History of Stratford* that the old place was still "one of the largest and most beautiful homes in Stratford, and now the residence of the James Albert Wales family. A walk through this curious mansion with its rich and modern furnishings, "is most interesting," Wilcoxson wrote. "In the great hall with the double staircase the walls are covered with old rose brocade in two tints with ivory trim. Oriental rugs in colors of old rose yellow and brown cover the polished floors. Against the walls are Chippendale chairs, an Empire sofa in old rose, a grandfather's clock and family portraits over the stairs. The extensive and beautiful grounds surrounding the old mansion extend from Elm Street to the (Housatonic) River, ornamented by a great many old, beautiful trees."

During the 1907 renovation the great room that had housed the Stratford Institute was transformed into three—drawing room, library and dining room. The walls of the drawing room and library, Wilcoxson wrote, "are covered with two-toned silk. The dining room walls are a tapestry of green trees on a blue background. These three rooms are in reality one great room, although separated by archways, supported by Doric columns. The detail of the exterior has thus been repeated throughout the interior. The house today has an atmosphere of the peace and quiet of a beautiful estate, and one finds it difficult to believe that within these very same walls once occurred the strange and remarkable manifestations that disturbed the peace and quiet of this old New England town."

In 1939, however, the Phelps Place had only a few more years to enjoy as an elegant private mansion. World War II caused shortages in domestic help, and increases in taxes that made many big old homes liabilities. And so in the early 1940's, Mr. Wales sold the Phelps House to Mrs. Maude Thompson, who operated a home for elderly people there until 1947 when she sold it to Mr. and Mrs. Carl Caserta, both registered nurses. For the next 20 years they operated in the old house the Restmore Convalescent Home, with 38 beds for elderly patients and a staff of four nurses.

Echoes of the old haunt now began to be heard. According to the Casertas, their nurses often reported mysterious noises in the night like distant sighs and whispers. And a cellar door that was always kept fastened had the eerie habit of swinging open now and then from no apparent cause.

Mr. and Mrs. Caserta, who are stolid, no-nonsense types, think it likely that the sighs and noises in the old house were caused by the wind and aged timbers contracting in the cold. And doors and their frames

can do queer tricks in their old age. But, two incidents *did* occur in the Phelps House during their residence there that impressed the Casertas —*profoundly*. Both happenings involved electric buzzers.

The old house is so large and rambling that it had been equipped with three sets of buzzers and buttons to call staff members in various parts of the house. One set was on the third floor, in the apartment occupied by the Casertas and their two-and-a-half-year-old son, Gary. Another was on the main floor near the duty desk. The third set was in the cellar. By pressing the proper button at any of these three stations a person could buzz either of the other two stations.

"The first of the strange happenings occurred after we'd been living in the house only a couple of months," Mrs. Caserta recalls. "After putting Gary to bed in his crib about eight o'clock one night, I foolishly arranged a blanket over a wall bracket of electric bulbs to shield the child's eyes from the light. My husband was away for the evening, and I went down to join the two nurses in the cellar, where we had some work to do.

"We three had been down there for half an hour, perhaps, working and talking, when abruptly the basement buzzer began sounding, loudly, insistently. We were so startled that all three of us dashed up to the

[144]

. . . suspended on a cord in the center of the room was a hideous-looking dwarf.

Opposite page: The Phelps House, photographed around 1939, one of the last years the old house was a private residence. Left: The Phelps House as it looks today. Notice the shattered windows and missing Doric column. This is the work of vandals.

main floor. After all, we were the only people in the house except the patients, who were too infirm to be up and about, and Gary who was too little to get out of his crib or to reach the buzzer button on the wall.

"After checking the patients and finding them all asleep, I started up the stairs to the third floor. Then I heard Gary begin to scream, *and I smelled smoke!* When I got to the third floor I found the blanket shading the lights had slipped down and caught fire from the bulbs. Holes were burned through it already, and the third floor was filling fast with smoke. I grabbed the blanket and threw it into the bath tub, and got Gary out of there. And we haven't learned to this day what set off that buzzer."

The second case occurred about two years later, and it also involved the boy, Gary, who now had his own room and small bed instead of a crib. One morning, around 1 or 2 o'clock, Mrs. Caserta was on duty alone, reading in the sitting room near the duty desk on the main floor. All the patients were asleep on that and the second floors, as were her husband and Gary on the third. The nurses were off duty and out of the house. Suddenly, Mrs. Caserta's reading was interrupted by the strident sound of the main floor buzzer.

"I quickly checked all the patients," Mrs. Caserta reports, "and all was quiet with them. Then I started up the stairs to see if Carl had buzzed me. Upon reaching the second floor I looked up, and there was Gary apparently walking in his sleep. Our boy was trying to scramble over the stair railing. He already had one foot over and was trying to pull up the rest of his body. The railing was at the top of a three-story stairwell. If Gary had come over it, he would have had a long, long fall all the way to the main floor.

"I ran to the third floor, grabbed the boy and pulled him away from the railing. When I looked into his eyes they showed no recognition of me, until I managed to shake him awake. Again, we don't know who or what pushed that button."

"If there's a ghost in that house, it's a good ghost, so far as we are concerned," Carl Caserta said not long ago. "When we moved out, it was like leaving a friend. That old place deserves better than it's got. It makes me so sad to look at the house, now that the scavengers and vandals and animals have got at it, that I won't go past it on Elm Street anymore."

The physical disintegration of the Phelps House began after the Casertas had sold it to the Alliance of Medical Inns, Inc., which operates a chain of convalescent hospitals in Connecticut, Rhode Island, North Carolina and Florida. Prior to selling the property, Carl Caserta had drawn plans for a new, 120-bed hospital building proposed for construction at the rear of the old Phelps House, which would be remodeled inside into offices and a nurses' home. The Zoning Commission agreed to allow the new owners to continue operation of a convalescent hospital in that residentially zoned area, provided the Phelps House was retained as part of the project.

The Medical Alliance management, however, preferred to delay construction until mortgage interest rates became more favorable, a company spokesman says. And so the new owners boarded up the "old haunted house" and waited. Lured by its mystique, vandals began breaking in. Then, the *Bridgeport Sunday Post* published a Hallowe'en feature about the "old haunted house in Stratford." After that, undesirable visitors began arriving by the bus-load and in motor caravans—college students, pseudo-psychic groups, hippies, kids—anxious to roam through the place, hold seances there and "wait for a ghost to appear."

It's doubtful if these intruders encountered a ghost, but they pretty well made one of the old house by breaking windows, punching holes in the walls, knocking down a chimney and destroying one of the large front

[146]

columns. The damage was such that the Medical Alliance, contending it would be impractical to repair it, petitioned the Board of Zoning Appeals for permission to raze the old mansion and build a completely new hospital. Local traditionalists squawked loudly for fear that another landmark was about to be sacrificed to "progress."

But, after a hearing last December 1, the Board of Zoning Appeals voted four-to-one to deny the petition. This meant that, if the owners expected to operate a hospital on that site, the old Phelps House must be a part of it. The Board sent a letter to the owners recommending that the Phelps mansion be made usable again.

A month later, the Alliance of Medical Inns announced that work would begin at 1738 Elm Street in March, to be completed by the end of the year, on a $750,000 hospital project. This will include a new, 90-bed "extended care facility" and the renovation of the old Phelps House. "The owners," the announcement said, "will undertake to restore the exterior (of the Phelps Place) to its original design."

And that is the story behind the big, old Greek Revival-style mansion that you can expect to see, for some years to come, if you should visit the Shakespeare Theater or happen to drive along Elm Street in Stratford, Connecticut.   □□

Ghost
Town

by
George Albert
Waldo

Here is a tragedy so heinous, a mystery so unfathomable, an abduction so strange, as to cause all who hear the tale to look askance, and shake their heads.

Have you ever tramped the trails leading from the White Mountains down onto the eastern bank of the Connecticut River? If you have, you will readily recognize the place I want to tell you about. There is a deep gouge dug out of the mountains where a small stream rushes through the rock bed. The water sprays and spirals as it leaves the black stones behind in its haste to join the river. Deep down into that ancient strata it has worn its path during a million years past. High along its sides rise the cliffs furred with evergreens which seldom see the direct rays of the sun. On bright days shafts of sunlight seep down into the undergrowth where newts and salamanders and snakes coil lazily and stuporously upon the shelves of projecting ore. A long, winding and much-decayed corduroy trail follows the convolutions of what fifty years ago was a busy lumber trail.

About a mile to the south the pinnacle of the mountain is crowned by a strange rock formation remarkably resembling an Indian's profile. The mountain rises an abrupt sixteen hundred feet at the water's edge. Strange tales are told of the early days in this region, which is uninhabited, although now three hundred years have elapsed since the advent of the white man in the New World.

Some distance to the north, perhaps a mile-and-a-half by modern reckoning, if the stranger follows the tracks of an abandoned railroad, he may still come upon the remains of an ancient village. Here, where once upon a time smoke curled from the chimneys of many happy homes, and the reflections of the evening sun were followed after dark by the gleam of tapers and tallow candles, stand deserted houses. Shingle-sided with slate roofs, and peaks sagging and the window ledges long since rotted by the heavy dews which descend upon the valley, these are the mute evidences of a once thriving rural community.

In these very houses a tragedy so heinous, a mystery so unfathomable, an abduction so strange was enacted as to cause all who hear the tale to look askance at me, and shake their heads.

In the days preceding the Civil War there were rumors rife in the locality concerning a band of wandering Indians, descendants of those tribes that originally inhabited the headwaters of the Connecticut. It is a fact proved by the students of Indian lore in our country, the same who can point out the sites of the old camp grounds of these tribes, that this region was a famous meeting place for powwows. Deep in the recesses of the hills are to be found even now the burial grounds of their braves. On more than one occasion I have visited a great open mead where mound after mound marks the interment of thousands of red men who succumbed to the smallpox. That was the scourge which these native Americans came to know as the WHITE MAN'S CURSE, and to fear more than his firewater and his flintlocks, because they looked upon it as being supernatural.

The period I have in mind was the time when immigrants came into the valley and opened a vein of copper which extended back into the hills. There on the shores of a lake overgrown with brushwood, one may still see the workings with its piles of slag, and the deep surface pits from which this valuable metal was extracted. The mule trails are still traversed by the curious who have little faith in the superstitions of the neighborhood. At the foot of the trail still stand the skeletons of more than fifty houses.

Officials of a mining company had sent their engineers in to select a site which would prove suitable for the erection of a town. Thousands of dollars were spent in laying out the project, and a small tram was introduced for the twofold purpose of bringing out the ores to the river and for transporting the workers from the nearest ferry to the small municipality. A community store was stocked and everything was in readiness for the miners and their families to move in. There were two hundred persons including the women and children.

Old records tell us, and ancient residents of the nearby towns have attested to the details, that while the preliminary surveys were getting under way, the construction was beset by many and unusual difficulties. As the first foundations were being laid, an Indian was seen to be haunting the neighborhood by night. On the following mornings the excavations were found filled in. Though watchmen were set at night, no one was able to describe how the day's work was undone. Later

But this time it was not the roofs of the houses that were missing . . .

several Indians showed themselves in the workings by daylight. In the wake of these strange visitations lumber would be found burning, and timbers split in manner unbecoming good building materials. At other times it was reported that kegs of nails and barrels of supplies suddenly would break themselves wide open and spread their contents upon the ground. What had been scheduled for completion in three months took the greater part of a year.

Finally, each night a roof would be removed from a finished house in the town; cleanly and completely it would disappear from over the heads of its tenants, leaving neither a splinter nor a broken slate to indicate in what direction nor by what forces it had been spirited away. One of my informants maintains to this day that he twice saw a huge black cloud gather on the horizon where the pine trees showed themselves against the blue of the sky, and in the form of a great tawny hand pass its fingers down the valley until it engulfed the superstructures of a building.

Conditions grew steadily worse after the immigrants moved in, and the nocturnal visits occurred more and more frequently. Indians were seen here and there throughout the settlement with but one exception. There was but one place in the village where they never had appeared, and that was in the plot of ground occupied by the tiny church, perched on a slight rise of ground to the north of town.

The pastor of the little flock began to feel that he might be able to learn some things regarding these disturbances if he could meet one of the intruders, and he at once moved into the home of one of his parishioners who had reported these occurrences most frequently. He had not long to wait, for during his second night there a marauder entered the gate-yard and the pastor challenged him. The exact words which were exchanged are not a matter of record, but the following day the minister had the church bell tolled and the people assembled. He said that the Indian explained the village had been built over an old burial ground of his tribe. In this cemetery there were the remains of many important chiefs who returned every night and sent him and other braves to warn the white man against building his "cave-of-many-rooms" over their sacred ground. He said that he was told to advise the white intruders to take their town to another location lest the Great Hand of the Evil Spirit descend from the mountain where the sun rises and remove all who remained, even as it had taken the roofs from off their houses.

When the good man had asked the Indian why it was that his church never had been the object of a visitation, he is said to have declared that the Great Spirits had directed that this was a bond to prove to the white man that even as the Indians had honored the sacred place of the intruder, they expected the white man to do likewise —and depart.

At these words a great silence hung over the gathering, until certain individuals, bolder than the rest, began to scoff at the story, saying that the pastor was "just entering his second childhood," and maintaining that all tales of spirits and Great Black Hands were the work of prattling old women.

Folks returned to their homes, and after a day or two of hushed discussions and placing of the family Bibles in the positions deemed to give the most protection against witches and other supernatural visitations, the whole matter was promptly forgotten. For a while there were no repetitions of the earlier misfortunes. The miners returned to their work in the pits, and housewives busied themselves with keeping their homes clean and putting up vegetables and preserves against the coming winter. The youngsters played in the village streets as usual and attended the Saturday and Sunday schools conducted by the old minister. All were lulled into a false sense of security.

And then . . .

It was late in August of that year. The diggings at the mines were just beginning to produce on a paying basis. About four o'clock on a sultry afternoon the sky became overcast. The sun's rays which filtered down through the trees were of an eerie orange color. The slight breeze which had been fanning the tree tops suddenly ceased. The orange hue deepened to a reddish vapor as though a Gargantuan shaker were pouring paprika down from the mountain top. At the mines a mile away the workers hastened to collect their implements and return home, but the sand banks which bordered the copper pits started to slide down. Ton after ton of sand and stones must have engulfed the poor wretches, leaving them not even the relief of an outcry. There were sixty-one miners in all.

As this catastrophe was enveloping the little group at the quarry, there appeared upon the eastern horizon a tiny speck of a cloud, black and sinister. It increased in size until it resembled a patch of soot pouring through the notch in the ridge of the mountain. As it passed to the river's edge it grew larger and larger and the uneven, serrated borders which it had exhibited took on the semblance of fingers; long tentacle-like digits which spread from one end of town to the other; from east to west and from north to south it poured down on the settlement and its inhabitants. Then as suddenly as it had appeared it was gone. A brisk breeze sprang up and the air cleared with that brilliant intensity which follows a summer thunderstorm. But this time it was not the roofs of the houses that were missing—it was the inhabitants themselves. Among all those dwellings marked by this searing hand, it was the little church alone which remained unscathed—as you may still see it to this day.

No explanation has ever been advanced. No one has ever been found who survived that red day in August more than one hundred years ago. The buildings still stand, to be sure, some leaning, awry and bat-infested, but no new tenants seek them out. The depressions which mark the mines in the nearby hills are still there to be excavated by those who pooh-pooh the legends. So far no venturesome soul has essayed to reopen the vein of metal. The Indian burial grounds are familiar to those who tramp through their sylvan fastness, the same today as yesteryear; but the spirits, or whatever they were, descend no more to the plains of that peaceful valley. □□

Section III

The Dark Side of Nature

Franklin's "Bloody" Apples

Franklin, Connecticut, used to be mysteriously reminded of a murder—every spring and fall. This is a story about apples, small, shiny, tasty apples . . . stained with blood.

by Joseph A. Owens

Franklin, a small town in eastern Connecticut, claims a juicy tale the likes of which never flowed from Ben's talented quill.

It's about apples, small, shiny, and tasty—and stained with blood.

The apples, known as "Mikes," could be plucked from only one tree in Franklin, the community of seven hills lying inconspicuously between historic Lebanon and the city of Norwich. This tree graced the Micah Rood Farm in the Peck Hollow Section, about one-half a mile from the stately Congregational Church.

For some 250 years this fruit bearer thrived in fertile soil near the Susquetomscot Stream, until uprooted by the 1938 hurricane. With the death of their lone source, "Mikes" went out of existence, but not the story surrounding their birth.

Here are the "facts."

Micah Rood settled in Peck Hollow in 1699. From his farm and orchard he harvested the necessities of life, little more. One December evening a peddler, on regular rounds in the tiny settlement, called on Micah, hoping to make a sale or two.

Dazzled by the display of goods, but not able to afford a purchase, Micah reportedly became crazed and thrust a knife into the heart of the itinerant businessman. He then carried the body outside and buried it beneath an apple tree.

With the arrival of warm weather this tree, which had always worn a spring coat of snowy white blossoms, was covered with red petals. Little attention was given the color change, but in August a wave of curiosity swept through town.

Young boys playing on the Rood Farm bit into some apples from the tree. Each apple contained a red globule in its center. The next day townfathers went to the farm, split dozens of apples open, and found the crimson clots.

Curiosity turned to fear when the peddler failed to pay his calls the following winter. It was remembered his last stop had been at Micah Rood's farm, and that since then Micah, a friendly outgoing man, had been morose and melancholy. And there were the apples. Was the spot caused by the blood of an innocent man trickling down into the roots of the tree? Was this direct incrimination of the guilty man?

While villagers whispered Micah lost the desire to live. His farm died quickly, but he lingered on. Records of the Congregational Church for 1717 show: "October ye first day. Ye society voted yt. each family shall give Micah Rood a peck of corn for sweeping ye meetinghouse one year."

Micah's death wait was long, his torture slow. A July 5, 1727, entry of the society notes: "The inhabitants do now, by their vote, agree to allow each man that watches with Micah Rood, two shillings per night. Also to those who have attended sd Rood by day, three shillings per day."

The end came on a December night. Micah Rood died a pauper as evidenced by this accounting of funds of the society: "December 17, 1728—to Jacob Hyde for digging Micah Rood's grave £0, 4s 0d."

But the unique monument to his reported crime grew, and for more than two centuries showered apples on the ground beneath its strong branches.

Stanley Armstrong, a selectman in Franklin for the past eighteen years recalls, "As a boy I gathered and ate my share of Mikes every summer. They were small and juicy like McIntosh apples."

The land on which the tree stood was rented and farmed for many years by the Armstrong family. The site is now overgrown with brush. Nothing remains of the Rood farmhouse or the apple tree.

Through the years several attempts were made by enterprising residents to cultivate other Mike apple trees from cuttings, but no one had the green thumb of Johnny Appleseed. "All the offshoots died," reports Mrs. Maude Manning, local historian.

The authenticity of the Micah Rood legend has never been seriously questioned. In 1869 the town's leading citizen Dr. Ashbel Woodward declared, "In face of the facts, who shall pronounce the story of Micah Rood a fiction, or think it too strange that nature should thus record her horror of human crime?"

Not present-day Franklin, whose people say with their eyes and lips, "Of course it's true. Ask any old-timer who remembers the taste of a Mike."

And a bowl of applesauce is tasty too!　　□□

In the Valley
of the Shadow of Death

by John Mason

August 28 was still and sultry. The leaves drooped from the trees. The grass lay motionless in the meadow—even the birds were still. 2000 feet directly above the Willey House the overhanging crags hung pitted and gouged and dry as dust . . . and then the rain came . . .

Just as folks along the Maine coast look out their windows around Thanksgiving time to see if there are signs of a storm like that which sent the Steamer *Portland* to its doom, so do people in the White Mountains look at the towering crags above Crawford Notch at this time of year and speculate, with a shudder or two, on the fate of the folks who lived in the Willey House many, many years ago. I am writing this story because at least a dozen readers have asked for it over the past few years. They all said, in effect, "The oldtimers know the tragic tale, but there are many youngsters who visit the White Mountains each year who have never heard what happened on that fatal August night, and we wish you would tell them."

The so-called "notches" of the White Mountains need no explanation. You all know that years ago, when the roads we glide over today were just trails, there was real and ever-present danger from falling rocks, landslides, turbulent streams, and in winter from snowdrifts, that defies the imagination. Only the hardiest of souls would attempt to get through the "notches" in winter. Some folks had to go through to get out of the mountains with their goods. In Benjamin Willey's book INCIDENTS IN WHITE MOUNTAIN HISTORY, he graphically described the mile-long line of sleds and teams winding in and out of the snow-filled mountain passes on their way to the markets of Portland and the outside world.

Even in those days there were tourists—rugged men and women who had scaled the highest peaks in Europe—and they were always protesting that better trails should be made, and more taverns erected for them to stay in.

At that time there wasn't a single house for a distance of 13 miles, from the old Crawford place to the Rosebrook house, and any traveler caught in a sudden snowstorm in a "notch" was sure to perish. It came as good news, then, that a small story-and-a-half house, with sheds and barn, was to be built on the barren stretch of Crawford Notch by a Mr. Henry Hill, an innkeeper. But travelers were so infrequent it failed to pay as a hotel, and the house was for many years unoccupied.

In 1825, in the fall of the year, Mr. Samuel Willey moved into the onetime tavern, with his family and two hired men, and immediately began to restore the place to its former coziness. The mountain gales had ripped shingles from the roof, which had sagged under the weight of winter snows. The windows were broken by flying sticks and stones, and the yard was filled with debris from the downpours and high winds. The men worked all fall and winter, patching up, painting, and enlarging the barn. They cut enormous piles of wood to keep from freezing, and only when absolutely necessary did they venture out of the notch for mail or provisions.

Each night the family would gather round the open hearth to roast apples, pop corn, and read the Bible, and many a weary traveler gave thanks when, through the swirling, screeching gale and driving sleet, he saw the faint gleam of Mr. Willey's lamp in the frost-covered window.

There was never a visitor at the Willey House who wasn't awed by the overhanging crags some 2,000 feet in the sky, right behind the house. Many tourists told Mr. Willey it was dangerous to live right under them; but, like many of us who get so used to dangerous conditions we fail to notice them any more, he just shrugged and kept about his work.

He did, however, have one warning—and had he heeded it there would have been no Willey House Disaster.

In June, after their first winter in the notch, Mr. and Mrs. Willey sat by the open window in the livingroom watching the mist (which rose like a long, thin veil from the mountain that now bears their name). Suddenly the whole top of the mountain shook and shivered. Then a crack appeared in the ledge, and a mighty chunk of earth and rocks broke away.

They heard a rumble and roar as the landslide tumbled down a thousand feet, tearing and smashing the giant pines like toothpicks.

The Willey House as it appeared shortly
before the bizarre event of August, 1826.

They were so fascinated and frightened, they couldn't move; but when the last echo died away and the dust settled, they knelt on the floor and thanked God that the slide had passed them by. A minute later another hunk of the mountain let go, falling on the opposite side of the house, piling up rocks and mud and tree trunks, higher than the tavern itself.

That night Mr. Willey hitched up the horse and kept the carriage ready with food and blankets; but there were no more slides and after a few days the Willeys forgot all about them.

"Such things occur only once in a lifetime," he said. "This won't happen again in my day."

That June had been a fair month, with clear skies and fluffy clouds. July was hot, August was hotter, and there was an ominous dry-stillness to the air that gave one a sense of impending danger. But the Willeys were too busy with their duties to notice such things.

For weeks the mountains baked in blistering sunshine. High on the peaks, above the treeline, the earth cracked open, and soil fell away around the roots of trees. The whole topside of that 2,000-foot mountain was pitted and gouged and dry as dust.

August 28 was still and sultry. The leaves drooped from the trees. The grass lay motionless in the meadow. Even the birds were still, and the farm animals, sensing danger, stomped in their stalls. The family dog whimpered, without knowing why he was afraid.

Then the sky became brassy as little whirlpools of dust rose from the trails. The trees stirred uneasily, and far off in the purple peaks came the deep, heavy roll of thunder. Low, black clouds darkened the valley and blotted out the mountains.

Then came the storm! No ordinary summer shower—a cloudburst! The lightning was blinding, and the successive thunder claps echoing from one peak to another made a continuous roar that shook the very earth.

(I can recall storms, in my childhood, that I thought lasted for hours. Actually they were short in duration, and I can remember how my heart used to pound when the lightning came in the midnight blackness of the countryside. If we could count to 10 before the thunder clap, we knew we were safe. Then there would be a different sound, a muffled boom that rumbled, and we knew the storm was passing. My father would raise the windows and I'd go back to sleep, lulled by the sound of dripping water and far-off, rolling thunder as the storm passed out to sea.)

In Crawford Notch, on that awful August night, there was no time to count between thunder and lightning. They came together. The rain didn't drip—it smashed in sheets against the mountain side, and fell in torrents on the Willey home. It poured down the chimney, slashed around the rattling windows, streamed in under the door. The whole house shook and swayed from the continuous concussion of power and fury.

Up on the cloud-covered crags, 2,000 feet above the Willey House, great masses of rain-soaked soil and tree trunks were tottering on the brink. Tiny streams had become roaring rivers. The cliffs were crumbling.

As the night wore on, Mr. Willey gathered his family about him —his wife and five children, the two hired men, and a little dog. He opened his Bible and began: THE LORD IS MY SHEPHERD. I SHALL NOT WANT. A shower of stones fell upon the roof. A sheet of lightning showed him the river was rising and creeping toward the house. HE LEADETH ME BESIDE THE STILL WATERS. HE RESTORETH MY SOUL.

Above the roaring waters and crashing thunder was another sound —a deep, heavy, hollow rumble, coming closer and closer, then the sound of 10,000 trees snapping like musket fire as a million tons of rock and earth broke away from the mountain peak and crashed headlong into the valley.

Mr. Willey opened the door, and a wave of muddy water swept across the floor. They were trapped—between the flood and the on-rushing avalanche!

With a child in each arm and the others following, Samuel Willey plunged outdoors into the churning debris. YEA THOUGH I WALK THROUGH THE VALLEY OF THE SHADOW OF DEATH I WILL FEAR NO EVIL.

The first man to reach Crawford Notch after the deluge was John Barker. It took him all day to ford the swollen streams in the flooded intervales. He was bruised from climbing over the rubble—covered with mud—and hungry. He sighed with relief when he saw smoke curling

*Crawford Notch in the White Mountains. The arrow
points to the site of the Willey House Disaster.*

from the chimney of the Willey House. But what destruction lay all
about it!

The yard was covered with silt, the sheds were gone, the barn a
shambles of splintered wood, and on either side of the house were
towering piles of stones and uprooted trees. The avalanche, sweeping
toward the Willey House, had struck a ledge and divided—one part
going to the right of the house, the other to the left. In front of the
house, it came together again, covering the meadow and field with
debris as much as 30 feet high in some places. The house was left completely unharmed!

Barker pushed open the door and went in. The embers of a fire
still glowed on the hearth, and around it was a circle of chairs. The

family Bible lay open on a table. He called—but there was no answer. The Willeys, he thought, had gone out to look at the damage. He dropped on the couch from exhaustion and fell asleep.

When he awoke it was dark, and he was conscious of a queer animal-like groan (or cry) coming from outside. He had no light, no means of rescue or protection, so he stayed where he was until morning.

The next day when he went toward the wreckage of the barn, he heard groans again, and peering through the timbers saw one of the oxen crushed under a heavy beam. The other ox was standing nearby.

As he released them, a searching party came up the trail, led by Mr. Willey's brother, Benjamin Willey. They didn't have to look far before they came on the mangled remains of Mrs. Willey and one of the children. Nearby, under the heavy boulders that fell from the cliff, was one of the farmhands. With a few boards pulled from the wreckage they made coffins and placed the three bodies in one big grave. By now it was too dark for further searching, so they retired in the Willey house that had been spared by the storm.

Next day the bodies of David Nickerson (the other farmhand) and the 12-year-old girl were located. The three remaining children, two boys and a girl, were never found. Were they buried under the falling earth? Were they swept away by the river? Or did they wander off into the darkness to die of cold and starvation?

Or did they—as some believed—become queer wild creatures of the mountains?

There are several theories offered as to why the Willey family left their home. Some think they were driven out by the rising waters or the avalanche, while others contend that Mr. Willey had constructed a small stone shelter, and was trying to reach it when overtaken.

In all probability it was the flood that drove them out, for while it seems impossible that the river should have come to their door, it is a matter of record that five miles below the notch, the waters did rise 25 feet in a very short time. There must have been a terrific amount of water pouring down those mountains as well as from the sky.

Visitors who went to Crawford Notch to look at the storm's damage were astounded at the great gaps torn in the mountain peaks, and the mile-long ugly scars showing that 30 slides had taken place.

In all the romantic and exciting history of the White Mountains, no story has been told as often as the Willey House Disaster in Crawford Notch, on August 28 after an unusually hot dry summer.   □□

The "Black Panther" Never Dies

by C. B. Colby

*One of the most persistent and intriguing wildlife rumors about
New England is whether or not the cougar, panther, catamount,
mountain lion or puma (to mention a few of his assorted names)
still roams the back country of this historic section of America.
Here are some of the facts to date on what biologists agree is the
country's most mysterious animal.*

One of the most persistent and intriguing wildlife rumors about New England is whether or not the cougar, panther, catamount, mountain lion or puma (to mention a few of his assorted names) still roams the back country of this historic section of America.

Almost every year new and "authenticated" tales of seeing, hearing or tracking old *Felis concolor* cougar appear in local papers. Some, upon expert examination, turn out to be outright hoaxes; some might be true; and some, reported by qualified and reliable observers, could conceivably be genuinely true. The trouble is that in the last case, reliable observers hesitate to report such sightings for fear of ridicule.

Let's look at some of the facts to date, and then discuss what to do IF you think you see a cougar—and how you may be able to convince yourself and others that you have seen what you thought you saw.

Historically and actually, the cougar once did roam all of New England and beyond, to the east into New Brunswick and Nova Scotia where reports still appear from time to time of these big cats being seen or tracked. Now it is a nagging conjecture on the part of wildlife enthusiasts and biologists as to whether these big felines are extinct or not, within our boundaries. They are officially recognized as being native to some of our western states and to Florida. Even the biologists who make range maps of this big cat can't seem to agree on where it is currently to be found.

The United States Fish and Wildlife Service, in reply to my query as to the possibility of cougar still roaming New England, simply states: "The question as you stated is still being argued," and mentions a record which states that *felis concolor* cougar occurs as a straggler into Maine from New Brunswick. They also mention the report of one being reported in Ossipee, New Hampshire in 1955, and the letter concludes with the intriguing comment, "the story is still open."

Maine's Carll N. Fenderson, Director of the Information and Education Division of Inland Fisheries and Game, reports that his Department does not have any evidence of the current existence of mountain lions in Maine. His biologists have followed, whenever possible, reports of sightings, tracks, etc., but to his knowledge none has produced any indication of cougars existing today in Maine.

Director Fenderson went on to say that ever since he had been with the Department it had received reports of these big cats being sighted. He believes that often a large fisher has been seen and reported as a "black panther." (A fisher is a member of the weasel family, about three feet long including a fourteen-inch tail. It weighs about eighteen pounds and is from dark brown to black in color.) Also, the tracks of the Canadian Lynx (*lynx canadensis*) are often mistaken for those of the cougar as they are exceptionally large for this comparatively small feline.

My old home state of New Hampshire, through Game Biologist Helenette Silver, reports many statements of cougar sightings, but invariably they have proved out as felis imagination, rather than felis cougar. Some have been reported as cougar nursing cows in a pasture; seen out of a window on a pitch black night; looking in a window. One was even reported on the other side of a barn from the window through which it was clearly "seen"! They have been reported as entering a barn and eating grain and vegetables, which is pretty far out for a man-eating carnivore.

One New Hampshire cougar was reported as having left tracks across a dirt road but, strangely, not on either side. These proved to have been made by a human hand in a big glove, with the maker's very human tracks carefully brushed away. Another Granite State panther, so close to a woman in a blueberry patch she "could have touched it," left tracks exactly like those of a deer. We have some odd-ball mountain lions up New Hampshire way!

Miss Silver concludes her report by saying she "believes in their possibility but not their probability."

A fine letter from a former conservation officer of New Hampshire, John S. Weeden, of Whitefield, New Hampshire reports at length on a sighting of his own near Dalton, New Hampshire, March 24, 1961. He had been called by a gentleman named Ralph Bedell of that town to help him drive off an animal "stalking his house and emitting a terrible scream every few minutes." Officer Weeden and his wife responded and did indeed hear the screams and see greenish eyes shining about two and a half feet above the ground, in the beam of his spotlight. Mr. Weeden also caught a fleeting glimpse of a second animal, brownish in color, bounding into the brush alongside a field a few seconds later. Officer Weeden states this animal was "much too large to be either a bobcat or a lynx." His wife had also sighted a big fawn-colored animal with a body about four feet long (but not a deer) bound across the road ahead of the car a few minutes earlier. They were then about a quarter mile from the Bedell farm.

When they reached the farm, they found a goat tethered in the

Above: The last authenticated cougar kill—shot by Alexander Crowell near Barnard, Vt. in 1881. Below: The Wardsboro "panther," or cougar. This specimen was killed near Wardsboro, Vt. in 1875, and is one of the last cougars ever taken in New England.

yard where it had been all day, an accidental but apparent lure for the animals. Later that night Officer Weeden was able to start some trained cat dogs on the trail of the two animals. They immediately took off into some rocky and almost inaccessible ridges in the area. The dogs turned up the following evening, one with deep claw marks an inch apart down one side of his head.

Here then is an authenticated report as recent as 1961, by an unquestioned expert on animals, who sighted what, to my mind, could only have been a cougar (or a pair of them). Although Officer Weeden hesitates to say in so many words that these *were* cougars, as he did not actually examine them at close range, he is certain the ones they saw were tawny brown in color, larger than either a bobcat or lynx with which he was familiar, screamed, and stood about two and a half feet high judging from their eyes. There are no animals which fit these known facts except the cougar.

Vermont has had its share of panther reports over the years, one being reported as observed through binoculars for several minutes from the Gore Mountain Fire Tower in northeastern Vermont a few years ago. Another is claimed to have been shot and buried in a pasture, location unknown. (This seems unlikely unless the hunter thought such a kill illegal.) The first recorded killing of a cougar in Vermont took place in the latter years of the last century near Bennington. Others have been authentically reported as killed in Roxbury, December 1821, in Weathersfield, January 1867, and in West Wardsboro in 1875. The last authenticated killing of a Vermont cougar was on November 24, 1881, when the famed "Barnard Panther" was shot by Alexander Crowell near Barnard. This big cat, shown in the faded photo purchased by the author in 1958 at Holden's antique shop in Brattleboro, measured seven feet in length and weighed 182½ pounds.

At the time of purchasing the photo I talked with Mrs. Holden about cougar in Vermont. She said it was too bad I could not have talked to a Mr. Henry Tanner, who used to live in Putney and who had seen panther near there several times within the past few years. Mr. Tanner, who had been a Florida game warden, was then living in California, but I did call a Mr. Ernest Parker, then Justice of the Peace and Notary Public in Putney. Mr. Parker reassured me that Mr. Tanner certainly knew a panther when he saw one and that he had told Mr. Parker of several sightings recently (1958), one in particular when the big cat had been spotted sunning himself on a flat-topped stone wall. Here again is a report by a qualified naturalist, of a sighting, or several sightings, by one who hesitated to report them for fear of ridicule.

When I recently wrote to Montpelier for official information on Vermont cougar and cited several of these sightings, my letter was returned with a brusque, longhand note at the bottom stating: "We don't have anything factual to send you. This information we have heard or read." So does Vermont dispose of her cougars.

No more than twenty have ever been officially reported as killed in Vermont since such records were kept. The most famous perhaps was the one once mounted over the sign of Landlord Fay's eatery which became known as Catamount Tavern near Barnard.

As for the cougar in Massachusetts, Howard S. Willard, Director of Law Enforcement, replied to my query that he had received no report of such cats being observed, and that there had been none for many years. With Mr. Willard's letter came a longhand memo from a Mr. Knurow of Pittsfield, Mass., who reported that an animal popularly identified as "The Thing" made a lot of news back in 1948 in the Pittsfield-Washington-Hinsdale area of the Berkshires. It was repeatedly identified as a "black panther." About this time another black panther was reported (according to the memo) in the Wilton, New Hampshire area

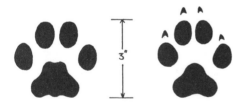

The wolf or dog track, right, has claw prints while that of the cougar, left, and Canadian Lynx do not. The cougar tracks can be over 20" apart while the Canadian Lynx stride is only about 6".

A cougar can grow to a length of 7 to 9 feet and
leap fifteen feet in height to climb a tree. It can
drop from a height of 40 feet and run away uninjured.

by a Conservation Officer named Charles Proctor. Wilton is about eighty miles to the northeast from where "The Thing" was reported. Could this be the same animal; and what happened to it after that? (The State of New Hampshire does not mention this alleged sighting by Officer Proctor.)

This same memo indicated that a pair of cougar roamed the Magalloway Region of Maine and New Hampshire in the 1920s. This apparently refers to the Magalloway Plantation region which straddles the Maine-New Hampshire line just north of Lake Umbagog, which is bisected by this same boundary line. Neither Maine nor New Hampshire mentions this in their replies to my query.

Rhode Island, in its official state publication, *Mammals of Rhode Island*, reports without hesitation that the only mountain lion to be found in Rhode Island today is in the Slater Park Zoo in Pawtucket. This publication reports that the old Boston Museum (which used to be located on Huntington Avenue) once had a mounted cougar, reportedly killed in Rhode Island in 1847 or 1848. This excellent booklet concludes its coverage of the cougar with the line, "It is almost beyond the realm of possibility that the mountain lion will ever again be seen in the wilds of Rhode Island." It is interesting to note that this scientific booklet on mammals is willing and imaginative enough to include the word "almost" in that last sentence. Even trained biologists can't be too sure when it comes to making a flat statement about these legendary cats.

Chief of the Game Division of the Board of Fisheries and Game for the State of Connecticut, Arroll L. Lamson had some interesting points to add to the legend. He states that a report written prior to 1842 by a Rev. James H. Linsley includes mention of a fine specimen of cougar killed in the northern part of Connecticut and exhibited in Mix's Museum (location unknown). Chief Lamson reports that today reported killings of livestock by cougar invariably turn out to be the work of semiwild dogs running loose. He concludes his fine letter with the line: "Our official stand here in Connecticut would be that these animals are extinct within our state boundaries."

So much for a partial report on past sightings, screams heard, and tracks spotted, as reported by the serious, the hoaxers, and the imaginative. For those of you who have yet to see or think you see a cougar, what should you look for to enable you to identify the animal with accuracy, or at least sufficient accuracy to warrant further investigation?

[173]

A cougar, being a member of the cat family, has a small head and short neck in proportion to the rest of his body. It can run from seven to nine feet in length, including a three-foot tail. Some cougars reach a length of nine feet! Visualize this in proportion to your 9′ x 12′ rug and you'll realize what a really big cat the cougar is! Bobcats and lynx average about three feet in length, including a short tail.

The color of the cougar is a tawny brown (color varies from light buckskin to grayish brown in various parts of the country) with white underparts and throat. The chin and upper lips are also white with a dark area where the upper lips merge with the cheeks. The ears are dark-rimmed on the back with white hairs inside the front opening. The tail, an unmistakable trademark of the cougar, is long, heavy and tipped with a dark brown or black end. There is no tassel as in African lions. All so-called "black panthers" are merely black mutations (freaks) of the normally colored animal, the same as there are black woodchucks, black squirrels, and black rabbits. A black kitten may appear in a litter of perfectly normal baby cougars.

Cougars stand about two-and-a-half feet high (remember the eyes Officer Weeden saw about this height above the ground) and weigh from 150 to 200 pounds. It is a mighty big cat! It is also a powerful cat, for it can leap fifteen feet in height to climb a tree, clear a fence, or a bank. It can leap down safely from a height of over forty feet and run off uninjured. It can drag a deer for many yards in ease, or over a fence with no effort.

The voice of the panther consists of growls, snarls, spitting noises, and its famous scream, which is enough to scare the daylights out of even a veteran hunter. It sounds like a human being in agony, or a woman in desperation and pain, and once heard it will never be forgotten I can assure you.

The tracks of the cougar are catlike with NO claw marks showing. They are big tracks, measuring over three inches in length. If they are in mud or soft snow they appear even larger. The tracks of the Canadian lynx measure almost as large, but those of a bobcat average about half this size, perhaps an inch-and-a-half. Although the tracks of a lynx compare in size with that of the cougar, you can easily tell the difference by the length of the stride (distance between tracks). Those of the lynx are about six inches apart when walking while those of the far larger cougar average almost twenty inches apart.

Should you see an animal resembling this description, or tracks which seem to match the data above, mark the spot well and contact your nearest game protector, conservation officer, or anyone qualified to pass judgment on the subject. If it is a sighting, write down all the facts as you remember them while still fresh in your mind, and have anyone else who saw the animal do the same for comparison. If you are hunting, don't shoot just to prove your point. A sight of one of these rare animals should be reward enough for any real sportsman.

I for one have a hunch that there are still some of these great and fascinating cats roaming the wild sections of New England, for they eat anything, literally, from mice to moose, and we have both of these. They are sly, expert at concealment, and have an inborn hatred and fear of man. It is no wonder they are rarely reported and even more rarely seen. Even in areas where they are known to be quite plentiful and are successfully hunted, they are about the most elusive of all game. Here in New England let's hang out the welcome mat instead of the no trespassing signs and hold our fire. Perhaps some red letter day we'll really know for sure whether old felis cougar is still as much a Yankee as he used to be. □□

Wings
Over Brattleboro

*Twenty observers described it as a violent bird war.
The author thinks it might have been a migratory
phenomenon resulting from a freak meteorological
event, but whatever the cause, it certainly was the
most extraordinary sight ever witnessed in New England . . .*

"Boston, October 11, we hear, that about the 20th or 21st Day of September, there was seen near Fort Dummer, the greatest Phenomenon that ever was seen in New England. Two large Companies of Pigeon Hawks, judged to be about 4000 in Number, headed by two large Eagles, one Eagle heading one Company and the other Eagle the other. They found themselves too large for two Companies and so divided themselves into 4 Battalions. They fought over from Fort Hinsdell to Fort Dummer, and fighting and fighting over and under one another from one Fort to the other for the Space of 4 hours, till one Company conquered the other, and chas'd after them. *This may be depended on, 20 being present.*"

This is, to my recollection, one of the earliest accounts of hawk migrations to be printed in New World literature, a possibility which fascinated me no end. Because I have live-trapped, banded, photographed, and fought (in self-defense), the various species of hawks and owls seen in my area of New York State, any reference to the birds of prey is likely to stimulate a conditioned response of enthusiasm. I first learned of the great flight from an article by John B. May in the October, 1956, issue of *Nature* magazine. Anxious to authenticate the report and to learn more of the history of the locale, I visited several of New England's finest libraries. The original description of the exciting scene appeared in the October 14, 1756, issue of the *New Hampshire Gazette*, and I was able to locate a copy in Boston's Massachusetts Historical Society. And in a visit to the Brattleboro area, I was able to find the fort markers and to establish interviews with several of its citizens who are well informed on New England folklore. New Englanders, I learned, are a proud people who find much revelation in discussing their heritage.

According to my findings, Fort Dummer was the initial settlement in the area of Vermont which was later to become Brattleboro. Obviously, the fort was constructed as a protection from the hostilities of the native Indians. "From the year 1720 to 1725," states Zadock Thompson, in his *History of Vermont* (1842), "a very destructive war was carried on between the eastern Indian and the New England provinces . . . and it was during this war, that the first civilized establishment was made, within the present limits of Vermont, by the erection of Fort Dummer." Originally built in the form of a blockhouse, a stockade was later constructed and several additional buildings placed within. In his essay, *Independent Vermont*, Charles M. Thompson contributes a romantic description of the scene. "Summer or winter, it must have been a picturesque sight; in winter, with the snow drifted high against its walls and blanketing the once sparkling river; in summer, with its rough logs hot in the sun, its plots of cultivated ground near the walls, its feeding cattle, and its sleeping dogs, its hens dusting in the roads, its leathery-cheeked, lean, sinewy, keen-eyed rangers chatting in the shade or going about their various occasions, and its Indians from New York who were encouraged to sell their furs there, and who, it was hoped, would help to protect it from the red allies of the French."

In regard to Fort Hinsdell (Hinsdale or Hinsdill), ". . . in 1742," as it is so recorded in the *History of Cheshire and Sullivan Counties, New Hampshire*, "Colonel Ebenezer Hinsdale built a fort and a gristmill on Ash Swamp Brook, north of Merry's Meadow." The two establishments, Fort Dummer and Fort Hinsdell, were separated by the Connecticut River and respectively positioned in a northwest-southeast relationship at a distance of slightly more than two miles.

As to the great hawk flight, a present analysis some 200 years since can only be a matter of speculation. Even so, there appears to be a sufficient number of parts to the puzzle to allow for a fairly accurate picture. To begin with, the anonymous reporter, possibly a militiaman, interprets the "Phenomenon" as a battle between "Companies" and "Battalions." For many years, I have witnessed large kettles* of migrating hawks not unlike the view described. It would be not only natural, but a simple matter for a layman of pioneer times to improvise a romantic interpretation of their intermingling actions. And when the soaring hawks followed one another beyond the line of sight, who was to deny that one had "conquered the other, and chas'd after them?"

The flight characteristics given in the description, ". . . fighting and fighting over and under one another . . . ," indicates the major part of the flight might have been something other than the species identified. While most hawks are capable of ascending in great circles, the group best adapted for soaring and most widely known for this habit are the Buteo (Buzzard)** Hawks. With broad deep wings and

---

* Kettle. A term used among hawk watchers to indicate a large mass of swirling hawks.
** Buzzard. Not to be confused with Vultures, a hawk equally adapted to thermal soaring.

short wide tails, the Buteos are made to order for thermal soaring. Thermals are turbulent and often violent upward movements of air due to great differences of temperature between the ground and the atmosphere. By continual adjustments to the set of their wings and tail, the hawks are able to circle for hours without once flapping their wings. The sport of flying engineless planes resulted from man's discovery of the secret of thermals.

Among the Buteos are such species as the Golden Eagle, Bald Eagle, Red-tailed Hawk, Red-shouldered Hawk, Rough-legged Hawk, and the Broad-winged Hawk. Because of their tendency to migrate together in considerable numbers, it is highly probable that the species seen during the flight of 1756 was the Broad-winged Hawk, *Buteo platypterus*. Not only one of the smallest of the Buteos, their size in comparison to the accompanying eagles is a logical explanation for their having been confused with a smaller species. The Pigeon Hawk, *Falco columbarius*, is a small falcon with narrow wings and is not known for soaring or migrating in large assembly. The historical account of New England by Zaddock Thompson, previously quoted, lends support to my conclusion. "The Pigeon Hawk is much less common than several other of the smallest species of hawk . . . This hawk is shy and watchful, seldom being seen out of the forest." He adds a bit of confusion to the discussion, however, when describing another species to which pioneers sometimes referred as a Pigeon Hawk. "This hawk is very common in Vermont, and generally passes under the name Pigeon Hawk.

. . . This is the Sharp-shinned Hawk. . . ." Was the Sharp-shinned Hawk, *Accipiter striatus velox*, the species seen by the observer at Fort Dummer?

The time of the year in which the great flight was observed, ". . . about the 20th or 21st Day of September . . . ," can be cited as one of our most important clues. ". . . the sky was literally darkened with Broad-wings, giving us a glimpse of the way it must have been any mid-September day a couple of centuries ago," stated Maurice Broun, a New Englander and former curator of Pennsylvania's Hawk Mountain Sanctuary. On September 16, 1948, Mr. Broun and his associates counted 11,392 hawks, mostly Broad-wings, in migration. For years, hawk watchers have climbed to the "lookout," an elevation of 1540 feet, to enjoy the sight of migrating hawks soaring the thermals above Blue Mountain. In 1968, 26,000 visitors witnessed a total of 29,765 migrating birds of prey, 18,507 of which were Broad-wings. Moving southward from their nesting habitat in northeastern United States and Canada, the hawks become funneled into two main lines, one along the east through Cape May, New Jersey, and the other slightly more west along the Kittatinny Ridge (Endless Mountain). Some pass the summit of Hawk Mountain at dazzling heights to appear as mere specks while others swoop in at

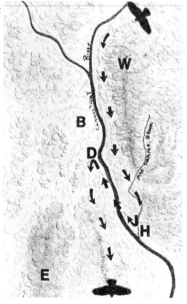

A *reconstruction by the author of the remarkable flight of 1756.* W = *Wantastiquet Mountain, 1390′;* H = *Ft. Hinsdale;* D = *Ft. Dummer;* B = *Brattleboro; and* E = *East Mountain, 1430′.*

breathtaking closeness, enough to observe the pigment color of their eye. Undoubtedly, a portion of these flights originate along the ridges of Vermont and New Hampshire ". . . the way it must have been any mid-September day a couple of centuries ago."

An examination of a topographical map for the Brattleboro area presents one with an opportunity for conjecture. The flight of 1756 might have followed a north-south path along the ridges of Wantastiquet Mountain, paralleling the Connecticut River. Theorizing a bit further, as the valley broadened and the elevation decreased, the birds lost advantage of the thermals and in the confusion circled about in search for another updraft. Moving in a northwest direction, they passed from Fort Hinsdale to Fort Dummer before catching a new air current on the west side of the river. The flight then continued southward along the ridges paralleling East Mountain. It might not have happened this way, but at least we have a picture of what could have occurred.

There is a possibility that the large movement of birds was the result of a freak meteorological event. We know that weather has a profound effect upon the manner in which migrations take place. Hurricane-like winds have sometimes forced migrating birds to span continents and large bodies of water, topography over which they might not normally follow. Hawk watchers are well aware of the effects of winds upon the movements of the birds of prey. In *Hawk Migrations and the Weather*, Broun indicates the poorest flights to take place during a low while the most phenomenal flights occur when the cool northwest winds batter the ridges. ". . . to be certain of enjoying a good flight of hawks at the Sanctuary," writes Broun, "one must hie to our heights on the heels of low presure areas passing to the north of us." Perhaps weather conditions had something to do with the phenomenal flight over Fort Hinsdale and Fort Dummer. A search for clues to this effect, however, has proved fruitless. Until more data is obtained, the theory must remain dormant.

Surely, the most startling movements of hawk populations in all history occurred unseen by human eyes. That the flight of 1756 was observed and recorded is a fact that should be appreciated. In the following years, when time allows for a return trip to an area through which hawks migrate, I shall be viewing the birds with new wonderment. My thoughts will be with their ancestral relatives who took part in "the greatest Phenomenon that ever was seen in New England . . . This may be depended on." □□

From the first sightings in the late 1950's, through the years of intensive tracking through New Hampshire forests, to the final and surprising solution of a mystery which baffled naturalists for more than ten years, the author describes the saga of · · ·

New England's
Brand New Animal

by Evan Hill

I t didn't make a man exactly happy to watch his dog be run out of his own pasture, chased yelping at a dead-hard run for half a mile toward the barn, not daring to break stride or glance back to see if the wild gray beast behind him was gaining.

Yet Leonard Gould, Sr., was calm enough as he stood in the doorway of his East Colebrook, New Hampshire, farmhouse watching his big three-year-old male collie hightailing it toward home.

The big animal chasing him—whatever it was—was gaining on Laddie when Gould waved his arms and shouted. Laddie spurted ahead faster; his pursuer slowed, then gracefully loped in a huge lazy arc back to where he'd picked up the chase, occasionally looking calmly over his shoulder at the dairy farmer.

For the last five years Gould and his neighbors have seen dozens of these animals—somewhat dog-like and yet certainly not dogs; somehow interested in humans and yet certainly wild. Some were as large as a big German shepherd. They were gray or reddish brown; some, especially the larger, older ones, were steel-gray, almost black.

The pups—and Gould had observed them closely as they gamboled around his tractor during haying time, catching field mice in the wake of the mower—resembled dogs. The adults looked a little more like foxes, yet not really.

Once, as Gould attempted to describe them, a man asked, "What makes you think they're not dogs?"

Softly Gould countered, "What makes you think they're not wolves?"

It was not the only time New Hampshire residents had asked that question in the last 15 years.

Sometimes the question was shrill, near panic, as country people—alarmed at the bloody deer-slaughtering techniques of these animals—telephoned game wardens to ask if it were safe to send their children to school. (It was.)

Sometimes the question was academic: were wolves returning to New England? (Perhaps, although only two of the 26 subspecies of wolves once common to the United States are still here and both are nearly extinct. In 1968, however, an 84-pound male timber wolf was killed by an automobile in upstate New York, the first authentic report of a wolf kill in the state since 1899.)

Most times the question was indignant: what in the world *is* the animal?

During nine years of scientific studies it was identified only as a "wild New Hampshire-type canid," although hunters and farmers reported seeing "coydogs," wild dogs, wolves and coyotes. Today it roams every New England state as well as upper New York and Canada. It is seen and killed in greater numbers each year. It has killed hundreds of deer, although not affecting the deer population. It has frightened thousands of usually unflappable New Hampshiremen, some by direct contact, more by rumors of the beasts.

During two cold New Hampshire winters it spooked hundreds of residents of Sullivan and Grafton Counties as if a pack of starving wolves were ranging the woods—which is what some residents believed.

One of the first sightings of the animal was made by Kneiland Wheeler, a rugged bear and bobcat hunter who lives in Springfield, New Hampshire (pop. 300), which probably contains more deer and bear than people. One night on a back road his headlights "caught a brown, shaggy animal about the size of a police dog." It whirled back into the brush, even as he thought it was a wolf. But he knew there hadn't been a wolf seen in New Hampshire in this century. He dismissed the thought.

But there were others who saw and heard, and didn't dismiss. They talked. There had been the strange howls up on Croydon Mountain, eight miles away, "like someone hollering." Searchers reported only

pursuing was much more than a rabbit killer.

"dog tracks." A beaver trapper told of seeing two strange wolf-like animals. Unearthly howling had frightened two tough French-Canadian loggers out of the woods on a bright summer day. A hunter saw "two coyotes in a field," but everyone knew there were no coyotes in New Hampshire. A farmer's wife telephoned game wardens about a fast-running, fox-like animal that could leap "ten feet at a time."

Game wardens were skeptical. For years they'd patiently listened to reports of a giant black panther who ranged the Connecticut Valley but left no tracks, and now they had another mystery beast. The howls, they said, were owls, or birds, perhaps; the "coyotes" were almost certain to be wild dogs. Don't worry, they said. But people did. They were uncomfortable. What they were seeing and hearing made no sense. Spasms of fear began to give some stomach stitches.

Then one cold moonlit February night, in 1958, a maple syrup producer named Kirk Heath heard strange goings-on in the pasture behind his house in Springfield. It was like nothing he'd heard before. It was a mixture of a howl and a yip, yet the yip was not truly a yip, not like a fox's. Quietly, he got his tape recorder and he hung the microphone out his bedroom window. For 30 minutes the reels spun quietly, recording the sound of a wild animal calling in the night. Then he telephoned his neighbor Kneiland Wheeler to ask him to bring his dogs next morning to hunt down the animal.

At daybreak Wheeler arrived with one of his half dozen dogs, a 70-pound cross between a redbone and a bloodhound. Heath got his own dog and they buckled into snowshoes.

The tracks, about four hours old, showed that the animal was trotting easily, plainly in the open, with no attempt to skulk along the edges of the field. It took a long, regular step, and from the depth of its track Wheeler judged its weight at about 60 pounds. He measured the length of the animal's pace. Twenty-eight inches, two inches shorter than his gun barrel. He looked up quizzically at Heath. His big Redbone-bloodhound paced out 24 inches.

Two miles farther, in a hemlock and balsam thicket, they saw blood and fur on the snow—the remains of a rabbit. Head and bones had been eaten. The animal had run down—actually overtaken—a running rabbit, and Wheeler had never known of a dog that could do this.

Within 100 feet they found where the animal, full with food, had bedded down for a few hours, and they unsnapped the leashes from their frantic dogs so they could follow the now hot scent. But the animal headed straight for a well-traveled, well-ploughed road and the dogs lost him there.

Next day Wheeler was out on snowshoes again, this time with a neighbor and his big blue tick hound. They tracked the animal nearly 15 miles through heavy snow that day, and near dusk its trail led them into the mouth of an abandoned mica mine. But the animal was gone. He'd started to lay up there for the night, but their arrival had driven him out. They'd started that morning with day-old tracks; now they were on tracks that were minutes old at most—a hot trail. But it was getting dark. The temperature was near zero and dropping as nightfall came on. They came out.

They were back at the mica mine shortly after dawn. The temperature was still near zero and the fresh tracks that had come out of the mine shaft the day before were now frozen. They moved ahead swiftly, the crust rasping against their varnished snowshoe webbing.

They paused at the edge of a long deer yard, a swampy, low-brushed area where deer—sometimes as many as 15 or 20—hang together in winter to feed on ground hemlock and tree bark.

There Wheeler saw what he later described as "the bloodiest mess I ever saw in my life." They now knew that the animal they were pursuing was much more than a rabbit-killer. The tragedy was clearly frozen into the blood-stained snow, in the fur and entrails, in the bloody tracks and the stiff carcass of a big deer.

The animal—probably only minutes after they had given up the hunt the previous day—had stalked four deer bedded down in the deer yard. It had leaped out, then slashed their throats and bellies as they ran. It had cut down one deer, and then gone on a killing rampage to rip at three more as they fled. The wounded deer, slashed and bleeding, had escaped, perhaps to die in another part of the forest.

Then the animal had returned to its kill, gorging itself only on the still-warm liver and lungs, and then glorying in rolling over and over in the snow. Its fur had bloodied an area nearly 20 yards square.

The dead deer had not been hamstrung—its hind leg ankle tendons had not been severed so that it would be crippled, helpless and unable to run, forced to stand immobile while its throat was slashed. It had been cut down while running, and Wheeler now knew the killer was

In August of 1960, Maurice Nelson, superintendent of Corbin Park (see YANKEE December, 1970—"23,000 Acres Inside a Fence"), killed "18 pounds of something that was not a dog and didn't quite look like a coyote." Here he holds it (or one of the others he shot a few days later), while Conservation Officer Jesse Scott looks on.

not a dog, for dogs hamstring their kills. Wheeler swore at the animal because he knew it had killed for pleasure, but it was no use to track any more that day. The crust was frozen and the animal was running on top of it, easily. And his trail was 18 hours old.

When word of the deer kill swept through Springfield, Grantham, and Newport, most residents thought immediately of wolves. "Wolves catch their prey by running it down in open chase," an encyclopedia reported. They can cover 25 to 40 miles in a night; appear in winter at places where none have been for years. They kill by grabbing a running animal from underneath, often killing an animal a day and eating only the tender parts; in one night two wolves killed 250 sheep, eating nothing. The people were talking wolf.

But not the State Fish and Game Department. When Kirk Heath took his tape recording to the man who was then the director of the department, the man snapped, "It's nothing but a dog."

His words were no comfort to residents. In one month alone 16 dead deer were found in the woods near Springfield, each with its throat or belly slashed, each with only its liver and lungs eaten. Kneiland Wheeler wore out his snowshoe webbing twice that winter as he hunted the animal, and found tracks that proved there were at least three of them roaming the woods; one, a large male. Springfield residents were long since past curiosity. They hunted the animal at every opportunity. On one Sunday 18 hunters were out after it.

Kirk Heath was playing his tape recording often. Radio station WMUR in Manchester, New Hampshire, broadcast it for tens of thousands of local listeners. A big game hunter said the howl sounded like a hyena, and Heath began to wonder if some exotic animal had escaped from a game farm or a traveling circus. A feature writer seriously suggested that atomic fallout might have caused mutations in wolf or dog or coyote.

On April 4—with still a lot of snow on the ground—a Springfield resident saw the animal crossing the meadow near his house. He telephoned Wheeler and watched the animal as he waited. Big, maybe 100 pounds. Confident, wandering through the open field, stopping now and then to sniff the air. Gray with a nearly white belly. Big pointed head. Pointed ears. Eighteen-inch bushy tail with black tip dragging along the snow. He knew he was seeing a wolf.

Half an hour later Wheeler got a shot at the animal's big white chest with his 30–30, at 150 yards. He missed, and that was enough for him. He had walked through his snowshoes twice hunting that animal. He'd frozen himself until he felt brittle, and he'd walked until his muscles ached. He'd missed countless $20 bobcat bounties while he'd been only minutes behind the creature and each time it had slipped away. Now he was through.

As spring came on, the howls diminished as with the melting snow, and Springfield lived in peace. The animal seemed to have disappeared. No one mourned the loss.

But on July 27, 1959—15 months later—Maurice Nelson, the superintendent of Corbin Park, a private game preserve seven miles away, heard strange noises—"like a dog fight"—behind the barn. He ran there, shotgun in hand, but found nothing. He recorded the event in his diary.

It was the beginning of a 16-month hunt on snowshoes, in snowmobiles and airplanes. It involved government bounty trappers, at least a dozen state conservation officers, bear hunters, fur trappers, and the advice of at least one Indian. (Advice not practical.) During the winter of 1959–60 the animals slaughtered at least 31 deer in the game preserve, using the same technique and the same dainty gourmet appetite they had in Springfield, but no animals were killed.

Early in August, while cutting brush, Nelson heard strange wailing howls. Armed with a .22 pistol he went about a quarter of a mile into the woods, mimicking the wailing animal, and causing it to answer. He headed for a nearby park road and waited, his pistol resting on a fence post, aimed at where it seemed the approaching animal would emerge to cross the road.

He was right. It came out, a perfect target as it stood at the edge of the rutted road, sniffing, waiting for Nelson to make another call. Nelson began the squeeze. But he stopped. A second animal came out to join the first, and then a third. Tawny, shaggy beasts, with black guard hairs, faces like coyotes, drooping tails, white chests and bellies. Alert. Sniffing.

Nelson changed his mind about tackling them with a .22 pistol. Quietly he slid into the brush behind him, and backtracked himself. When he was clear, he ran a half mile to his house to get a shotgun, hoping the animals would still be there when he got back.

They were. He fired. One fell. Two fled. That night he telephoned Jesse Scott, the local game warden, to say that he had just killed 18 pounds of something that was not a dog, and didn't quite look like coyote. It wasn't anything he'd seen before in a lifetime in the woods of New England. Next day the newspapers called it a coydog, a hybrid mixture of dog and coyote.

On August 25, Nelson shot two more, a 17½-pound female, and a 15¾-pound male. These bodies were taken to the New Hampshire Fish and Game Department biological laboratories for study, as the first had been.

Nelson shot the fourth—a 24-pound male—four days later, and Jesse Scott, not entirely satisfied that the animals really were coydogs, took the dead animal to a veterinarian, who discouraged the coydog label.

After that Nelson and the conservation officers called it a coyote, although they really didn't think it was. Neither did New Hampshire biologists. The biologists began to call it by the loose Latin catch-all *canid*, which was certainly safe enough because the dog is a canid and so is a fox and a wolf and a coyote.

Traps were set in the park—50 or 60 or a hundred of them, no one knows how many—and in October the fifth animal was caught. It was a 25-pound female.

That was all for five months. Nelson and Scott had their fingers crossed, however, for they had killed only young animals. Where were the old ones? The big ones that Wheeler had tracked outside the park?

At the end of February a government trapper, previously successful with wolves and coyotes in the West, was brought in by the Fish and Game Department. This time he was a failure.

Nelson's diary on March 8 says: *Talked to coyotes for two hours while Jesse and two other conservation officers tried to sneak up on them. No results.*

Diary—March 26: *Coyotes howled at woodshed. Took shotgun, but they were gone. Called Jesse and Glen Higgins.*

Higgins is a bobcat hunter from Hinsdale, New Hampshire, who owns a scrappy dog with a reputation for following anything. Nelson told him over the telephone, "I don't want him to get killed," and Higgins replied, "I have a lot of faith in that dog."

The next morning that dog, Rusty, a red tick hound, started tracking from the corner of the woodshed, tugging at the chain leash on Higgins' wrist. Nelson was with them. Both men were on snowshoes. Six miles and five hours later they were on top of Moose Mountain with the webbing coming out of Higgins' snowshoes. It had been tough work, but Nelson and Higgins felt a little smug. Below them six armed men were stationed at strategic spots—the logical and only spots the coyotes would approach as soon as Rusty flushed them.

When they reached the hot scent of the spot where the animals had been bedded down—there seemed to be three of them—Higgins turned Rusty loose. He leaped off barking, flying over the crust.

The animals went where Rusty chased them, and where Nelson and Higgins knew they would go. But the men below didn't see them; didn't hear them. The animals slipped through like ghosts in a fog.

In the first week of April, a Massachusetts cat hunter tried, and Nelson's diary recorded: *No results. The coyotes win again.*

But April 9 was Bonanza Day. It was Saturday and Glen Higgins was back with Rusty. There was a heavy crust in the woods, strong enough to support dog or canid, and enough new snow for perfect tracking.

Top: The original litter of Eastern Coyotes—captured in the Blue Mountain Forest, N.H., by Glen Higgins and Maurice Nelson in 1960 (see text) —were raised by Walter and Helenette Silver, game biologists for the N.H. State Fish and Game Department. For the first few months, they were allowed to use the Silvers' fireplace for a den and even at that age they could handle a pretty good bone! Bottom: Eastern Coyote female from this same litter, as she looked seven years later. She's hunting mice while tethered on a 50-foot chain.

Higgins turned Rusty loose and the two men followed. There was no sound. Rusty was running silently, probing, hunting through patches of drifting fog for something to bay about. But all that morning he was a quiet hound, for he had nothing to say.

Then, on the side of Croydon Mountain, a new track joined Rusty's and followed it and the men knew that now a canid was tracking the hunting hound. They went on faster, and then Nelson stopped suddenly.

"Glen," he whispered, looking down at the two animals' tracks. He beckoned. Higgins came back.

"Look," he said, pointing at a scattering of fresh brown earth on top of the new snow.

Higgins understood immediately. The earth could have come only from a spot sheltered from the winter's heavy snows—from an animal's den; and it could have gotten there only one way—on the fur of the animal now tracking Rusty. They backtracked the animal, and within 50 yards found the source of the tell-tale earth—a crevice beneath a big granite outcropping.

Nelson kneeled and peered down into it. He reached and felt among the leaves, then turned to his partner.

"Come here, Glen," he called. "There's more coyotes here than you've ever seen in your life."

There were five black, fuzzy pups, newly born, their eyes still closed and their umbilical cords still dangling from their bellies, perhaps only a day or two old. They were identical. Their heads were tan, their tails tipped with white.

Nelson wanted to kill them, right there, right then. He couldn't forget the nearly three dozen deer that had been slaughtered in the park by the parents of these pups, and he didn't want to run any risks of survival and escape. He'd had enough of them.

But Higgins said, "Aw, let's bring 'em out and we can kill 'em later if you want."

Nelson stripped off his black sweater and tied the sleeves together to make a woolen basket. He arranged the squeaking animals in it and tucked the bundle inside his shirt. He went back to his house.

Nelson never did kill the pups. Instead he telephoned Jesse Scott, who took the litter—three females, two males—to Walter and Helenette Silver, game biologists for the New Hampshire State Fish and Game Department. They were to live with and study the canids and their offspring for seven years and two months.

Meanwhile, Maurice Nelson was now even more eager to get the mother of that litter. He didn't want her to produce more pups. The animals were still killing; in one day he found seven slaughtered deer in a five-mile stretch.

Three days after the litter was found, three adult animals were sighted together, and for the first time Nelson knew that there were more than two. He redoubled his efforts. A Fish and Game trapper brought pieces of the cloth the pups slept on and vials of their feces and urine. But these did not lure the mother back to her den which had been heavily staked out with steel traps. The older animals were not fooled.

Then Nelson called in Ken Flint, one of the best trappers in New England, and gave him clear instructions: get those animals out of the park.

During that spring and the next fall Flint drove a Land Rover and a Jeep more than 5000 miles over park roads and trails, tending trap-line. He baited with muskrat gland scent, and with wolf and coyote urine ordered from Montana.

On April 24 he caught a 40-pound male in an open field at the foot of Croydon Mountain. Later he picked three coyote toes out of a trap, and still later the coyote that had lost the toes.

The known remaining wild canid—a large adult—vanished from the park shortly afterward. Only the captured litter remained, now being raised and studied by the Silvers, as much a biological mystery to the nation's wildlife experts as their deer-killing parents had been to Kirk Heath and other residents of Springfield.

None of the dead animals shipped to game biologists had been identified. There was opinion—lots of it, wild dogs, coyotes, wolves, coydogs—but it had no scientific basis, and New Hampshire wildlife people continued to call the animals canids until they knew what they were talking about. But now—with the captured litter—there was a magnificent opportunity to study the animals as they grew.

As the pups put on weight—some reached more than 50 pounds—they clearly resembled the animals shot and trapped in Corbin Park. They were obviously relatives of the beautiful brute that had caused Kneiland Wheeler to walk through his snowshoes twice.

Clearly they were not domestic dogs; nor offspring of domestic dogs gone wild. Although they were friendly and affectionate and never vicious or dangerous, they were wild animals. But what kind? They resembled a large coyote, or a small wolf, or a German shepherd. But resemblance is not identification. Their fur was russet and gray with black guard hairs; their chests carried a splotch of white, and they wore a wolf-like ruff or cape across their shoulders. Their tails were long, bushy, and tipped with black. They had heavy heads, with large, pointed ears and a long nose that was broader than a coyote's but narrower than a wolf's. Yellow eyes. Large feet. Long legs.

While their voices were higher than a wolf's—something that Kirk Heath's tape had proved—they paced like wolves (coyotes trot) and when the captive males became fathers, wolf-like, they washed and cleaned their pups and taught them to eat. A visiting naturalist observed that they resembled the southern or red wolf (*Canis rufus*).

When the animals reached maturity, the Silvers began to breed them to each other—50 offspring were born—to see if they bred true. They did, thus eliminating the possibility of recent canine hybrids. Bred to pointers, they produced a litter resembling mongrels; bred to collies, their pups looked like barnyard collies.

In 1963, the National Science Foundation granted $38,000 to study and identify the animals. The New Hampshire Fish and Game Department was to attempt identification through behavior and growth of the animals. Thus the Silvers' breeding of the litter. Barbara Lawrence, curator of mammals at Harvard University's Museum of Comparative Zoology, was to supervise and adminster the grant, as well as to attempt identification through skull and body measurements.

The information-gathering stage was completed in 1967, and the captive animals were destroyed. The evidence was complete.

Now at Harvard and in Boscawen, New Hampshire, the scientists compiled their statistics, digested their findings, and came to conclusions. The verdict was in with the publication, in two scientific journals, of the two independent studies. The identification of the animals was identical. The Silvers reached their conclusions from close observation of the behavior and growth of the animals. Barbara Lawrence, publishing her findings in collaboration with William H. Bossert, reached conclusions from cranial studies.

They are not wolves, not coydogs, not dog-wolves, or wild dogs. They are not hybrids.

The Silvers write that the "data favors the acceptance of predominantly coyote ancestry for these animals. . . . It is likely that they have evolved from the coyotes, but have been partly dependent on the acquisition of some dog and/or wolf genes."

[194]

". . . the New England animals are examples," write Lawrence and Bossert, "of a rapid evolution of a race of coyotes characterized by large size and more powerful teeth suited to preying on large mammals."

Both reports indicate that the animal, which both suggest be called *Canis latrans*, var. or Eastern coyote, is invading the empty "predator niche vacated by the gray wolf in the late 19th century." It ranges throughout the Adirondacks, the St. Lawrence Valley, New Hampshire, Vermont, Massachusetts, and occasionally into Connecticut.

Before publication of the scientific findings about the animals, Helenette Silver became disturbed by newspaper reports of the animals' viciousness in attacking deer, and by the fear such reports have bred throughout New Hampshire.

Having studied them closely for seven years, she and her husband probably know more about the animals than anyone else, including the men who have hunted and trapped them.

The Eastern coyote, she says, is "no threat to humans. They are no more dangerous than a rabbit."

Of course, they are dangerous *to* a rabbit, or to a deer. Kneiland Wheeler and Maurice Nelson can testify to that. □□

COYOTES IN MAINE

Although coyotes and other feral dogs have been seen in Maine for many years, they seemed to really "settle in" about 1968, coming in from both New Hampshire and Canada. Specimens were taken in Upton in 1968 and 1969. Others have been shot or trapped in West Paris, Turner, and towns in that area.

From Canada, the newcomers, now known as the Eastern coyote, took a southerly route to extend from Jackman (where they are most numerous) at least as far as the Starks. The animals have been shot by hunters or farmers in Kingfield and Concord; at West Forks one was struck and killed by a motor vehicle, and they have been seen in many other towns. During the spring and summer of 1970 there have been new pups seen with females. No specimen has been taken, but most of those who have seen the animals at close range describe the type identified as the Eastern coyote. A group described as blunt-nosed, shaggy, and honey-colored, constitutes an exception.

COURTESY MRS. BEATRICE MAKI

Section IV

Devils, Witches
and Vampires

"The most gruesome episode in American history," wrote John Fiske, describing the great witchcraft scare that swept over Salem, Massachusetts, in the year 1692. Other historical writers have applied their own pet adjectives to it: "Shocking," "Infamous," "Regrettable," "Barbaric," "Inexplicable."

It was all of these things and more, apparently. For behind the outward acts, the accusations, trials, convictions, torturings and executions that are so well documented, there was a tangled web of motivation that has not, even today, been entirely unraveled.

The painting "Trial of George Jacobs for Witchcraft in 1692" shows the accusing fingers of young girls pointing at their innocent victim. Such juvenile hysteria was the cause of the Great Witch Delusion.

Juvenile Bewitchery

by Paul Chadwick

The first on-the-spot mystery that every student of Salem witchcraft encounters is that of the old village itself. Where is it? What has become of it? Did it disappear long ago in a malediction and a puff of sulphurous smoke?

The man at the gas station in Danvers, Massachusetts, where we stopped to make inquiries wasn't at all helpful.

"You're in the wrong place, Buddy," he said positively. "This is Danvers. It always has been Danvers as far as I know and it always will be, I guess."

He was wrong, of course. Danvers, we verified later, includes an area that was once called Salem Village. It was made into a separate township in 1752.

But the gas man awed us by his brisk and light-hearted approach to American history. Salem itself, six miles away, was really the "Witch City," he told us, the Mecca of demonically inclined tourists, the place we were looking for.

"That's where you want to go, Mac," he said brightly.

We didn't, though. Not yet. We wanted to stay right there in Danvers and slowly unravel the tangled skein of mystery that would eventually lead us to Gallows Hill.

It was fitting, therefore—so much so as to seem almost eerie—that the next place we stopped at was the little Yarn Shop diagonally across the street from the Danvers Historical Society. The Society building was closed unfortunately. But the Yarn Shop was open. There was a pleasant-faced lady inside, shelves of bright-colored yarns all around her.

What better place, we thought, to begin any yarn, factual or fictional, than in a yarn shop? The proprietress was a "find," too. Our ears pricked up immediately when she said her name was Mrs. Richard E. Putnam. For one of Danvers' many claims to distinction is that it was the birthplace of General Israel Putnam, as well as of little Ann Putnam, a ringleader in the circle of girls who "cried out" against innocent persons, sending them to their doom.

Mrs. Putnam was willing to do anything she could to make our pilgrimage a success.

"How many witchcraft victims were burned?" we asked as a test question.

We knew what the right answer was, of course. But we waited expectantly and, sure enough, Mrs. Putnam didn't fail us. She had her historical facts at her fingertips even if the gas man didn't.

"None!" she said vehemently. "That's only a popular notion. No witch suspect was ever burned in Salem or anywhere else in New England."

"What method of execution was used?" we inquired.

"Hanging—except in the case of poor old Giles Corey who was pressed to death under planks and stones."

So much for that. Now about first causes.

"Do you think that the bunch of teen-age girls who met secretly in Reverend Parris' parsonage started it all, Mrs. Putnam?" we asked.

She shook her head and a far-away look came into her brown eyes.

"No, I don't. There were a lot of different reasons for what happened. The girls were only a part of it."

We knew just what she meant. History books and musty old records of the great witch hunt had impressed names in our minds until they had become like living people again. The centuries slowly dissolved and familiar forms took shape.

Doc. Griggs, the well-meaning but sadly limited Salem Village physician! Was it he who had started it all when, unable to cope scientifically with the odd convulsions, cataleptic rigidities and rantings of the young, hysterical females, he'd given it as his opinion that they were bewitched? Was it the influential, highly educated Cotton Mather with his fanatical belief in witchcraft who might have set the stage? Was it Tituba, the West Indian slave woman, with her voodoo antics in front of the girls who was most to blame? Or was it just the temper of the times that had made things ripe and ready for a violent outbreak of witch hysteria?

The storm, we knew, had seemed to come with the suddenness of a New England thunder squall. One year Salem Village had been a busy, prosperous little community. The next it had writhed and quivered in the grip of fear, its farms neglected, its gardens sprouting rank weeds, its citizens obsessed by horrid thoughts of the Prince of Darkness.

Actually, though, that Devil's brew of mad superstition had had to simmer before it could boil. And simmer it did all through the chill winter of 1691 when little Ann Putnam and her friends met surreptitiously in the Parris kitchen, in what is now called Danvers, to listen wide-eyed to Tituba's tales of demons and witches. It simmered as Cotton Mather's busy pen and fertile imagination concocted vaporings about invisible horrors that did not exist, and as learned barristers split legal hairs over just what laws would best control the rising tide of witchcraft in the Bay Colony. It even simmered in the petty quarrels over boundary lines and property rights in Salem Village itself and in factional disputes inside the meetinghouse that the Reverend Parris did nothing to abate. The skeins grew more tangled every hour. The tension mounted day by day. But who can say what contributing cause was the greatest when the outbreak finally came?

"All the Putnams are related way back," said Mrs. Putnam. "I'm sure of that much. But go see Mr. Charles Tapley. He knows more about local history than anyone else in Danvers and he'll be glad to talk to you."

We followed her suggestion and found that Mr. Tapley, a cultured, affable Danvers businessman with a long and aristocratic New England heritage, was not only a mine of historical information, but was also the author of a very fine book called *Rebecca Nurse, Saint But Witch Victim*. This volume tells the story of one of old Salem Village's most beloved "witches," a martyr to truth who died on the gallows rather than confess falsely that she had consorted with Satan. Mr. Tapley is the former head of the Danvers Historical Society, ex-President of the Bay State Historical League, and one of the vice-presidents of Essex Institute.

When we asked him about Gallows Hill he mentioned the controversy that had once flared up as to whether the witch victims were hung at the bottom or at the top. No one really knows for sure even today, he said, though the evidence seems to point to the summit as the place of execution.

Mr. Tapley volunteered to take us to the least visited yet most

[201]

significant spots of the witch delusion. And no student of Salem witchcraft ever had a more patient, knowing and reliable guide than he
turned out to be.

We told him we especially wanted to see the site of the old
parsonage where Tituba and the girls had gathered in the kitchen, also
the meadow behind it where the witches from all over Essex County
were said to have met for their unholy *Sabbaths*, cackling like birds.

"I'll show them to you," said Mr. Tapley.

Presently we stood at the end of a little, grassy lane, leading off
Hobart Street between a stone wall and a hedge. Looking through this

*"Accusation of a Witch," inlaid in
wood. Courtesy of the Essex Institute,
Salem, Massachusetts*

*Which hill is "Witch Hill?" The au-
thor finally found Gallows Hill and an
old stump they call the "Witch Tree."*

[202]

to a tree at the far end we saw the very spot where the old parsonage had once stood. Almost reverently we walked forward till the meadow stretched away in front of us.

For this is the holy of holies, the shrine of the great American witch delusion, if such an evil thing as belief in witches can have a shrine. It was on this exact square of earth, in the low-ceilinged, smoky kitchen of the house that once rose here, that the slave woman and the girls worked themselves into a state of nervous tension that led to horrible and damning fantasies later on.

Little Ann Putnam with her sickly body, her pixyish face, her

All save Giles Corey hung for their "crimes." Corey was pressed to death beneath planks and piled stones.

"Witchcraft Victims on Way to Gallows." From a supplement of the Boston Herald. Courtesy of the Essex Institute.

precocious thirst for occult knowledge was there. So also were Abigail Williams, Mercy Lewis, Elizabeth Booth, Mary Walcott, Susanna Sheldon and three or four others. While kettles simmered over the fireplace, trouble for Salem and for all of the Bay Colony simmered between those four walls. Yet neither Tituba nor the young girls can be blamed entirely. They were victims, too, in a way—victims of ignorance and of man's inhumanity to man. Victims of frustrations, hungers and indwelling forces beyond their understanding or control.

Looking down at that historic spot, we could almost see them: young, fanciful, eager, gathered in a tense circle, their faces straining in the semi-darkness that smelled of spices and wood smoke, while Tituba presided over them like some high priestess of magic. What color she must have brought into their drab little Puritan lives! What excitement she must have given them! What delicious tremors of fright and fascination must have chased up and down their spines!

Some of them surely sensed that what was being done and said in that shuttered room was forbidden according to their Puritan codes— but the hypnotic enticement of the mystical, the unknown, was like strong wine to their imaginations. They must have enjoyed every minute of it even while they shuddered. They must have thrilled to it because their lives were so empty of more wholesome pleasures. So perhaps we should pity them, not condemn them. Yes, even though they were shortly to become the human instruments who would send innocent men and women weeping to the gallows.

Next we visited the First Congregational Church of Danvers on the corner near the site of the old parsonage where Hobart Street swings sharply north. Across from it is the "new" parsonage where once stood Ingersoll's tavern, or ordinary, in which some of the first witch trials were held. This church, though it is the sixth built on this location, is not on the site of the first original meetinghouse. That was down the street a bit. It was thought best when the old meetinghouse was finally destroyed never to build another house of worship on that exact site again on account of its associations with witchcraft.

We crossed the street to the "new" parsonage, built in 1750, and had a pleasant and instructive talk with the present pastor, the Rev. Adrian Aeschliman and his wife. Pastor Aeschliman is worth visiting just for himself. He served America in the 10th Mountain Division and has the distinction of being the first ski chaplain.

"This church has no historic continuity with the past," said Rev. Mr. Aeschliman. "Not with the witchcraft delusion, at least. That could never happen again."

He went on then to tell us something about Joseph Green, the young pastor who came to the meetinghouse right after the witchcraft outbreak had ended and did so much to heal the wounds and comfort the congregation by his wisdom, kindness and tact. It was Pastor Green who in 1706 read Ann Putnam's humble confession of guilt in the great witchcraft delusion and had this "lost sheep" taken back into the fold shortly before she died.

Now that we'd seen the site of the old Parris parsonage, the very seedbed of witch hysteria, we resumed our travels and visited that other, truer shrine in Danvers, the home of Rebecca Nurse, whose ageing body swung from the gallows on July 19, 1692 along with those of four other persons accused by the little girls of being witches: Susanna Martin, Sarah Wild, Goody Good and Elizabeth How.

Rebecca Nurse and her companions were not the first "witches" to be executed. That distinction fell to Bridget Bishop, a more flamboyant lady with a taste for flashy dresses and lace and a reputation that was not exactly spotless. People had been whispering about Bridget Bishop for years, criticising her clothes and the way she ran her two taverns. When the circle of teen-age girls and other witnesses accused her of being a witch she was tried, condemned and finally hanged alone on June 10, 1692.

But the execution of Rebecca Nurse was an even more unjustified and heart-rending affair. She was an elderly lady of spotless repute, pious, hard-working, self-respecting, honest and beloved by her friends and family. It stirs the resentment and compassion of everyone who knows her story that she should have been subjected to the indignity of a search for "witch marks" on her person, then tried, convicted and executed in her old age after such a blameless life.

Her house even today seems to reflect something of her staunch and simple spirit and of the pathos of her death. Here is the land she loved, the rooms she moved in, the grass she walked upon, the old well

A fragment of the "Examination of Rebecca Nurse" at Salem Village in the handwriting of Rev. Mr. Parris.

from which she drank. It is one of the best preserved, most lovely and oldest houses in the township. Below it, on the peaceful flatlands, is the old burying ground where her loving sons brought her body after the execution. The exact spot where she lies is unknown. They were taking no chances that witch-hunting vandals might desecrate her grave. But an impressive granite monument to her memory was raised by her descendants in 1885 with these apt lines of Whittier upon it:

"O Christian martyr, who for truth could die
When all about thee owned the hideous lie,
The world redeemed from superstition's sway
Is breathing freer for thy sake today."

The house and picturesque grounds belong to the Society for the Preservation of New England Antiquities. Its caretakers and tenants are Mr. and Mrs. George Gordon.

Mrs. Gordon, a graduate of Middlebury College, freely discussed what it has meant to her to live there for the past fifteen years. She came to it originally so that her two children could have lots of fresh air, green grass and sunlight.

"What do you think of the witch delusion?" we asked her.

"Looking back from our times," she said, "it is very hard to recontruct the feeling of those days. Almost everybody believed in witches then, even well educated people."

She went on to tell us about the different reactions of different visitors to the house.

"Some tourists actually shrink and shudder," she said. "They seem to think that Rebecca Nurse really was a witch and really did something evil. Others, better informed, know that she was a brave religious martyr who died because her conscience wouldn't let her distort the truth. She could have confessed to witchcraft and saved herself. Only those who refused to confess were hung."

We asked Mrs. Gordon about her job then. How did she like it?

"The great variety of the visitors who come here make it very interesting," she said.

There are close to thirty thousand living descendants of Rebecca Nurse, she told us, and about fifty of them visit the house every year. School children from Danvers visit it, too, and study American History at first hand. This, thinks Mrs. Gordon, is one of the finest contributions to present-day living that the old house makes.

On our way toward Salem proper, and a look at Gallows Hill, we stopped in at the Danvers Chamber of Commerce and met Mr. George Merrill, who is a descendant of Rebecca Nurse on his mother's side. From him we got a hint of the rivalry that exists today between Salem and Danvers over the matter of the witchcraft scare.

"Salem likes to call itself the 'Witch City'," said Mr. Merrill with some asperity. "But the whole thing actually started and ended right here in Danvers."

We were aware of that now, so we didn't argue.

"What do you think of it all anyway?" we asked.

"I think Tituba got those poor kids excited with her voodooism. I think she worked on them first, then on the grownups, till a lot of 'em were sort of possessed."

"You mean she lighted the fuse that started the witch hysteria?"

"Yes. But when the blow-up came I guess a combination of circumstances had a lot to do with it."

Once again, as with Mrs. Putnam, we agreed. An ignorant slave

[207]

woman couldn't be made the only culprit. Neither could those nervously keyed up, semi-hysterical adolescents. Even Cotton Mather was sincere in his beliefs. So were the judges, Hathorne, Corwin, Sewall and the rest. They thought, while the witch scare lasted, that they were doing a fine public duty in jailing and executing Satan's disciples. Many thousands of alleged witches had only recently been put to death in England, Germany and France. Mr. Merrill seemed to think, just as we did, that the whole sorry business was no one person's fault. It was an indictment of mankind's own, home-grown stupidity, blindness and fear.

Thoughtfully we left Danvers and headed for the Salem town line and distant Gallows Hill. Here again we ran into difficulties. Some cities share their historic treasures gracefully. Salem doesn't. The points of interest are scattered far apart for one thing. And the many one-way streets set confusing traps for the motorist.

There's no chance of getting from point to point as the crow flies. You have to be patient and hope for the best. Even the friendly cop, giving us directions, admitted a little sorrowfully that there was one spot on the way out to Gallows Hill where we might "run into a little trouble."

We did—lots of it. Traffic swirled around us in all directions as madly as the witch suspicions of old. "Do not enter" markers blocked the very streets we coveted most. Finally we made it, though, rejoicing when a white sign on a side street announced: GALLOWS HILL BALL-GROUNDS.

Then we came to the hill itself, or rather a series of low, rocky summits, all contained in what is now called Gallows Hill Park.

Even this was confusing. Which hill was the right hill? Where was the exact and awful spot where the carts stopped, the victims climbed out and the nooses were adjusted?

Nobody seemed to know. The teen-age ballplayers on the field at the base of the hills were apathetic when we questioned them. Several thumbs jerked lackadaisically in different directions.

"Over that-a-way."

Two children, a girl and a boy, playing on rusty old barrels beside the ballfield offered to guide us to the "Witch Tree," however. That was a new one. We'd never heard of it. Sure enough, though, there it stood on a hilltop all by itself; a bleak, high, grim-looking stump with a few leafless branches and with one forlorn woodpecker hole near the top. No bit of stage setting could have seemed more appropriate. Yet we looked at it skeptically.

"Is that really the stump of the gallows tree?" we asked, making quick mental computations as to how long exposed wood fibers might survive the battering of three centuries.

The oldest of our guides admitted that it mightn't be.

"There used to be other trees," she said. "There was even one in my cousin's backyard on the edge of the park. But this is what they call the Witch Tree now."

We saw where tourists had chipped off bits of wood for souvenirs. But the tree wasn't good enough for us. We had a thirst for historical fact, not poetic fiction. By means of a photograph in Samuel Chamberlain's *Historic Salem in Four Season's* we finally located the *real* Gallows Hill. It is to the right of the ballgrounds as you enter the park.

There, under a murky, rainy, lowering sky, YANKEE's cameraman took his photograph the next day. The clouds seemed almost to be shedding tears for what had once been perpetrated there. We remembered what Mr. Tapley had said about the question of whether the victims had been hanged at the bottom or at the top. It didn't seem to matter much now. In any case, the dark ledges of felsite cried out their woe, the ground under our feet was surely a little holy because of the nineteen men and women who had gone to their deaths rather than betray their consciences. First Bridget Bishop. Then Rebecca Nurse and her group of five. Then John and Elizabeth Procter on August 19, along with John Willard, George Jacobs, Martha Carrier and the white-haired Reverend George Burroughs who had faultlessly recited the Lord's Prayer just before the noose had cut off his breath. It wasn't until eight more victims were hanged on September 22, 1692, that the Bay Colony came slowly to its senses and the great witchcraft delusion began to abate.

It seemed fitting after leaving Gallows Hill that we should go into the teeming and busy city of Salem and visit two men who are trying their best in a small way to rectify the wrong that was done over three hundred years ago.

These men are Judge Robert W. Hill and his assistant, Mr. John A. Serafini. This year, and for several years previously back to '45, they have introduced bills into the State Legislature the aim of which is to "reverse the attainders, judgments and convictions for witchcraft of Ann Pudeator and others."

So far they have not succeeded. Their bill passed the House in 1954 but was defeated in the Senate. "Screwball legislation," its opponents call it. "An unnecessary rewriting of history," say others. "A possible menace to the tourist trade."

But his Honor Judge Hill and Mr. Serafini do not see it as any rewriting of history or any block to tourist dollars. They have a client, a Mr. Greenslit, who is desperately anxious to have his beloved ancestor cleared. The bill is a good one, says Judge Hill. It should go through, notwithstanding the fact that Colonial lawmakers did issue a public apology and clear some of the witchcraft victims' reputations in 1711, even awarding damages to their families. No complete clearance has ever been made by U. S. lawmakers, however.

"What will be accomplished if the bill does finally pass?" we asked.

"Nothing," said Judge Hill honestly, "except to put on public record for all to see that the witches were improperly convicted. We believe that would be a good thing all around."

Thinking it over on the way out, we found ourselves agreeing with Judge Hill. "Screwball" or not, it would seem that the bill should receive the Commonwealth's hearty indorsement if it makes even one descendant of the witchcraft victims feel easier about his ancestor, or one of those brave martyrs to truth rest easier in the grave. The nineteen men and women who were hanged by the neck until they were dead, and the one who was pressed to death under rocks and planks for refusing to confess falsely that he was trafficking with Satan, gave their lives in a cause which eventually helped to rid men's minds of an ugly, barbaric form of superstition. It is up to us alive today, we feel, to do what little we can to show our appreciation and to prove if possible that those blessed innocents did not die in vain. □□

The "Vampires" of Rhode Island

by Nancy Kinder

*Could you possibly believe that Mary E. Brown
was the victim of her "convicted vampire" sister, Mercy?
Their family and friends did—and that's the truth!*

The vampire is considered to be a type of undead spirit. Legend presumes it to be a living corpse which comes from its burial place to drink the blood of the living. Belief in the vampire is nearly universal. Almost all people have legends concerning this repulsive creature.

The vampire has been more greatly feared than witches, werewolves, or any other legendary demon. Sentiment against the vampire ran so strongly in Europe that a painting depicting a blood-sucking ghoul entitled "Vampire" by artist Edvard Munch was considered "objection-able" enough to be instrumental in the closing of the Verein Berliner Kunstler exhibition of 1892.

Although the vampire did not play an important role in the forma-tion of American folklore, it was not overlooked. On the contrary, Noah Webster defined vampires as "blood-sucking ghosts or reanimated bodies of dead persons believed to come from the grave and wander about by night sucking the blood of a person asleep." Two cases of suspected vampire activity are reported to have occurred in Rhode Island.

There is a legend that, prior to the American Revolution, there lived in some rural part of Rhode Island a young man named Snuffy Stukeley. It is said that he married and settled down to the life of a peaceful farmer. He was industrious and clever. He prospered in both property and family. The legend is that his farm was as productive as his wife, the lady contributing fourteen children to the Stukeley family circle. The children grew and some were already adults when Stukeley encountered an ominous omen.

The omen came in the form of a dream, perhaps more aptly de-scribed as a nightmare. In his dream he saw an orchard quite similar to his own. In the dream, however, exactly half of the trees had died. The vision worried him. He felt that it must have some symbolic meaning and the fact that he could not imagine what the meaning might be bothered him even more than the dream itself.

Shortly after his dream of the orchard, his eldest child, Sarah, sick-ened and died. She was laid to rest in the family cemetery. Soon a sec-ond daughter became ill and perished. The illness of the second child was accompanied by something quite unusual. The second child com-plained that Sarah came every night and sat upon some part of her body causing her suffering to increase.

One after another the Stukeley children fell ill and died until there were six dead. All complained of painful visits from Sarah during their illnesses. Then a seventh became ill. By this time Mrs. Stukeley was also complaining of nightly visits from Sarah.

Obviously something had to be done. Stukeley and some of his neighbors suspected Sarah of being a vampire. So with the aid of their friends and neighbors the Stukeleys exhumed the bodies of the six dead children. The hearts of the corpses were to be cut out and burned upon a rock in front of the Stukeley house.

The six Stukeley bodies were examined. Five of the bodies were well on their way to becoming part of the earth they had so recently trod. Sarah, however, was in quite an incredible condition. Her eyes were open. Even her hair and nails had grown. The clincher was that her heart and arteries were filled with fresh blood. Therein Sarah gave herself away. Everyone knew that fresh blood in a long-dead corpse was a definite sign that the body was inhabited by a vampire. In fact, all conditions of a vampire were present in the body of Sarah Stukeley. She had been the first to die and all of the others had complained about her with great enmity. Her heart was therefore burned and all of the bodies were returned to their graves.

The seventh victim died shortly thereafter. It was generally accepted that he was too far gone when Sarah's heart was burned. At last peace came to the family. Stukeley's wife was no longer bothered by Sarah's apparition and Snuffy Stukeley's prophetic dream of losing half his orchard was symbolically fulfilled with seven of his fourteen children dead.

The second case of vampirism was far more recent. In the Chestnut Hill Cemetery in Exeter, Rhode Island, in back of the Baptist church, one may still view the graves of some of the members of the Brown family. There are three graves of relevance to this story, those of Mrs. Mary E. Brown and her two daughters, Mary Olive and Mercy L. Brown.

They apparently died of tuberculosis. Mrs. Brown succumbed on December 8, 1883. Six months later, on June 6, 1884, Mary Olive Brown, at the age of twenty, shared her mother's fate. These deaths left George Brown with one son and several daughters. The son was Edwin A. Brown. He lived in West Wickford and was reportedly a husky, strong young man, not subject to disease or illness.

Several years passed. Edwin was employed as a store clerk when he suddenly became ill. He departed for Colorado. While Edwin was away trying to regain his health, his nineteen-year-old sister, Mercy, also became ill and was carried away to her grave in January of 1892.

Edwin returned to Rhode Island in failing health. He contracted tuberculosis. His condition became worse. His family and friends held a council to decide what was to be done about him.

The family and friends unanimously agreed that it must be a vampire that was sucking his blood and causing his loss of strength. They further concurred that a vampire was very probably the cause of the other deaths in the family. They also considered it likely that the demon was living in the grave of one of the departed Browns. They advocated the exhumation of the guilty corpse.

It was necessary to find out which body was harboring the ghastly ghoul. They then decided that it would be simpler to disinter all three bodies and examine them for signs of the vampire.

Finally Edwin consented to the plan. In March of 1892, armed with various digging implements, the friends and family of Edwin Brown dug up the graves of Edwin's mother and sisters.

When the bodies were viewed, Mrs. Brown and Mary proved to be skeletons. No abode for a vampire in those two.

Mercy, on the other hand, had only been buried for a few months. Ash had not gone to ash, nor dust to dust. There was blood found in her heart and it was therefore assumed that the vampire had made her body his permanent dwelling. Her heart was burned to ash in a fire lighted on a nearby rock in the cemetery. The bodies were then returned to their graves.

The object of burning the heart was not merely to destroy the evil creature that inhabited the body of Mercy Brown, but also to provide an antidote for the afflicted Edwin. The doctor prescribed for Edwin the ashes of his sister's heart dissolved in medicine. It evidently was not particularly effective because Edwin Brown perished shortly thereafter as had his mother and sisters before him. □□

Left: The gravestones of Mary E. and Mercy L. Brown. Mercy died in January, 1892, and was buried. Two months later, her body was disinterred—ash had not turned to ash, and blood was found still in her heart.

The Man Who Knows

by Emeline K. Paige

"I'll do what I can—" the big man said, and turned from the telephone.

Requests for help were not uncommon to his experience, so it was no surprise that an acquaintance in Philadelphia, whose daughter was missing, should call him—in Florida—to ask for the kind of assistance that *only he* could give.

Concentration clouded the tall man's face for a few minutes, then he picked up the telephone again. "Tell the police to look in the river fifteen feet from the boathouse, near the left bank . . . they will find your daughter's body there . . ."

. . . and Peter Hurkos hung up.

In a comfortably air-conditioned office in Texas half a dozen men watched as a large map was spread on the floor. There were three stones on a desk's glass top, each picked up on land recently purchased. The big man glanced at the map, holding one of the stones in his hand. Almost casually he placed it on the map, then did the same with the second stone.

"I'll have a beer," he said, nodding to one of the men. After a slow swallow he set the third stone on the map. "There is oil here at 15,000 feet, here at 4,500 feet, and here at 11,200 feet," and he pointed to each stone in turn.

Peter Hurkos had made one mistake: drilling found the oil to be only 11,000 feet below the surface under the third stone.

It all started one day in Holland. The bandaged head moved slightly on the pillow. The big man had been in the hospital in a coma for three days—since a fall from a ladder knocked him unconscious.

ESP, like weather forecasting, is sometimes apparently possible. Blind luck, you say? Perhaps, but in the case of Peter Hurkos the odds on chance are ONE in 629,000,000,000,000,000,000 times . . .

Slowly, his eyes opened. At the next bed a nurse was assisting a patient about to be released after recovering from an injury sustained in an automobile accident. As the eyes of the two men met, the bandaged one said, "Good morning, Mynheer Burgmeier." The other, looking around quickly, replied, "My name is not Burgmeier. It is Joop de Vries."

"No . . . you are Hans Burgmeier, a bank teller at a bank in Rotterdam. I see you putting money into a bag and hurrying away . . . and an automobile accident . . ." The other snapped the cover of his suitcase and hurried from the room.

The nurse began to strip the vacated bed. "What made you call Mynheer de Vries 'Mynheer Burgmeier'?" she asked, not certain that Peter Hurkos was fully conscious, for his eyes were closed again.

"That is his name."

"How do you know?"

"I don't know . . . but it is so." After a minute or two the patient spoke again, this time with some anxiety. "And you, Nurse Zelder—you must be very careful. I see you on a train, and you may lose your valise—"

Thoroughly startled, the nurse moved to the side of the bed. "How do you know my name?"

"I don't know—"

Turning away, Nurse Zelder pulled the bottom sheet from the empty bed and a folded paper fell to the floor. It was a driver's license, made out in the name of Hans Burgmeier, its description fitting "Joop de Vries."

Nurse Zelder rushed to the office of the Director, showed him the

Placing stones on a map, Hurkos can forecast the location of an oil well and the depth at which oil will be found.

license and repeated the brief conversation between the men. While the Director informed the police that their bank robber had just left the hospital, Nurse Zelder tried to tell him of the injured man's warning to her.

Impatiently, the Director muttered: "Delirium!"

"But Dr. Pieters, this morning on my way here by train from Amsterdam *I did lose my valise!*"

Peter Hurkos—a big man, 6′3″ and not looking overweight at 228 pounds—does not know why or how he knows what he knows . . . why the smallest detail, of no seeming importance—such as the third button on a man's vest being sewn with blue thread instead of black—appears on the radar screen of his mind. He doesn't know how he can take a photograph selected at random from two or three hundred on a table before him, hold it in his hand and know at once where the pictured person is, what he is doing, and the state of his health. His information is as accurate when he is blindfolded as when his eyes are open.

Maria Hurkos, young, attractive Belgian, and a licensed pilot for both day and night flying, would be just as happy if her husband did not greet her after a simple shopping expedition with, "You bought a green dress with a silver belt for $35, and tried on two others before you chose this one." She has no opportunity to surprise him with a new necktie for his birthday, a new hat for herself, or even a new kind of dessert for dinner.

Some call it "extra sensory perception"; some call it a "sixth sense." Whatever it is, it enables Peter Hurkos to solve riddles, to see around corners, and—most important—to right wrong. Working with the police of 27 countries, speaking five languages besides his native Dutch (he has learned English in the past ten months and speaks it with a slight Scottish accent), this man is at home anywhere in the world because nothing is new or strange to him.

In his bulging scrapbooks are clippings, pictures, citations. One of the latter bears the crest and seal of Spain's Franco; another, highly prized, is signed by the Archbishop of Mechlin and was presented at the request of Pope Pius XII. His files hold hundreds of letters from men and women whose lives have benefited in one way or another through the exercise of Peter Hurkos's "sixth sense."

Living now at Glen Cove, on the coast of Maine, overlooking Penobscot Bay, Peter Hurkos has spent nearly a year giving laboratory demonstrations of his remarkable ability to *know* almost everything about other people. These tests will help medical science to understand more of the extra sensory perception so highly developed in this Dutch house painter.

For those with respect for figures, it is of interest that in certain tests in which Peter Hurkos made a perfect score, an electronic brain shows that the odds of accomplishing this by chance are ONE in 629,000,000,-000,000,000,000 times.

Listening to opera recordings, painting a little (pictures, not houses —and with great speed and dramatic color), working on his boat, and cooking, are things for his spare time. He receives as many as 1200 letters a week from people who feel that Peter Hurkos can help them.

When the telephone rings it may be Boston or Buenos Aires . . . and when he leaves from the airport four miles from his home, he may be heading for Cleveland or Cairo.

Peter Hurkos can't say "No—"

Instead, he says, "I'll do what I can!"   □□

"It was much as he could do to get out before he got drownded . . ."

The Witch of Colebrook

by *Colonel Richard Stevens*
Illustrated by Mark Kelley

Whether or not you believe in dowsing, please consider the events herewith described as strictly factual. As to the quoted statements . . . well, they were made!

As I bounced along over the narrow dirt road I thought about the man I was going to see. His reputation was that he "had shot more game, caught more fish and told more and bigger lies than anyone this side of Texas."

I had important business with him. He was, so his reputation went, a water witch, and I wanted to find water I could pipe into my camp at Big Diamond Pond. I also wanted to see the old man in action. I knew that if he were a water witch there would be none better—to hear him tell it.

He was now working as a cook for a farm crew and was mixing up a batch of biscuits when I arrived. I went out into the pantry and talked with him. Yes he could find water, in reply to my query. We chatted on. "Of course I hain't got no license to practice it," he said.

". . . with most folks the stick flops down.
With me it shoots up."

I made haste to assure him that I could easily overlook the deficiency and would not turn him in. "I've made quite a study of it," he said. "I've found water south as far as Manchester and north to Shausheyville" (Chartierville, PQ). "No I never had any failures. It's the electricity in me that does it. I thought once or twice I might lose it. I was to the hospital, and they give me shots for something or other. They punched me so full of holes I had to wear a raincoat to keep the blood in. I thought the juice might run out the holes but it didn't. Another time I got my hand and arm sawed open over to Walter Klebe's, and I thought that might take the power from me, but she seemed to work all right after. I allus planned to get one of them scientific divining rods, they call 'em, but I hain't got around to it yet. I hain't done much of it lately but they used to keep me pretty busy.

"I remember down to Ernest Simses. He got me to go down there and I worked the ground and drove a stake, and told him to dig down seven feet and six inches and he'd have a good flow of water. I went home and he dug down a ways and got sick of it. He saw me in Colebrook and says, 'I thought you said there was water there.' 'There is,' I told him. 'How far did you dig down?' 'Seven foot' he says. 'You go home and dig down where I told you and you'll find water. Seven feet and six inches,' I told him. Well I went down with him and we went out to the hole and he jumped in. He got the water. He drove an iron bar down in the bottom of the hole and the water pressure drove her right up over my head. It was much as he could do to get out before he got drownded.

"Then there was Sam Young over to Beecher Falls. I put in the stake for him but he thought he knew better and when I went home he dug somewhere else. He met me later and said he didn't find no water. I went over and looked around and told him to dig where I said and he'd find his water down five feet and four inches. He dug down and found a vein all right. It come out of the hole, a stream big enough to run a sawmill." He meditated, smoking his pipe. "The next day a spring about a half a mile below him, where half the town got its water, dried up. He had a lot of trouble over that.

"Yes, I can tell you whether it's hard or soft water, how deep down it is. That is, within six inches. Whether you got to go through ledge or dirt to get it and what size vein it is."

"Can you tell whether the vein is running water or not?", I asked.

"Wal it's got to be running to find it," he answered. "It's the friction of it running that makes the electricity. A man's got to have a charge of electricity in him to be able to find it. That's the reason you got to walk with your legs spread as far apart as you can spread 'em when you're finding water. It gives the juice a better holt. With most folks the stick flops down. With me it shoots up." (It *would* with him . . . he'd have to be different from other people.) "I use apple, hazel, or even birch. Anything that's got the sap up in it.

"I'll come over and find you some water."

"That's fine," I answered. "Can you come now?"

"Aiyah, I can, but twon't do no good. Too wet now. Wait till we have about three weeks of dry weather. There's water everywhere now but you want a good vein that won't dry up. Come up when it's dry and we'll go over and give her a whirl."

A couple of months later I went over to see him. "This is a good time," he said. "Dry enough now."

We covered the hillside behind my camp just "studying the lay of the land." Then he cut a forked stick from a hazel bush. He took his grip on it and, with his long-legged, lanky build, spread his feet wide apart and started pacing carefully. The rod did not move for some distance, then started to flicker. "Edge of the vein," he said. The rod popped straight up. "There she is, down 12 feet and under a ledge. I can tell it's a ledge by the way she pulls and I know it's 12 feet down because it's 12 feet from where I caught the first twitch to where she went right up." We moved along but the best he could do for me there was "good soft water, 10 feet down and under a ledge."

We moved to another locality. "There's veins all through here," he said, "but they're deep." He found a number of places, mostly under ledge, and a few where he thought the digging might be better. Finally he picked a spot where "the vein's nine feet down and no ledges in between." I marked the spot and took him back home as he had to get dinner for his crew.

I hurried back and started digging. About two feet down my pickaxe struck rock and I soon uncovered ledge. I thought to myself, "Why did that old fraud go through all of that talk and tell me those things, when he knew I was coming right back to dig." Just then I found a hole in the ledge and uncovered more. I went down in the hole another foot and struck ledge again, but—trickling from a crack in the rock was a small stream of water. I went no farther but cleared out the hole and had a serviceable little spring.

The next time I saw my witch I told him his divining was poor. "Didn't you find water?" he asked. I admitted that I had found some and told him what I had run into. He claimed he couldn't understand what was wrong with the place, so we went out and looked at it.

"Aiyah," he said. "Just as I thought. You see the big vein, down nine feet give me the electricity. The leak you found is coming straight up so, of course, I couldn't notice that. The crack it came up through was just big enough so I couldn't feel any ledge between me and the water. And she won't pull if she's coming right at a fellow. I admit I got my faults but being wrong ain't one of them." □□

Village of 100 Witches

by Maria Dabrowski

Such a wave of relief swept the cape when Tammy Younger died that she was given a silver-plated coffin and an expense-paid funeral . . . but what about Witch Wesson and all the other "girls" in Dogtown?

In the heart of Cape Ann, a windy spit of land a few miles north of Boston, lies one of America's few deserted villages. A weird, lonely moor which was once the site of a thriving village of more than a hundred honest, Godfearing farm folk today breeds only legends of witches and ghosts, buried treasure, howling dogs at midnight, and pirates. An overgrown trail from the village of Rockport, Massachusetts leads up and up to Dogtown Common where today you will find a high, almost barren plateau covered with great glacial boulders the size of houses, larger than the houses which once surrounded them. Coarse grass blows in the wind off the ocean, here and there is a yawning cellarhole with a worn granite doorstep before it. A broken stone wall which once enclosed a neat garden tumbles among blueberry bushes.

Early settlers of Cape Ann chose this high tableland for safety from the pirates who roamed and ravaged the coastline below. After the Revolution, when there was no longer danger from British privateers or Barbary pirates, the farm folk of the settlement moved down to the harbor to enter the more prosperous trades of fishing and shipping. When a new road was cut along the shoreline from Gloucester to Rockport, Dogtown was left high and dry and by 1830 was a deserted town lying in tumbled ruins.

Dogtown men have left their mark upon America's history. Descendents of the early settlers rowed General Washington across the Delaware; Dogtown's Isaac Day was a gunner on the Constitution. But the most colorful part of Dogtown's history began after the Revolution with the taking over of the empty houses by the derelicts of Cape Ann Villages—a weird assemblage of the "tetched" and very poor who eked out a miserable existence by scratch gardening, blueberry picking, and fortune telling. A few of the original settlers remained in the village—respectable widows of sea captains who kept huge dogs to guard them from their new and less-respectable neighbors. It is from these animals the settlement got its name. As their owners died the dogs roamed wild over the moor, howling at night or baying at the moon. The majority of the squatters were toothless old women, certain of whom were famous for the evil eye and predictions. Each week these old crones would go down the hill to the harbor and demand free supplies of fish or oil or salt, and woe betide the merchant who dared refuse them—they would belabor him with sticks and curses and "vile langwich," or terrify him with dire predictions.

Among the witches was Easter Carter who was once a respectable

English woman. She made her living nursing but also picked up a few pence telling fortunes. Easter had pride and scorned her neighbors for subsisting all summer on blueberries. "I eats no trash," said Easter. She was proud that she lived in the only two-storey house in the settlement. Upstairs lived a curious mulatto woman known as Old Ruth, Tie, and John Woodman. Tie was one of the many freed slaves that were common to the region in the early eighteenth century. She always wore men's clothing, which was an amazement in her day, and made her living building stone walls, hauling wood, and doing other rough men's work. Nearby lived Aunt Becky Rich who sold a "dire drink" for spring fevers, brewed from foxberry leaves, spruce tips, and wild herbs. Aunt Becky peddled her brew in the village below and would say as she entered a house: "Now, ducky, I've come down to bring a dire drink, for I know you feel Springish." The young people of the village of Rockport in a spirit of derring-do would sometimes go to Aunt Becky's house for fortune telling and a supper of boiled cabbage and cornbread. (Remindful of another horrid New England meal—the infamous breakfast served in the Fall River home of Lizzie Borden that fateful, torrid August morning nearly a hundred years later—cold mutton soup!)

Young witches of the settlement who cast different sorts of spells upon village men from respectable families and sailors who visited port, were Moll Jakups and Judy Rhines, who were no better than they should have been. And there was Granther Stannard who in his younger days was proud captain of a vessel engaged in foreign shipping; he was then properly known as Captain Morgan Stanwood. When his sailing days were over he took ownership to a little clay and sod hut known as "The Boo" where he cobbled shoes and acted as local dentist until be became convinced that his legs were made of glass and he could no longer stand on them. Granther was known to be a good cook, perhaps not a strange accomplishment for an old sea dog who'd sailed womanless across the world for many years, and not so strange as the accomplishments of Sammy Maskey who was brought up by his grandmother to turn a neat hand to housework. He took care of his grandma, old Sarah Phipps, and wild Moll Jakups in her old age until town authorities came to take them away to the poorhouse. Sammy wore a shawl over his head and a long apron over his trousers and went about Rockport and Gloucester villages doing housework and washing and ironing. He particularly relished a job "nussin' " which kept him in the village for a spell. After his nursing duties were over for the day he'd go calling and pay for his cup of coffee by telling fortunes from the coffee grounds. Sammy never went anywhere without his knitting.

Queen of the Witches, as she loved to be called, was Tammy Younger, famed far and wide for her evil eye. It is said that Tammy could hex a load of logs right off a wagon if none was yielded her without argument, or that she and Aunt Luce George would bewitch the oxen till they stood "with their tongues run out" and couldn't get over the hill till a toll was paid of a generous supply of well-cut logs for the cold winter ahead. Tammy and Luce's house had a little window at the back overlooking the road, which they could run up by a rope and leer through, ready to hex any load they heard approaching from the woodlots. Tammy was a fat old woman with two walrus-like tusks in her upper jaw. She was a great favorite of seamen and buccaneers who always made for her house for fortune telling and a round of rum whenever their ships came to port. Tammy was a witch not without a witch's honor even in her own household, for when she died at the age of seventy-six, the inmates of her house refused to go to bed until her coffin was removed, even though Mr. Hodgkins, presumably the minister from the village below, stood in a corner all that rainy night with Tammy's coffin "ready for polishing." Such a wave of relief swept the Cape when Tammy died that she was given a great funeral and her coffin ornamented with silver plate, paid for by the gratefully bereaved. There is a rumor that gold was found buried in Tammy's cellar after her death, and that nearly a hundred years later a picknicker, digging in the cellar ruins, found a beautifully decorated enamel snuffbox with a full-rigged ship on the cover, gift of an English sea captain who came to Tammy to have his fortune told. But the most feared witch of Dogtown was Peg Wesson, who was said to ride a broomstick.

The last inhabitant of Dogtown was Black Neil Finson. By 1814 only six houses of the original sixty or more were still standing. Black Neil was favored by the ancient witches who took pity on him and gave him shelter, and he outlived them all. He lived first at Moll Jakup's house until it fell into the ground and then he moved to Judy Rhines' cottage.

After Judy died the cabin fell in and Neil boarded the cellar over and burrowed in. Judy and Moll were ladies of ill repute in their youth, and the old man was certain there was gold buried in their cellars. He spent fruitless years digging for their treasure. In 1830 the town Constable went up to get Neil and brought the dirty, starving, nearly frozen old man down to the village poorhouse. A week later Old Neil was dead "of sheer comfort."

In 1845 the last of the houses was torn down and as the years passed grass grew up in the little lanes, and saplings sprouted strong in the shelter of the cellarholes. Wild roses, bayberry, thistle, and blue aster set their seed in the door yards. Many, many years ago Thomas Wentworth Higginson described a walk through Dogtown which might have been written just today: ". . . three miles inland we found the hearthstones of a vanished settlement . . . an elevated tableland overspread

Tammy Younger could, if none was yielded her, hex a load of logs right off a wagon.

with great boulders as big as houses and encircled with a girdle of green woods and another girdle of blue sea. I know of nothing like that gray waste of boulders. It is a natural Salisbury Plain, of which icebergs were the druidic builders. In that multitude of monsters there seems a sense of suspended life; you feel as if they must speak and answer to each other—the silent nights, but by day only the wandering seabirds seek them, on their way across the Cape, and the sweetbay and green fern imbed there in a softer and deeper setting as the years go by."

The coarse voices of rum-soaked buccaneers, the cackle of Peg Wesson, the shrill imprecations of Tammy Younger are displaced by the sound of an occasional falling stone or the lonely cry of a seagull wheeling overhead. When the sun goes down there is no more eerie, romantic, and awesome place in all of New England than Dogtown Common.

□□

Dogtown . . . "is an elevated tableland overspread with boulders as big as houses."

Section V

Things They Left Behind

Wareham's Haunted Violin

by Herb Arral

Harold Gordon Audworth is not a superstitious man but he has yet to come up with a natural explanation for a violin that makes one sound and causes others . . .

The fact that a Joseph Hornsteiner violin was made, probably, for a king, about 1769, is enough to make it an instrument worthy of note. When that instrument is capable of causing strange and unexplained phenomena when played makes it even more interesting.

Such is the case of the Hornsteiner violin owned by Harold Gordon Cudworth of Wareham, Massachusetts. The instrument itself is a beautiful creation of the German master violin maker, having 365 separate inlaid pieces. Most of these pieces comprise a well-executed design on the back of the violin.

The fact that the instrument has this inlay causes appraisers to believe the violin was made especially for a king whom Hornsteiner wanted to please—which makes it a collector's item.

Harold Gordon Cudworth has prized this violin in his own collection of some 50 instruments for better than 20 years.

"I have especially prized it since the first time I played it after I acquired it some 20 years back," Mr. Cudworth said. "I was playing the instrument, which has a deep resonant sound, at my mother's home in Wareham, when suddenly a rumbling noise occurred, seemingly coming from the area of the kitchen sink. At the time I was playing 'The Broken Melody,' written by the well-known English cellist Van Biene."

As Cudworth lifted his bow, the "rumble" ceased. Picking up the melody where he left off, the disturbing noise was again heard, louder and more intense. At this point, the violinist investigated but could find no reason for the rumbling. He retired that evening thinking little more of the incident.

However, he was to be reminded of it again when, two weeks later, he was practicing for a concert and played upon the Hornsteiner, choosing "The Broken Melody" as his number.

"This time the rumbling noise came from above, on the upper floors. Again I paused and again the noise subsided. There was nothing but stillness as I stood before my music stand listening. My mind was not playing tricks on me because my mother also heard it and wanted to know if I could identify the noise. I could not."

When the disturbance resumed with the playing, both mother and son believed the noise upstairs was caused by their cat. They merely looked at one another when the cat was seen curled comfortably behind the kitchen stove.

Several months went by before this particular violin was again picked up and played. As he practiced, Cudworth decided to again try "The Broken Melody."

"On this occasion," he told us, "nothing unusual happened as I played. I laid the instrument aside and started to repair a broken lamp. I just started working on it when I heard the latch on a door behind me rattle. It was one of those old-fashioned latches one sees in old houses. I turned but saw nothing unusual. The latch remained stationary."

Mr. Cudworth finished repairing the lamp and started down the stairs when he halted near the half-way mark. The door to his room, above his head, slammed shut!

"I turned quickly. The door to my room was ajar just as I had left it."

Harold Gordon Cudworth is not a superstitious man and offers no explanation of these strange sounds. He merely states what happened and leaves any explaining to others. He sincerely wishes he could reason them out.

On another occasion, shortly after playing "The Broken Melody" on the same violin, Mr. Cudworth started to remove his wristwatch in preparation for bed when the latch on his bedroom door worked up and down as if someone were on the other side of the door and wanted in —or else wanted to let the violin player know there was someone there.

"The strangest part of it was," said Mr. Cudworth, "there was no one on the other side of the door when I opened it."

Another time the concert player was asked by a father to give violin lessons to his daughter in New Bedford. At the finish of the lesson, the father requested Mr. Cudworth to play a tune. With a twinkle in his eye, Mr. Cudworth told us he chose the haunting melody out of curiosity.

"As I played, both of us heard the front door open and shut several times, each succeeding time being louder and more forceful. The student's dad went to the head of the stairs (we were on the second floor) and called to his daughter to stop slamming the door.

"Both of us were informed by someone below that his daughter had left the house several minutes previously. The informant had heard the noise as well but was sure the front door had not been opened or closed."

Harold Gordon Cudworth chuckled. "I guess he's still wondering what caused the noise, as well as I," he said.

Sometime during the past five years, Mr. Cudworth played the same melody for a woman living in Rochester, Massachusetts.

"She asked, when I finished, that I please not play that tune again, whatever it was, because she said it made her feel 'funny.'"

Within the last year this 61-year-old violin player and collector raised his bow to the quivering strings and once again played "The Broken Melody" at a home in Mattapoisett, Massachusetts.

"I was asked to stop playing when the man of the house noticed a couple of pictures on the wall started swaying, pausing to the left before swinging back to the right."

At the present time Mr. Cudworth has more or less retired the violin in preference for another in his collection. However, he told us that the violin is in perfect condition except for the need of a new finger-board, a repair he intends to make.

There are times when he plays this piece by Van Biene when nothing unusual happens, which, he says is all right with him.

"I am not superstitious at all," he states, "I do not believe in ghosts; but I do wish someone could explain the odd happenings this combination of violin and tune cause." □□

THE WINCHESTER HOUSE:

You'd have to be very rich and a little eccentric to build a house with 160 rooms, 40 staircases, 2000 doors, 47 fireplaces and a 6-acre floor plan, but that's exactly what Sarah L. Winchester was . . .

Left: *This photo of the Mystery House was taken some time prior to 1894 and shows the beautiful gardens, now a mass of weeds. At this stage, building had hardly begun!*

Below: *With regal gesture, Mrs. Sarah L. Winchester sits for her only known portrait.*

A Blueprint to Madness *by Josiah E. Dewey II*

"Sarah dear, if our house had not been finished, I would still be with you. I urge you now to build a house but never let it be finished, for then you will live." This spiritualistic message, which Sarah L. Winchester received from her husband during a seance held some time after his death in 1881, touched off a building spree that lasted for over thirty years and produced as the end result one of the strangest and oddest

[239]

structures ever built in this country. Built entirely without plan or form, it stands today a massive jumble of towers, balconies, gables and odd-shaped angles, a maze of 160 rooms, halls, passageways and stairways, many of the latter leading nowhere; chimneys that stop at the ceiling and go no farther, winding stairs that lead to no place, a monument to the spiritualistic belief of a remarkable though eccentric woman.

To learn the why and wherefore of all this one must go back into New England history over 150 years. For over 100 of these years the name of Winchester has been synonymous with guns and rifles. One of the greatest, if not THE greatest, success stories of New England manu-facturing, is the tale of Yankee shrewdness shown by Oliver Fisher Win-chester. Born in Boston with a twin brother on the 10th of November 1810, these boys were the youngest of five children by their father's third wife. Obliged to go to work at the age of seven to aid in supporting the large family, Oliver was later, at fourteen, apprenticed to a carpenter and in short time became a master builder. In 1830 he removed to Baltimore, Maryland, where, after a period of contracting and constructing, he went into the retail clothing business. About 1834, he married Jane Ellen Hope of Portland, Maine, and it was while living in Baltimore that his three children were born: Ann Rebecca, William Wirt and Hannah Jane.

Some time later he became interested in the design of men's shirts (a far cry from guns) and, hoping to improve their fit, he decided to return to New England and engage in their manufacture. Up to this time, men's shirts had hung from the collar band and were not very com-fortable or well fitting. Winchester changed the design so that the shirt would rest on the shoulders more and hang less from the neck band. One of the first to solve this problem, he began the production of shirts in New Haven, Connecticut, shortly before 1848. The venture was an immediate success. He then began looking around for something in the manufacturing line in which he could invest some capital and further exercise his shrewdness and acumen.

About this time, in many of the New England industrial towns, skilled mechanics were busying themselves trying to perfect a breech-loading rifle. Men such as Tyler, Hunt, Jennings, Smith, Wesson, Colt, Kendall and Christian Sharps were all at work on this problem and many new types of rifles and ammunition were marketed that began to spell the end of the muzzle loader. Oliver Winchester became an investor in this gun program and between 1857 and 1880, the year he died, the company that he formed to manufacture guns and ammunition, The New Haven Arms Company, later The Winchester Repeating Arms Company, enjoyed a success unequaled up to this time. On December 10th, 1880, a month after he reached his seventieth birthday, he died at his home in New Haven. His son William Wirt, who had been associated with his father's enterprises many years, was expected to follow his father's footsteps but had become very ill with tuberculosis and, at a reorganization meeting of the company officials held on March 2nd, 1881, he was too ill to attend.

In his stead, William W. Converse, brother-in-law of Sarah Winchester, became the company president while William Wirt (Sarah's husband) was elected its vice-president. Later, in this same month, William died a little over three months after his father's passing, leaving his widow Sarah with a small child. The Winchester Company was largely a family controlled affair with the common stock closely held. Out of the ten thousand shares outstanding, 4440 shares were held by Oliver's widow, 777 shares by Sarah and 400 shares by Mrs. T. G. Bennett who was Oliver's daughter, Hannah Jane.

Shortly after the death of her husband, Sarah Winchester lost their only child. This double tragedy nearly unbalanced the mind of the wife and mother and she was put under the care of a physician for some time. She took up spiritualism in an effort to mollify the memories of the past but, her health failing, she progressively became more upset and her doctor told her she would have to remove to another area, begin life anew and take up some hobby which he advised her to "pursue vigorously." Under date of June 19th, 1886, the land records of Santa Clara County, California, show that Mrs. Sarah L. Winchester, widow of William Wirt Winchester, bought and paid for some 44 acres of land within this county (in San Jose) and an eight-room house thereon and that, subsequently, she added about 116 acres bringing her holdings to about 160 acres.

Here then was set the stage for the pursuit of the hobby she had chosen: that of building without cessation for the rest of her natural life and, until her death on the 5th of September 1922, the sounds of hammer and saw, of plumbers and electricians, were heard during every hour of each working day. From the time of her purchase of the California property until she died she was never without the help of carpenters (sixteen at one period) and other artisans who built, altered and removed portions of the house she occupied. The house as she left it

The house, a "hodge podge" of bell towers (left), cupolas (above), false stairs, and doors that led nowhere, cost approximately $5,000,000. It would probably cost ten times that amount today. Opposite page: From above, the roof lines suggest a village or a town; certainly not a widow's domicile.

really defies description. The original eight-room house she purchased in 1886, had increased to 160 rooms—a real "hodge podge" of cupolas, false stairs and doors that led nowhere, cupboard doors but with no cupboards behind them, beautiful rare wood paneling throughout the main floor with mystic numbers in its pattern, mostly thirteen; porch posts, pilasters and stair newels all installed upside down.

After the death of her mother-in-law in 1897, Sarah was assigned 2000 more shares of the Winchester stock and during most of this period her income was approximately $1000.00 a day. From 1869 to 1914

to stockholders reached a high of 79%. . .

the percentage of profits paid out in dividends to the stockholders, with the exception of six years, was said to have been never less than 21% and in some years reached a high of 79%. This substantial income from the Winchester Company enabled Sarah to satisfy any whim she may have had with regard to the purchase of building materials. Also her local investments in California real estate augmented her already huge income. Small wonder then that she always bought the best.

Some of the leaded glass doors within the mansion cost as high as $2000.00 each. The leaded glass windows, not flat like conventional leaded glass church windows, were made wavy in pattern and built with optical glass imported from Holland and furnished by Tiffany's of New York. Some of the "bulls eyes" in the windows were true lenses which give one an upside-down view when peeking through them. One stairway in this remarkable house, in which the total rise is under ten feet, has forty-four treads and nine 180 degree turns. Each step has a rise of but two inches. One room with three hot air outlets from a central heating plant also has four fireplaces. This probably could be explained as a place where Sarah retired to quite often to treat the arthritis which plagued her late years. Her private shower was provided with nozzles at her shoulder height (she was very small, less than five feet in height) so she would not get her hair wet while showering. The control valves for this were outside the shower stall and provided with a thermometer so she might adjust the water at the right temperature before entering the stall.

There are forty-seven fireplaces in the house, some of which have no flues to the outside, probably blocked off during some of her reconstruction work or because the 1906 earthquake shook them down and they were not rebuilt. The front door to the main part of the house cost over $2000.00 and through it she never admitted visitors. She was a recluse and wished no company. It has been said that even President Theodore Roosevelt, a friend of her father-in-law, wishing to visit her, was admitted through a back door. She designed the laundry on the ground floor and had made enameled iron set tubs with the "rub board" and the soap dish cast right into the metal.

There were in this mansion three elevators, one electric and the other two hydraulic, thirteen bathrooms all with clear glass doors and one had the tub in the center of the room. She also had a white satin room with but one small window, always curtained, a seance room perhaps. Some of the other oddities were water faucets projecting from under second story windows, inside windows barred while outside windows are not. There were windows with sashes of different lengths that were impossible to lock since the meeting rails did not jibe, yet she had them equipped with bronze locks made by the Winchester Arms Company.

In the light of cold logic many of these eccentricities can be explained but to do so would remove the aura of mystery and, since the present owners wish to commercialize it to the fullest, the guides who take parties through the house at $1.50 per person leave out any explanations from their spell and thus, in a measure, perpetuate this rambling pile as a "Mystery House." After her passing, Sarah Winchester's remains returned to New Haven, Connecticut, there to rest beside those of her husband. The Yankee was in her blood and though she deserted this part of our country for a time, she finally returned, as many do who have the love of New England in their souls. Her house today stands stark and bare (the heirs removed all furnishings)—a monument to Sarah L. Winchester and her spirit world.　　□□

The
Marble Mourner

by Geoffrey Elan

Detail of statue of John P. Bowman

The amount of time and money spent on a memorial is a personal thing, but how about a structure requiring the services of 125 sculptors, granite and marble cutters, masons and laborers, containing over 750 tons of granite, 50 tons of marble, 25,000 bricks, and 325 barrels of English Portland cement?

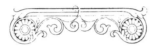

There is nothing unusual about a cemetery on a hill in a typical New England town. Cuttingsville, Vermont has one and it could be said that the village is fairly typical of New England. But in passing Cuttingsville's cemetery, motorists have been known to gasp, swerve wildly from side to side and then draw to a shaky halt. The sight that causes this unusual consternation is a ghostly, white-clad figure of a man about to enter the doorway of a huge, garnite mausoleum that dominates Cuttingsville's otherwise typical cemetery. Motorists need not fear. The figure is not a ghost and he will not move. He hasn't moved since 1881!

The figure that today startles motorists is nothing more than a life-size, marble statue of John P. Bowman, the man responsible for the construction of the Laurel Glen Mausoleum. The statue is poised on the granite steps, the hands holding a wreath and a key to the massive door, the head cocked in anticipation, almost as if it expects to hear voices from within. Some say that before he himself was placed within the tomb, Bowman did indeed have this expectation, for inside lay the bodies of his wife and children.

A self-made man of but little education, Bowman was in the tanning business most of his life and manipulated his money with such skill and honesty that he soon found himself wealthy beyond his fondest dreams. Having moved from Vermont to New York State, his business was conducted there and his private residence was evidently something to behold. A happy marriage was blessed with a first daughter, Addie, who unfortunately died an infant. A second daughter, Ella, brought joy and gaiety to the household, but tragedy again struck when she died at the age of twenty-three. The tragedy was further compounded when her mother, Jennie, passed on seven months later. Bowed by grief, John Bowman brought the remains of his family back home to Cuttingsville for burial.

Not content with the usual New England headstones for his family, Bowman vowed to build a tomb that would withstand the centuries. After considerable research he hired the architectural firm of C. B. Croff of New York City and in 1880 proceeded to construct one of the most remarkable mausoleums Vermont has ever seen.

The structure required the services of one hundred twenty-five sculptors, granite and marble cutters, masons and laborers. It took over a year to build and contained seven hundred and fifty tons of granite, fifty tons of marble, twenty thousand bricks and three hundred and twenty-five barrels of English Portland cement. The interior was as beautifully decorated as the exterior was solidly constructed. The entire floor is a marvel of colored English encaustic tile and the walls and ceiling are splendid examples of the marble cutter's art. The two far corners of the interior are faced with plate glass mirrors which, when one stands between them, reflect and re-reflect, giving the optical illusion of a long, colonnaded gallery. The catacombs, containing the bodies of his family, make up the rear wall of the mausoleum and are engraved with their names and dates of birth and death. Standing on pedestals are busts of Bowman's wife and younger daughter, while between them is a life-size statue of the elder daughter who died an infant. Upon his death in 1891 a fourth statute, of Bowman himself, benevolently gazing upon his family, was placed within the tomb.

Bowman never gave a reason for placing the life-size statue of himself outside the tomb. Since it was placed on the steps some ten years before his death, he must have passed it daily in the course of his devotions within the mausoleum at a tiny altar constructed for the purpose. He saw it also from the doorway of his large summer residence across the road, a residence in which he was the only member of the Bowman family. Strange behavior, perhaps, but who is to say what is strange in the pursuit of a memorial to one's family? □□

Right: The magnificent interior of the mausoleum contains the family busts and a life-size statue of Bowman's oldest daughter.

Below: Exterior of the Laurel Glen Mausoleum with another life-size statue of Bowman, himself, guarding the entrance.

Westford's Knight in Stone

by Lawrence F. Willard

An 1873 English translation of the Zeno narrative indicates that Harry Sinclair, the Earl of Orkney, led a 14th century exploring party to the Western Atlantic. Was it this party, then, that left this portrait on the rock in what would one day be the Commonwealth of Massachusetts?

If evidence uncovered by Frank Glynn, Assistant Postmaster of Clinton, Connecticut, is to be believed Europeans were wandering around Massachusetts a century or more before Columbus made his famous voyage.

Glynn, an amateur archaeologist, has long been interested in such things as the underground stone beehives in Acworth, New Hampshire, and in Upton, Massachusetts, and other stonework of ancient and unknown origin scattered throughout New England.

Archaeologists from many amateur societies as well as archaeological students have puzzled over such interesting finds as the North Salem, New Hampshire ruins. Here excavations have revealed an acre and a half of underground walls, some still standing and supporting roofs. Some of the masonry weighs from 15 to 25 tons, and is similar to some found in Europe of a very early period. (See Mystery Hill Caves, page 258)

Other ruins on the Maine coast and the famous stone tower at Newport, Rhode Island, are generally believed to be the work of Norsemen or Vikings, although some researchers think the Newport tower may have been built by early Basque fishermen as a lighthouse. (See Who Built the Old Newport Tower?, page 266) Leif Ericson's annals record that his Vikings landed and established a camp in North America in 1003, but the location is not known.

This recent discovery by Glynn in Westford, Massachusetts, may provide more definite information as to who was at that particular spot, anyway, and approximately when. He believes that an image punched into a rock ledge, apparently by blows from an ironworker's tools, is the portrait of a Scottish nobleman in the full armor of the 14th century.

The existence of this image came to Glynn's attention following the publication of a book, "Merlin's Island," by Prof. T. C. Lethbridge of the University Museum of Archaeology and Ethnology, Cambridge, England. Glynn was interested in Dr. Lethbridge's beliefs that there were probably frequent voyages made to America from the British Isles, principally by Irish missionaries, dating back to before Leif Ericson and his Norsemen.

Glynn wrote to Dr. Lethbridge and a lively pen friendship began. Glynn sent his friend all the books he could find on the subject of early visits to America. One of these was a book by W. G. Goodman, "Greater Ireland in America," which contained a drawing of an image found on a rock in Massachusetts.

Goodman, an amateur archaeologist of long standing, and many-times president of the Lowell Historical Society, had interpreted the drawing as representing an 11th Century Norse "broken sword." Dr. Lethbridge on receiving the book from Glynn recognized that the drawing clearly showed a hand and half-wheel pommel sword of Medieval European vintage. He wrote to Glynn and urged him to rediscover the ledge.

"Strip back the dirt and see if you don't find something like this," Dr. Lethbridge said. He enclosed a sketch of a knight of the 14th Century.

It took Glynn two years to locate the ledge. Goodman had died and his reference to the ledge being only one of "in Massachusetts" covered a lot of territory. About 7:30 one evening in 1954 Glynn and his small daughter, Cindy, stopped in Westford. In reply to their usual inquiries, they were told that there was an unusual Indian drawing on a rock less than a mile from where they were. Glynn wasn't, at the moment, interested in Indian works of art. It took Cindy to prevail upon him to see what it was.

"The sword jumped right out at us as we looked at it," says Glynn, "we had found the right ledge at last."

On weekends Glynn began digging and as Dr. Lethbridge had thought, there was more to the drawing. For years the residents of Westford had proudly shown, as an authentic relic of Indian days, the picture to visitors. Old-time residents remembered climbing on the rock when they were youngsters. They had been intrigued by what appeared to be the figure of an Indian Chief about 20 inches high. The "Indian" turned out to be the hilt of a sword and a bird crest, probably a hunting hawk or falcon, perched on a jeweled helmet. The entire figure, when uncovered, was life-sized.

Glynn connects punchmarks in the rock with chalk lines to reveal the strange, life-size figure of a Scottish knight, who may have been an explorer in the 14th century.

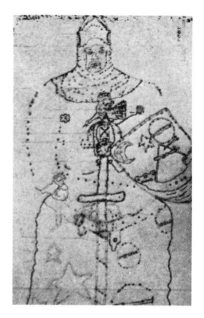

Frank Glynn's drawing of the mysterious figure he found in Westford.

Glynn made drawings of the figure and later made plaster casts of it. He described his find in the January Bulletin (1957) of the Eastern States Archaeological Federal in which he said:

"It now appears possible . . . there exists on Westford Hill a rough, life-sized portrayal of a late 14th Century knight in full length surcoat."

Glynn's tracing shows the features of the knight's face in an open-vizored helmet, shows crest, long sword with scabbard, a dagger in the knight's right hand, and a shield with emblems on his left arm.

"In whole, or in part," says Glynn, "the figure seems referable to the class of monuments known as the Military Effigies."

It was customary Medieval practice to mark the spot where a knight fell. Glynn reasons:

"If we went on an expedition, we wouldn't take an undertaker and a tombstone cutter along, but we would have an armorer to repair our weapons. If one of our chief men fell, we'd turn to him. Accustomed to working these symbols in iron, he might try to reproduce them by a series of punches in stone."

Glynn has produced experimental marks similar to these on the ledge. He used blacksmith tools: pointed punches, pee dee hammer, and a flat-headed hammer with a thick, blunt claw. These tools could have been found in the kit of a 14th century traveling metal worker or armorer.

The location of the figure is logical, Glynn believes. He refers to the probable path of visitors to the eastern shore of Massachusetts. If a party sailed up the Merrimack River, the hill then and now would be about a day's hike inland. Here is a logical high point from which to view the country.

Clues to the identity of this early landing party were gained by study of the emblems on the shield held by the figure on the ledge. Clearly evident are a star and crescent, a large round brooch, and small boat with furled sails (sometimes used as a symbol of journey's end).

"It was when we began to work out the trademarks on the shield that the hair began to rise on the backs of our necks," says Glynn. "Dr. Lethbridge did not at once recognize the brooch emblem, but investigation with aid from the Lion, King of Arms, the official Herald of Scotland, revealed that the design had been on the shields of several branches of the Orkney Sinclairs, a Scottish family."

An 1873 English translation of the Zeno narrative indicates that Harry Sinclair, the Earl of Orkney, led a 14th century exploring party to the Western Atlantic. Was it this party, then, that left this portrait on the rock in what would one day be the Commonwealth of Massachusetts?

Glynn thinks it is likely. However, he admits that this is speculation. He hopes that professional archaeologists who have now begun to examine the ledge may find still more information.

"There are plenty of mysteries in this field," says Glynn, "which we may never find the answer to. A number of years ago a clay object at first believed to be a peace pipe turned up in the excavating of an old Indian campsite in Clinton, Connecticut. It seemed on further examination that it might be a Roman lamp. We sent it to Cambridge University, England, for examination by experts on antiquities. They reported that it was a terra cotta lamp made on either the Island of Crete or the Island of Cyprus about 350 to 400 A.D. How did it get into the Indian dump? We will probably never know. The site was destroyed by teen-age arrowhead hunters before we could tell whether there was evidence to suggest that the lamp was deposited in Roman times."

Glynn makes no guess as to how the lamp got to America, though he points out that the Romans had ships 250 feet long . . . bigger than Columbus used.

"So much of this business is speculation," says Glynn, "that it's a wonderful thing when we make a find like the knight on the rock. For every discovery like this there are dozens which work out to nothing. Little by little, however, we are finding out something about these early visitors to our shores." □□

Mysterious Rock Carvings:

"Read these lynds and ponder . . ."

One afternoon in late 1786, a group of North Brookfield, Mass., citizens gathered in the tavern to discuss the fearful news that their neighbor Israel Allen had smallpox. They decided he would have to leave the area immediately and suggested a cave near Sucker Brook.

It is said that Allen did not flinch at the sentence presented to him by the village doctor—he would no doubt have supported the decision had the victim been another townsman. So, within the hour, Allen set out on foot for the cave which was to be his home until his death two years later.

The next winter, a hunter heard ringing and hammering sounds coming from the cave. Allen, now all but out of his mind, was recording his plight on the stone wall of his "home"—though the exact words he wrote were not discovered until someone found his body inside the cave in 1790.

The laboriously pecked-out letters are still legible enough to puzzle the casual visitor to the cave today. They read, "I Had the Small Pox April 19, 1788 I. Allen." Several feet below are the words, "Read these Lynds and Ponder . . ." *Courtesy of Bernard Quinn*

Four Unique Examples . . .

Now a word from the Abenakis . . .

In the town of Embden, Maine, on the west bank of the Kennebec River, is the only known work of the Abenaki Indians. This consists of a remarkable petroglyph, "pecked" into the rocks as if by an artistic robin with a very durable bill. The rocks once extended far into the river, but were partially blasted away years ago as the log jams they created were dynamited by the river drivers.

The pictures have never been translated—in historic times, that is. Some who have studied them think they tell of battles. However, the Abenakis (People of the Dawn) were peaceable.

Those who think the carvings are prehistoric base their reasoning on the fact that the tomahawks and bows and arrows indicate the work was done before the introduction of firearms. The crossed lines are considered part of a map, such as junctions of rivers or streams, rather than religious crosses.

A really close study of the ledge shows that the carvings could have been made over a period of many years. They surely do not appear to be the work of one artist. (The drawings shown in the photograph above have been chalked.) *Courtesy of Beatrice Farrand Maki*

John Davenport's Rock . . .

In the southeast corner of Weston, Mass., lies a much-weathered boulder on which are carved the worn initials: "JD." According to map maker Edward G. Chamberlain of the last century, "In 1639 Governor Winthrop and Rev. John Davenport had an 'Outing' up the River" (meaning the Charles River). He goes on to say it was John Davenport who carved his initials on the face of a stone overlooking the river.

Two years earlier, Davenport, a Puritan clergyman, and a London merchant, Theophilus Eaton, were apparently advised by Governor Winthrop to explore this area to find a suitable place for a new settlement. Not finding one, they sailed to the present New Haven, Conn., where they founded a colony in 1638.

If Chamberlain's source is accurate and Davenport indeed visited the Weston area again a year later, could the initials have served as a claim to the land, in the event Davenport decided to settle there instead of New Haven?

None of the known property owners in the nearby vicinity had surnames beginning with "D" and the initials, some 7½" high, are known to have existed before 1895.   *Courtesy of Thomas M. Paine*

The Round Swamp Mystery . . .

Charles Nye and Sal Pry lived in Sandwich, Cape Cod, in the late 1700s. It is said that their togetherness often took them to an idyllic spot on a ridge overlooking Round Swamp. Eventually, Charles went to sea to earn the money to build a house for Sal Pry. When his voyage was over, they were to be married. However, after four years of waiting, Sal was married to another.

Shortly thereafter, Charles returned. He took the news badly; in fact, he withdrew from the world and built a cabin deep in the woods—near Round Swamp and his memories of Sal Pry. There he spent day after day carving strange figures, letters, and symbols on the rocks and old logs.

So much for the legend. It is certainly a plausible explanation for the five (perhaps there are more) carvings on rocks located deep in the woods on what is now Otis Air Force Base property. When the rocks were discovered by two hunters back in the 1860s, however, tourists flocked to view what the ancient Vikings had carved! Nonetheless, old-time residents of Sandwich were pretty certain that the figure, such as that shown below, was (and still is) one Sal Pry.

Courtesy of Sumner Towne

Mystery Hill Caves

by Michael Oren

*Eskimos? Stone Age men? Irish monks? . . . No-
body seems to know, but somebody, with a plan,
moved an awful lot of rocks in North Salem, New
Hampshire. And what about that sacrificial stone?*

Up in the New Hampshire backwoods stands a pile of rocks put together like an ancient fort. In recent years its weatherbeaten walls
have seen a new kind of skirmishing. Professors, postmasters, priests and
a retired insurance man from Hartford have been taking verbal potshots
at one another. Each thinks he knows who piled the rocks in place and
is dead sure that all other theories are wrong. Among their candidates
are Eskimos, Stone Age Men, and a band of roving Irish monks.

Recently the Governor of New Hampshire snipped the ribbon that
formally opened this rocky battleground to the public as the "Mystery
Hill Caves." Anyone who cares to trek over to North Salem, in the
southeastern corner of the state, can now see the evidence and decide
for himself.

But what's there to see in a rockpile? Well, these rocks are very
big—as large as seventy-five tons—and somebody has done a fantastic
amount of work prying, levering and actually hoisting them up in the
air to build walls and a kind of stone igloo called "beehives." Next to
one of the beehives is a waist-high stone table sitting on four piles of

rocks. It is ten feet long, weighs four-and-a-half-tons, and has a deep groove running around the edge and off at one end. Some people think this groove was meant to catch blood, and they call the table the "Sacrificial Stone." There is a ledge a few feet above the stone that would make a handy place for watching sacrifices.

The beehive next door is a T-shaped affair with a couple of small closets and a long, low shelf built into the stone walls. It has a fireplace and chimney to make it cozy, and what seems to be the figure of a running deer has been scratched into one of the rocks. At the cross in the T is a small square hole in the wall through which one can peek out under the table. Those who speak of the "Sacrificial Stone" call this hole the "Oracle Tube." It is customary procedure for the ghost of a sacrifice (human or animal) to utter a few oracular words as it departs this world. For refractory ghosts a man hidden in the beehive could yell through the tube with much the same effect to observers on the ledge. One recent investigator tried yelling in Latin, and the effect was absolutely bloodcurdling.

Whoever put these stones together apparently never heard of mortar, for there has been none used in the whole square acre that the site occupies. Not only did the builders dress their stones and lug them up the hill, but they crisscrossed the area with long masonry drains, filled in chunks of the site with earthen ramps and interlaced the buildings with corridors and a broad plaza. They were up to something, all right, but what? And who were they?

Here is where the assorted professors, postmasters and the like were stopped cold. For these ruins looked like nothing ever built by Vikings or Indians. In fact, nobody even knew what they were used for.

After some thinking, our various protagonists came up with some varied answers. They decided:

(1) The ruins were entirely the work of an old-timer named Jonathan Pattee, who liked to move stones. Local tradition backed this up, and most of the professors wound up in this camp for lack of any proof to the contrary.

(2) Some other Early American built the place to store turnips and other root vegetables so they wouldn't freeze in the winter. The remaining professors gathered under this flag.

(3) A bunch of Irish Culdee monks from Iceland set it up not quite a thousand years ago and held religious ceremonies there while they Christianized the Indians. Hartford insurance man William B. Goodwin wrote a book to prove this view.

An artist's conception of a sacrificial rite as it might have been performed by Stone Age men. This was Goodwin's theory, but many people have tried to disprove it.

Below: The so-called "sacrificial stone" weighs 4½ tons. The object in the center is a foot rule. "Distinctly not a picnic table," said one visitor when he viewed the stone.

by the ancient cubit . . . 20 inches ± ½ inch.

(4) Stone Age man built the site a few thousand years ago and used it to worship the underground gods. An archaeologist (the postmaster) is currently digging the site under this assumption.

(5) It was built by the Eskimos. Nobody seems to know who suggested this and nobody wants to take responsibility.

Proving any of these theories has had its difficulties. Jonathan Pattee, for example, certainly lived on the site. In the 1820's he built a house there. At the very least he threw a roof over some existing walls and stuck on a chimney. But would any man in his right mind have built the whole affair?

On the other hand, who says Pattee was in his right mind? Some of the professors are sure he was crazy. He had a brother who just happened to have been a carpenter and housewright; this brother was declared insane. So one or the other of them may have done it for exercise.

Jonathan Pattee has become something of a neighborhood hero. One story has it that he was a moonshiner who played tag with the federal agents among the rocks. The town history refers vaguely to the time Lafayette paid him a visit on his last tour of America. Oddly enough, an old brass naval button made in Paris was recently dug out of the ruins.

After Pattee the site came upon evil days. The nearby towns of Lawrence and Andover, Massachusetts carted away perhaps forty per cent of it to serve as curbstones. In the 1850's someone seems to have fixed it over as a station in the Underground Railroad for fugitive slaves escaping into Canada. Then for a long period it stood almost neglected.

In 1937 insurance man Goodwin bought the site and began to dig. Archaeology had been his hobby for a long time. He had studied the Vikings and dug up some old ruins in Jamaica, and had written books about both of them. He knew of some other odd stone ruins in New England—about fifteen of them—but North Salem was the most spectacular. It was also the hardest to explain.

Goodwin was familiar with the old Norse sagas, particularly the parts that told of voyages into the far unknown west. Some of these trips wound up in a place called Great Ireland. Goodwin carefully studied Irish history. His eye fell on a sect of monks called Culdees, who may have established outposts in Iceland. Culdees and Norsemen never did mix well, and Goodwin decided that after a while the monks gave it up and ran away to America. They arrived almost a thousand years ago, well before Columbus even left sunny Italy.

The leader of a Culdee colony was called an Ab. He had a long beard and, if the ruins are any test, certain talents as an engineer. The North Salem Ab slept on the stone shelf in the beehive and used to yell into the "Oracle Tube" during ceremonies. His followers put up a number of odd stone structures around New England, keeping themselves busy in between times by Christianizing the Indians. They wore white robes and used to wave flags and chant loudly when in a pious mood.

In 1946, after much digging and calling in of experts, most of whom disagreed with him, Goodwin published a book called The *Ruins of Great Ireland in New England* (Meador, 1946). Through this book march an intriguing succession of Norse and Irish characters like Wolf the Worsh, Tuathal the Legitimate, the Saints Ninian, Drostan, Kentigern, Finbae and Comgall, and a short dark mysterious people called the Firbolgs. The evidence that they have any connection with North Salem, however, is open to question, and in fact it has been questioned many times.

Goodwin's work attracted many visitors to North Salem, among them a number of clergymen from Boston who had been invited by a local Irish brewer. The site had certain possibilities as a shrine, they thought, and made Goodwin an offer for it, which he refused. But there is a story that before he had even bought the ruins, a party from the Archdiocese of New Hampshire had blessed them and taken some artifacts which it deemed to have a religious significance.

What truth is there in the report that the Archbishop of County Kerry in Ireland once offered $100,000 for the site under certain conditions? Unless the Church had inside information, it seems to have had more faith in Goodwin than did all the professors put together.

Goodwin had many critics but his real arch-enemy was Professor Hugh O'Neill Hencken of the Peabody Museum in Cambridge, Massachusetts. Hencken was one of three Harvard professors with whom Goodwin carried on a running fight for several years, the other two being historian Samuel Eliot Morison and the anthropologist Ernest Hooten. Morison had wanted an article on North Salem for the *New England Quarterly*, and he sent Hencken to investigate. Goodwin was most cordial. Not only did he invite Hencken to work on the site but he threw open to him his immense library of supposed Irish and Norse antecedents. Hencken, who is a specialist in early Irish archaeology, looked it all over carefully. He dug up the stump of a white pine growing in the ruins and decided that it had started to grow between 1652 and 1769, before Pattee's occupation. He was circumspect in giving opinions, but Goodwin was encouraged.

As soon as the article appeared, however, it turned out Hencken had gone over to the Pattee camp. Goodwin took the news hard, and not at all quietly. He smelled a conspiracy against him, and he said so. But Hencken did not recant. Instead he published another article repeating his views.

When Goodwin's book appeared in 1946 the preface promised a complete account of "the bitter and totally uncalled for attacks made on me by some of the Harvard University faculty and the plain unvarnished reason for their cowardly manner of expressing themselves to do me the utmost harm." Without hesitation he went on to explain that "any attempt to create a new interest in antiquities and particularly to ask for pecuniary aid ran counterwise to those archaeologists who have fields of endeavor abroad, and not at home in these United States or Canada, and needed such aid for their own researches in Europe, Asia, Central and South America, as well as aid for their Museums with which they are directly connected."

This blast managed to cut relations between the camps, and no more work was done on the site for several years. In 1950 Goodwin died. Were the North Salem skirmishes at an end? Not quite.

Four years later, the Executive Director of New Hampshire's Planning and Development Commission, Ernest L. Sherman, heard of the site and Goodwin's claims for it. If there was any truth in them, he thought, it was downright considerate of the Irish—having beaten the *Mayflower* by over 600 years—to have set up headquarters right on his doorstep. Boston was less than fifty miles away. A little publicity would bring swarms of tourists on the pilgrimage to North Salem. Now it was really important to find out who built it.

So Sherman rounded up a number of people who had been interested in Goodwin's sites, including the Arctic explorer Vilhjalmur Stefansson and the Curator of Anthropology of the American Museum of Natural History, Dr. Junius Bird. Dr. Bird had sunk a couple of tests pits in North Salem several years before at Goodwin's invitation. Now he was asked to direct a new investigation. Sherman's group, which called itself the Early Sites Foundation, engaged an anthropologist and three graduate students to do the actual spade work.

In the spring of 1955 this expedition encamped at North Salem and dug for six weeks, which was as long as the Foundation's money held out. Hundreds of old nails, buttons, and pieces of glass and china were uncovered, but not a single one could be dated prior to the American Revolution. However, the Foundation did manage to turn up an old document alleging that Pattee was "fond of root-cellars," a kind of colonial icebox. It then filed a number of reports suggesting that most of Goodwin's ruins were really root-cellars. Peace seemed to have come at last to the North Salem battleground.

As it turned out, these reports were more like truce papers than a peace treaty. Hardly were they issued when one of the Foundation's directors noticed how much North Salem resembled certain sites in Malta and other parts of the Mediterranean. These places were used to worship underground gods in the late Stone and Bronze Ages. North Salem is full of drains and hand-cut fissures which would be handy for pouring offerings into the ground and for practically nothing else.

So this director, Frank Glynn by name, resigned and started to dig

A number of theories have been offered: stone age man built the site for worship; it was a sort of colonial ice box; the intriguing structures were the remnants of an ancient Eskimo village; and some one has gone so far as to suggest that it was part of an underground railroad . . . (?)

on his own. Glynn is the postmaster of the story; he is Assistant Post-master of Clinton, Connecticut. He is also president of the Connecticut Archaeological Society.

Up to the present time a highly unusual potsherd and a layer of stone chips have been uncovered by the new dig. The chips were under Hencken's pine stump, which means they must have been knocked off before Pattee's time. Some of the larger stones have been measured: twenty-eight out of a random thirty-three measurements turned out to be divisible by the ancient cubit (20 inches ± ½ inch—the length of the forearm) rather than by feet. A few of the bricks brought up earlier have been found to be adobe, or unfired clay, a practically un-known occurrence in colonial New England.

Is Glynn about to claim victory? Hopes are high but he carefully keeps his head down as he pushes his trench across the hilltop. What he would really like to find is the skeleton of a Stone Age man. This gentleman could speak louder to science than all the investigators in the history of the site.   □□

Many people think the deep groove running around the edge of the stone table served as a channel for the flow of blood.

Who Built the
Old Newport Tower?

by Richard Morgan

The Newport Tower—Viking relic or Colonial windmill?

*The controversy surrounding the origin of the Old Newport
Tower has raged for more than a hundred years and we're not
much closer to an accepted answer now than we were then . . .*

The most controversial building in America is one of the least impressive structures you ever saw. It is a squat ungraceful cylinder of lime-mortared fieldstone, 26 feet high, with semicircular arches between eight chunky columns, and no roof, standing in the middle of Newport, R. I., in a small park.

There are a few small unframed windows scattered seemingly at random in the part above the arches, and these, combined with numerous niches on the inside, make it an admirable shelter for Newport pigeons, which is its only function at the present time. Before Newport was built up, the tower, on a high point of land, commanded a fine view of the ocean; now its windows look out on taller houses.

It is highly unlikely that you would stop your car to gaze at such an uninspiring sight, unless you had heard about it in advance. There is nothing grand in its proportions, nothing romantic in its location, no sign hinting at an unusual origin; and yet this little stone ruin is said by some, and vehemently denied by others, to verify definitely perhaps one of the greatest and most intangible of all our legends—that the Vikings colonized America.

For more than a century now, an occasionally scholarly, often fanatic, usually bitter dispute has raged about the old round tower. Over 100 books, articles and pamphlets have attempted to throw light on its origin and purpose. The Irish, the Portuguese, the Dutch and even ancient Druids have been suggested as the builders; but there have actually been only two theories that hold water—the Norse and the Colonial.

It seems impossible that two such opposite viewpoints could co-exist, and the fact that they do, each championed by men of such unswerving conviction that nothing the other side produces can convince them, indicates how little is actually known about the tower. With each new article, each impressive new name added to the ranks of one, bringing forth rebuttals from the other, public opinion has shuttled between the two like a tennis ball. Except in Newport, where most people continue to call it, as they always have, and probably always will, "The Old Stone Mill."

As James Edward, managing editor of the Newport *News* and author of the Publicity Commission booklet *Newport Story*, says, "Newporters don't get very excited over anything, especially over familiar things." And the Old Stone Mill has been a familiar sight to them since at least 1675, when, most of them believe, it was constructed by Governor Benedict Arnold as a windmill to replace the wooden windmill of Peter Easton which was blown down in a hurricane that year.

[267]

". . . archaeology is a fairly exact science."

Evidence for this is contained in Arnold's will of 1677 which refers to "my stone-built windmiln"; this together with a deed to the Jewish cemetery 10 months earlier mentioning "ye stone mill," is the earliest accepted reference to a stone tower in Newport. But while most practical, or unimaginative—depending on your viewpoint—people simply assume that Arnold built the tower as a windmill, Norse theorists, the romantics, point out that although Arnold used it as a windmill, there is nothing in his will or elsewhere, to show that he built it. In their opinion he was simply putting the old ruin on his property to intelligent and timely use.

Right there you see the seeds of the dispute, and why it is so impossible for either Norse or Colonial school to build an airtight case. Arnold didn't say, "the stone windmiln which I built," nor did he say, "the old stone tower which I made into a windmiln." Either one of these simple statements would have shut up the other side in the controversy. As it is, there is almost no limit to conjecture.

But Arnold isn't the only one to blame for failing to set the picture straight for future generations; nobody else wrote anything about the origin of the tower either, until it was much too late to learn the truth from those who knew. Peter Easton received a property grant from a grateful town when he built the first windmill, which was duly recorded in the town records; Arnold apparently received nothing, not even a passing mention. And yet certainly it was a most unusual structure to build at that time as a windmill, not only a technically difficult and complicated undertaking, but unlike any windmill ever built before.

But this is getting ahead of the story. As a matter of fact, if anybody ever even wondered about the tower before the early 1800's, there are no records to show it. Except for indistinct and unrealistic mutterings a few years previously, the controversy didn't get underway until after 1837, following the publication of *Antiquatatis Americanae*, a mammoth work by a Dane named Charles C. Rafn, in which he traced Norse vestiges in America.

For eight years previous to its appearance, Rafn, secretary of the Royal Society of Northern Antiquaries at Copenhagen, had been in correspondence with Dr. Thomas H. Webb, secretary of the Rhode Island Historical Society, in an attempt to unearth evidences of Norse settlement in southern New England, which Rafn had fixed upon as the location of Vinland.

Webb responded with information about all sorts of unexplained inscribed rocks along the coast, which, although much of it was misleading, served to convince Rafn. On the strength of these relics, plus astronomical evidence in ancient texts, Rafn committed himself on southern New England as the Vinland of the sagas in *Antiquatatis Americanae*. Unfortunately, the inscriptions on the rocks were not Norse, as it turned out.

In 1839 Webb again wrote Rafn, mentioning for the first time the Newport Stone Mill, questioning its construction by Arnold, and hinting it had long been the object of speculation. Enclosed with the letter were two drawings by F. Catherwood, a famous illustrator of the time. It has since often been asked how such an accurate artist could have made such inaccurate drawings in this particular instance, because the impression given was of a much more sophisticated structure than the humble little Newport ruin.

Partly because of the glorified drawings, and partly due to suggestion by Webb, Rafn bit again, and in 1839 published a supplement to *Antiquatatis*, in which he set forth for the first time the theory that the Newport structure was built in the 12th Century by Eric, Bishop of Gardar in Greenland, as a church.

To back this contention, he pointed out the similarities between the arches and columns of the Newport building (Webb had given him the idea that the upper part was added in Colonial times), and various European churches of the 12th century. Rafn thus began the prototype method, which has been so extensively used by Norse theorists ever since.

The possibility that the Norse had discovered America long before Columbus was a new and eagerly seized upon concept in this country, and with Rafn's book as ammunition, the Norse theory grew powerful overnight.

Numerous converts rushed into print and Henry Wadsworth Longfellow composed a highly romantic poem called "The Skeleton in Armor," in which a skeleton adorned with metal ornaments found in Fall River becomes the Viking bold who built the Newport tower as a bower for his lady love. The skeleton turned out to be a dead Indian wearing some skimpy brass trinkets bought from the English.

But in 1847 the Viking theory began to fall into disrepute, helped along by a sizzling exchange of letters printed in Newport and Provi-

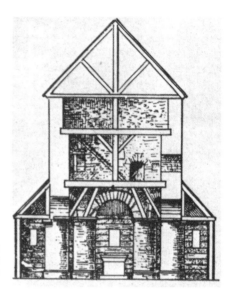

Right: Old Mill restored as Norse round church. Below: Supposed Gilbert Stuart painting of mill, around 1770.

dence papers between "One of the Oldest Inhabitants of Newport," and "Antiquarian." In this exchange, "Antiquarian," of the Norse persuasion, goaded "One of the Oldest Inhabitants," a staunch Arnoldist who later revealed his name as David Melville, to fury with incredible inventions of Norse relics in various parts of the country, and quotes of nonexistent scientists who had pronounced the Newport ruin Norse.

It was actually a practical joke by two Newporters, masquerading as an antiquarian from Brown University, which was exposed by Rafn, after Melville indignantly forwarded him one of the letters. Besides bringing discredit upon his tormentors, Melville produced what Arnold theorists had long been awaiting—a prototype mill for the one at Newport.

In fact he intimated there were hundreds all over Europe. According to him, Arnold was born and brought up in Leamington, Warwickshire, England. Near this town stands the Chesterton windmill, a stone structure built in 1632, with six columns, very similar in appearance to the Newport mill. He had come across an illustration of the Chesterton mill in *The Penny Magazine*. Melville pointed to the obvious conclusion that Arnold had built his mill in imitation of the structure he had

A close prototype for the Newport Tower—
St. Olaf's Church, Tonsberg, Norway, 1200's.

[271]

known in his youth. The use of open columns was to reduce back eddies of air. That Melville was nearly as free with the truth as "Antiquarian" was only proved much later.

When a few years later, in 1858, the eminent historian John G. Palfrey backed this solution in his *History of New England*, the Norse theory was buried as far as the public was concerned.

Especially in Newport this seems to have been taken as the final word; they had never veered far from their original thinking anyway. The tower was planted with vines and almost literally dropped from sight until 1879. It was even recommended by a local architect that the ruin be torn down as an eyesore. To suggest that the Catholic Norsemen had founded America was not considered very good form in a part of the country that prided itself on its Protestant background.*

Despite the ascendancy the Colonial theory of the origin of the Old Stone Mill enjoyed from the 1850's all the way into the early 1900's, the Norse theory was being quietly but steadily developed and refined. Scholars both here and abroad were deeply interested in it, and as thinking on the subject became more and more logical, the wild conjectures that so often characterized writings on the structure were gradually weeded out, leaving a residue of solid thinking, reinforced by new discoveries in history.

It's time now to take a look at the rival theories as they stand today, after 115 years of development. The Arnold theory, being the conservative one, that merely had to be defended, backed by the few known facts has not progressed too much, but better reasons why it should have been built in Colonial times are now given. An up-to-date statement of Arnold opinion comes from Herbert O. Brigham, librarian of the Newport Historical Society, who prepared an unusually objective booklet summing up both sides, titled *The Old Stone Mill*, concerning which a friend said to him, "You walked a tightrope, and never fell off."

The latest thinking among the Arnold theorists is that the governor probably did not build the stone tower as a mill, but for a watchtower and possible defense. He had moved to Newport in 1651, from Providence. During that period the first war between the Dutch and English occurred, and a second one broke out in 1664 during which the Colony of Rhode Island took defense measures and caused beacons to be erected along the south coast.

* *The Norse were devout Catholics for over five centuries.*

While no mention is made of any defense structure on the hill where the Stone Mill now stands, Brigham considers it possible that Arnold, the biggest landowner and the wealthiest man in Newport, built the tower privately as a lookout and strongpoint. The impression he has gained of Arnold from historical sources, is that, "Arnold had three fads: he was a stone enthusiast (some say his house was of stone); he had a fear of somebody (he kept a watchman), and was avid about buying land."

Another theory Brigham brings up to account for the building of a stone mill is that it was sort of a WPA project during King Philip's War in 1675, when many settlers from devastated areas took refuge on Aquidneck Island, one of the safest places during the time.

"Possibly," says Brigham, "Arnold's idea of a combined fortress, lookout and mill took root and the settlers aided Arnold in erecting the building. To these people, it was a commonplace matter, hence the few records that are extant give no clue to its construction."

Another proof Arnoldists produce is the similarity of construction in other stonework in Newport of the same period. Finally, most Arnoldists would echo Brigham, who maintains, "There's not one single Norse artifact in New England."

In turning to the fully developed Norse theory, the first impression is amazement at the really extraordinary amount of research that has gone into its construction. In 1942 Henry Holt and Co. published a whole book, *Newport Tower*, by Philip A. Means, a distinguished student of Latin-American architecture and history, summing up everything that had been said before, and adding many new ideas. Means had become interested in the Stone Mill in the mid-thirties, after reading a provocative monograph by D. E. J. Allen. In order to prepare himself for his undertaking, he first steeped himself in medieval history, civilization and architecture. Backed by friends, he traveled throughout Europe examining ancient source materials, and medieval architecture. As an indication of how much research went into his book, the bibliography runs more than 27 pages.

In its first chapter, Means set about destroying the Arnold theory with obvious impatience, hurling accusations of "lying," and "making an ass of himself" right and left. He demolished the story previously spread by Melville that Arnold had been born near the Chesterton Windmill—Arnold had actually been born in Ilchester, Somerset, nearly a hundred miles from Leamington. As the Chesterton mill was built by the famous architect Inigo Jones two years before Arnold left England, Means doubts that he ever saw it. And even if he had, Means continued, the Chesterton mill had actually been built as an observatory, and wasn't converted to a windmill until long after Arnold died. This revelation effectively knocked the props from under the theory that the Chesterton mill was the prototype for Arnold's mill, so that it appears there is no other windmill prototype in the whole world.

After stating the two rival theories and dealing thoroughly with their development, most of the rest of Means' book is devoted to proving that the Norse could easily have had a settlement along the New England coast any time between the 10th and 14th centuries, and then minutely examining the dimensions and construction details of the Old Mill and proving their close parallel to Norse round churches of the 12th century.

These similarities include double-splayed windows, loopholes, the arches and columns, the fireplace with two flues running through the wall to the outside—much more primitive than fireplaces built in Arnold's time—and the two stories that were evidently once a part of the Newport Tower.

Eight-column round churches which most closely resemble the Newport tower are: Great Hedinge Church, Denmark; St. Olaf Church at Tonsberg, Norway; and the Church of the Holy Sepulchre at Cambridge, England. Means pointed out they not only bore close resemblances in design and form, but also in dimensions and orientation. The columns of the Newport tower, like the round churches, are oriented according to the *true* points of the compass, apparently determined by the North Star, rather than by later magnetic compasses. Means' conclusion: Eric Gnupsson, appointed Bishop of the Greenlanders by King Sigurd in 1112, who was known to have gone to Vinland a few years later, could have constructed the Tower in memory of the Church of the Holy Sepulchre in Jerusalem, the inspiration for all round churches, with which the Norse were familiar as a result of their participation in the Crusades.

Although Means' reasoning was not conclusive, and he himself said many more facts would have to be brought forward, and much more research done, calling particularly for archaeological excavation, his book convinced a lot of people. But Hjalmar R. Holand was even more convincing in *America 1355–1364*, which came out in 1946.

Holand, a Wisconsin man of Scandinavian descent who has spent most of his life in Norse research, chiefly to defend the validity of the

The Chesterton windmill, thought at one time to be the prototype for the Newport mill.

Kensington Stone, found in Kensington, Wisc., in 1902, and now accepted as a genuine Norse runestone, believes the tower was built by the royal expedition of Paul Knutson to Vinland in 1355 to 1364, in search of the settlement that had vanished from the western coast of Greenland.

Since there are features of the tower unique to both Norway and Sweden, Holand theorizes that the building is a composite of the ideas of both nationalities. It was both a fort and a church. New details in the Newport Tower brought out by Holand include: a long niche that could have held a portable altar, the medieval-style second-story entrance reached by a ladder, which Means had treated as a window.

Obviously it is impossible to present all the substantiating evidence for the Norse theory, when whole books have been written on the subject. But it would seem fruitless now anyway, because the Arnold school has had, since 1949, almost irrefutable proof of its claim that the Stone Mill is Colonial and nothing more.

Beginning in 1948, the long-recommended archaeological excava-

[275]

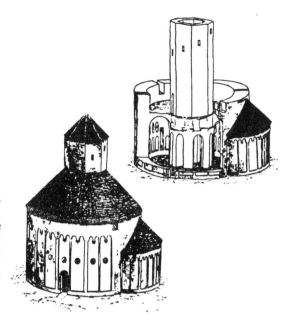

Right: Another prototype for the Newport Tower, at Ostergotland, Sweden. Below left: Österlars Church, Bornholm, Denmark, has many construction features similar to the Newport Tower. Below right: The largest of the openings in the old mill bears close resemblance to second-story doors of fortified Norse churches.

tions were undertaken under the auspices of the Newport Preservation Society, and under the close supervision of the Park Commission, which had long resisted the proposal. A young archaeological graduate student, William S. Godfrey, Jr. did a very thorough job in two consecutive summers. He found the original annular trench dug to receive the footings for the columns, and a few artifacts. None were Norse. He did find, however, Colonial artifacts in the bottom of the trench, and even right under the columns themselves.

There were three main items that Godfrey felt proved the point: a square-heeled footprint at the bottom of the original trench, beneath which was found a fragment of a clay pipe; a fragment of Colonial pottery among the stones of a footing, and a layer of Colonial brown earth, containing a gun flint and other artifacts, passing under four of the columns.

Godfrey comments in a recent letter:

"When the excavation began, I was more than half convinced of the Norse origin of the structure, but the Colonial evidence . . . was so consistent, the Norse evidence so absolutely absent, that I had no choice but to alter my original views. Although I will not place any bets on the original use of the Old Stone Mill, there is no doubt in my mind that it was built by the early settlers of Newport, perhaps by Arnold."

So that settles it. Or does it? As a matter of fact, it doesn't. Godfrey's report may have swept off all the fence straddlers onto the Arnold side, but he didn't even budge the hard core we spoke about at the center of the Norse school. Those who continue to claim Norse origins for the Stone Mill have of course lost much prestige, and the most unregenerate of them are labeled crackpots by the Arnoldists particularly, but as Mrs. George Henry Warren, president of the Newport Preservation Society says, "Now, as far as we're concerned, the matter is just as much up in the air as it was before." Mrs. Warren had the idea that "if it could be proved to be a Viking relic, then it would be the first Christian church in the Western Hemisphere. It would be a national shrine."

That train of thought is what the rival Historical Society terms "wishful thinking." Herbert Brigham, the scholarly looking elderly librarian of the Historical Society, whose soft voice conceals a sharp wit, comments, "Local people don't like to spoil a legend." He himself regards the archaeological findings as definite. If they had been Norse, he maintains, some relics would have been found. "You'll leave a trail after two weeks," he says, "no matter what. You'll break a cup or something else, but you'll leave some signs." Brigham had always inclined toward the Colonial theory.

John Howard Benson, outstanding monument designer and letterer, is another Newporter who has been deeply interested in the mill controversy. Armed with copious notes and slides, he delivered many lectures on the subject. Although his talks were non-partisan, Benson admits that he definitely favored the Norse theory, until the excavation findings changed his mind. "Archaeology," he points out, "is a fairly exact science." However, he still can't find any prototype for the mill, and he doubts that it was constructed as a mill.

James Edward, newspaperman, still thinks the Norse theory is a nice idea. "I sort of hope it's Norse," he says wistfully, "because it would be much more colorful and interesting. It would mean Newport has probably the oldest European building in America."

A few years ago he had proposed putting up a colorful sign to direct people to the old ruin, illustrated with a Norseman in full getup. He was turned down. "It's very strange, the conservatism of some of the old residents," was his comment.

There's also an underlying division, apparently, between those who want to boost Newport, and those who shun publicity. A very outgoing, jovial real estate and insurance man, who is another Newport booster, Richard C. Adams, with an office less than a hundred yards from the Stone Mill, also likes the Norse idea, although he says, "I don't think there's a chance it's Norse. So long as it's talked about, that's the main thing." Adams is a past director of the Chamber of Commerce and secretary of the Preservation Society.

There was only one person we found in Newport who still believes completely in the Norse theory. He is an architect named John Perkins Brown, who lives in an old Victorian house near Ocean Drive, within sight of a poor replica of the Stone Mill that was built in the last century as a water tower. Brown, a book collector and antiquarian in his own right, was a friend of Means, who died before the excavations; he has many of Means' reference books and manuscripts. He still maintains, "I think the whole thing is against its being built when people say it was." He and Means, he says, "always held the theory of an ambulatory surrounding the tower. They dug the trench in only one place outside the tower, and I think they just missed the ambulatory wall." He thinks Godfrey's trench may have gone right through the doorway of the ambulatory. It will be difficult ever to prove or disprove this point, as the Park Commission has forbidden any further excavations.

The excavations didn't convince Brown, nor did they change Hjalmar R. Holand, who is sticking by his arguments as developed in his book, *America, 1355–1364*. In a recent letter he resounded his war cry: "Against this lone statement [Arnold's reference to "my stone-built windmiln"], which is of no value in seeking the purpose of the builders, there are a dozen arguments, which each in turn proves that the Tower was not build by Benedict Arnold or any other colonist, and that it was not planned as a grist mill."

There is one more authority to be consulted before leaving the controversy about the Stone Mill—Kenneth J. Conant, Professor of Architecture at Harvard University, honorary president of the Archaeological Institute of America. An erudite, kindly man with a gentle sense of humor, Prof. Conant sounds convincing. Pointing out that "the 17th century English colonists were still building in the medieval style," he comes out in favor of the Arnold theory. He lectured on the mill in a course in American architecture, and one of his students made an accurate model. The student attached a framework to the sockets that are set into the tower, and Prof. Conant says, "I could see that it was framed for a mill, rather like the Chesterton Mill. Not only that," he sums up, "but it was badly framed for a fort." But the Chesterton structure was not designed as a mill. Well, Conant doesn't think this one was, exclusively. Rather, "I think it was conceived as a Pavilion."

It is very remarkable, Prof. Conant concedes, that the Newport mill should have so many points in common with Norse architecture. "The actual fabric is medieval," he admits, "while the statics of the building are Norse. It so happens that the only arch left from medieval Norse construction in Greenland is like that." But, Prof. Conant regards the excavation as conclusive.

Perhaps more facts about the origin of the Old Stone Mill in Newport will come to light in the future, and the problem will finally be solved. The excavations proved to the satisfaction of most people that the tower is Colonial. But it seems that there is still room for doubt, and that someday, as the process of uncovering ancient documents continues, the solution of the Newport enigma may prove the legend of the Vikings in Vinland. Meanwhile, Newport pigeons have a distinguished residence. ▫▫

The Mystery Trenches of Millis

by Warren Carberg

*What were they . . . boundaries or fortifications? And who
built them . . . the Redmen, or the Norsemen,
or the English settlers?*

They are filled with the rotting leafmold of perhaps sixty or more generations—these mysterious trenches that trace a dim trail through the little-frequented woods that fringe South End Pond in Millis, Massachusetts.

The decaying leaves and primal stumps of oak and beech might be black gold to the gardener who chanced to find them, but to the archaeologists they are a perennial puzzle.

Were they built as fortifications by a shadowy race of Redmen along the west bank of the Charles, or by a colony of Norsemen, as one Harvard professor maintained? Or did they serve the more prosaic purpose of town boundaries of the very early English settlers who eked out a precarious living here in the mid-seventeenth century?

The trenches have been explored during the past fall by local archaeologists, Francis Porter and Wilbur Roache. Both succeeded in digging their way through mold and roots to a depth of almost five feet. In the leafmold of the trenches they found living beech trees twenty inches in diameter, growing out of still older stumps.

Almost one hundred years ago, one Harvard professor expressed the conviction that the trenches had been built by 300 Norsemen some 1100 years ago. But a later investigation revealed the trench system to be so extensive that the Norsemen during their brief stay could have built only a small part of them, if any at all. The most probable theory at this point is that they were constructed by the Nipmuc Indians or those who immediately preceded them.

Enclosed by trenches and brook, river, and swamps, are some seven or eight miles of territory. It is believed that in this patch of land there must be an immense burial ground, for outside of the Ohio Valley no such extensive works is known in the entire United States. The general plan, as near as can be ascertained, is that of an immense triangle subdivided by trenches, making each of the seven hills which they encompass a formidable encampment. It is believed large enough to accom-

Above: Archaeologists Francis Porter and Wilbur Roache dig into one of the trenches, now clogged with leafmold.
Left: In February of 1676, the Indians massacred many whites in the area—possibly in an attempt to defend these trenches. A stone house was then located at the bottom of the foreground slope. In attacking it, the Indians set fire to a cart loaded with flax and rolled it down this hill toward the stone house (no trace of which remains today). The cart swerved into the large rock shown by the arrow and lodged there. Several Indians tried to free it but they were shot by the colonists and the stone house was saved.

modate 2,000 people. Their construction is planned as carefully as the works of any modern engineer. In some places stone embankments have been found extending 2,000 feet. Several places have been found where the arrow makers, the blacksmiths of their day, toiled. Chips from arrow heads permeate the ground for several hundred feet.

The land is crossed by the old King Philip Trail, which passes through Mendon, Uxbridge and Douglas until it joins the Pequot Trail in Connecticut.

Some have speculated that the Indians considered the area sacred and for this reason decided to kill or chase off the whites occupying the area back in February of 1676. The resulting bloody battle marked the first successful defense by the New England settlers against Indian attackers during King Philip's War.

Until they are tested by the modern carbon fourteen test, the exact age of these mysterious trenches cannot be determined. □□

Section VI

Hopes, Horrors and Dreams

CITY OF GLOUCESTER. 1892.

A Hand Aboard the Horton

by William P. Deering

The fate of the Henrietta Horton is not known, but all Glouces-
ter believes she sank in collision on Georges in March of '86. If
so, she sailed from home to the white haven of death and she
went short-handed by one man.
God keep me from the devil and all his works! I, who write these
lines, saw that recent sailor rejoin his vessel in another March
gale, twenty years after she was lost.

Tide ripples, making the water coldly bright, danced around the bows
of the *Henrietta Horton*, moored, ready for sea, tug fast a'port at the
sea-end of Phalen's wharf. A rising land breeze strummed in her rigging,
then hastened ahead, cabin boy of Aeolus, to escort her out to sea.

The tug whistled and Captain Abijah Horton, towering aft, bawled,
"Cast off." Mooring lines, released by loungers, slatted aboard.

The cook, gripping the wheel, said uneasily, "Cap'n, he didn't
make it."

Captain Horton eyed him frostily. "No," he said.

"Mebbe, sir, we could wait a little."

The captain's face, rugged as if carved from his native Cape Ann granite, did not relax.

Bleakly he asked, "Do the winds wait on the sins and follies of man? Does the tide wait? No? We wait not one jot or tittle more than they. My brother knew we sail with the tide. Where, then, is he in this hour of duty? In some saloon, in some foul den of Beelzebub, you may be sure.

"I know your mind, John, you would spare my father. Yes, this well may be the last straw to break the back of his patience. I hope not, but if this results in his casting William adrift, on my brother's head rests all the guilt and blame."

"Aye, sir." The cook spoke sadly.

"Mains'l halyards, haul, lads," the captain shouted. "We'll drop the tug off Ten Pound Island. Five dollars in pocket equals five quintals in the hold."

They sprang to it smartly.

Big Ted Thomaston allowed no sodden drinking in his saloon up near the head of Phalen's wharf. Now, he was rebuking a man who entered, hurled his sea-bag into a corner, and demanded whiskey.

"No whiskey here for you, William," Tom said curtly. "You've had enough. Why'nt y' get aboard? She sails on the tide and Bije won't wait."

"Will so," the fisherman mumbled, and then, "Aah let'm sail. But," cunningly, "I'm all ready. I'll be aboard." He pointed to his bag in the corner.

Big Ted was aware of this odd new business doctrine, that the customer is always right, voiced recently by a merchant prince in Boston, and, generally speaking, he favored it, but for his saloon he held to a few reservations.

Well, there are standards that submit to no compromise. One is the dictum that a sailor must be aboard his ship at sailing time.

"Pick up your bag and get aboard, you scut," Big Tom said fiercely, "before I kick you half way to Duncan Street. There'd be no drink for you at this bar today if your name was President Harrison."

Whining about injustice, the fisherman obeyed. The cold March wind sponged away the fumes of alcohol a little and he looked anxiously down the wharf for his vessel, but great sheds concealed her.

Afraid, he hastened down the pier past the stored hogsheads of pickled fish but when he "opened up" the wharf-end no sturdy masts arose above the cap-log, no bustle of embarkation milled about. However, down the harbor, off Ten Pound Island, he saw the *Horton* casting off from the tug.

To the man's despair, the utilitarian little schooner seemed fairer than any dream boat in the great world afloat.

"Lord, she's gone, she's gone," he moaned. "I'm on the beach!" It seems he was talking aloud. Loafers, lingering on the cold wharf-end, regarded him apathetically.

Afraid to go home, he must have stayed on his debauch for near four weeks and, by then, the schooner was "Given up."

The day she was posted as "Lost," old Commodore Horton, stern, white-bearded, patriarchal, sought his son through waterfront dives, found him, reviled him, cast him adrift.

"Had you been with your brother, drunken dog," the biting, controlled voice intoned, "you might have aided in saving our vessel, or died in honor. Go now, and join him. You are no son of mine, nor do you bear the name of Horton."

I went Georges hand-lining in the 90's and 1900's and, by the Lights of St. Elmo, it was a trade fit only for men, especially in winter. Cotton mittens on our hands, woollen nippers around our wrists to take the bite of the icy lines, we stood at the rails, fishing, while ice from spindrift and an occasional mean sea coated everything. But when we were "on fish," yanking them in, that was joy. How they would fight! Drag your arms right out of the sockets—seemed so. That took backs and biceps. That took men.

Generally was a fleet on the bank: mainly Gloucester but some Boston and Cape Cod. We often lay double-anchored, and rivalry— my good gosh!

This formation sometimes caused terrible tragedies, when an anchor dragged. A schooner adrift in the fleet becomes a catapult of death. Out of the smother she strikes her victim and the shrieks of the drowning compete momentarily with the screeching gale.

That, probably, happened to the *Horton*.

Legend grew until no Gloucesterman would anchor in certain areas of Georges Shoals. There, men said, the *Horton* perished and there the ghosts of her crew haunted the scene of their agonies. Men said that,

Abijah would lead his dead on board . . ."

come starlit August or maddened March, the flukes of any vessel anchoring there, stirring up the bottom around the *Horton's* bones, awoke horror and disaster. At one bell in the midnight watch, Captain Abijah would lead his dead on board, climbing over the knightheads, silently pacing the deck; beards wagging solemnly, stumbling aft, each ghost peering into the faces of the watch as if seeking, vainly, for something precious and long-lost; vanishing over the stern.

Fortunate such a vessel if she ever made port and, certainly, her luck was gone forever.

Do I believe that? Look, I'm modern, I've been to school, I ain't saying.

But one character on the waterfront paid the ghosts of the *Horton* no nevermind. We called him Leghorn Larry. He had sailed to Leghorn and liked to gab about it. Signed on under that name, too.

When topmasts came down, as vessels changed from Mackereling, South Channel, Ipswich Bay, to "Winter Georges"—Larry always showed seeking a berth. I've been shipmates with him and he was a character.

Always drunk, when ashore, he would quit a saloon at a whisper to "go aboard" on sailing day. The vessel that carried Old Larry had at least one man who never missed the tide. He always seemed old. Habits he had and clothes he wore appeared to belong to an older generation—such as stocking-caps when at sea and sea-boots when ashore. He was a good man in a dory or on cod.

By 1906, though, he was really old. Captains don't like to sign ancients, so it grew difficult for him to get a vessel. Finally he would hang around the wharves, hoping that some crewman would fail to show at sailing time. He was often signed on this way.

That's how it was that mid-March afternoon, when the beautiful clipper schooner, *Castile and Aragon*, big Dan Maginnis, master, lay at the sea-end of Phalen's wharf, tug fast a'port ready to drop down the harbor with the tide. All hands were aboard except one and he was up town drunk; still he might show.

Old Larry stood, shivering, on the wharf. He had asked for a lay and darned if he didn't blubber, whine and beg: "Cap'n, I gotta go. I gotta. I gotta be on Georges on St. Patrick's Day."

"Wait on the wharf," Big Dan said. "If that so-and-so ain't aboard, he can stay ashore and be damned to him."

The tug whistled, ripples around our forefoot showed the tide's turning. Big Dan called, "Cast off."

Larry threw the lines and jumped into the main rigging. I was standing where he hit the deck and this is what I heard him say: "God is good to sinful man. Praised be His Holy Name." I heard him plain. Make any sense of that?

We set sails, cast off from the tug before we were opposite Norman's Woe, and, just as our canvas got drawing, snow blew up and never left us until the big gale on Georges.

The *Castile and Aragon* was a wonderful, beautiful, sailable vessel and, on the ocean chop she seemed like stepping a fancy minuet.

We picked our anchorage in the bank fleet but fishing was poor and, by the third day, the snow was heavy. We shifted, had better luck, but, by nightfall, there was a real tough blow.

"Two man watches," Big Dan said, "two hour stretches that ain't bad. Say, it's St. Patrick's Day."

About one bell in the midnight watch, Old Larry and I went on deck. I left the smelly but cheerful fo'c's'le reluctantly but Larry seemed right happy. Once on deck he went for'ard and I aft. First I slid the companionway hatch cover over.

Winter Nor'easters on Georges are really *something*—seas surging endlessly, cross-waves breaking, vessel tossing like a chip, for all she's fast to two mud hooks. Seas heave for a second into your riding lights' feeble circles, and are gone, bigger ones always following. Snow is in solid walls, icy and stinging. Five minutes and your oiled clothes are armor, a bearded man's face rimmed with steel. Wind! Think of any possible comparison and this is worse. Better hang on, sailor, this wind is pushing like a great, hard, hostile hand. And, that night we even had lightning.

The storm was pounding us from sta'b'd and I went back to stand by the main rigging. What did I expect to see? Nothing, but there are duties that a man just has to do.

But I saw something, oh, aye, indeed! A terrible flash of lightning, just as a cross wind blew aside the swirling snow, disclosed a valley through the opaque mountain of the storm and down this channel a schooner, bare-poled and adrift, was driving before the Nor'easter right at us. I saw that she was an old-fashioned blunt-nosed boat and that she was poised to hit us dead amidships and cut us down, like a splitting knife slicing a mackerel.

I yelled to Larry, but my voice was torn away to port. I jumped to the after companionway, threw back the hatch cover, and shouted, "Deck ho! Schooner sta'b'd, close aboard!" Then I raced for'ard. The fo'c's'le cover was snugly in place, so Larry had not heard me. I slid it back, yelled my alarm. Might not be too much point in the lads making the deck but no sailor wants to drown like a gray dock rat in a wire trap.

Back at my post, I saw the fellows tumbling up from below, Big Dan first, and, at the main rigging, Old Larry was standing, of all places, on the rail, steadying himself with a hand hold on a ratline. He was peering into the smother off there, where, I knew, the stranger, bringing us death, was swiftly approaching.

Another flash, and I saw her again, but she was falling off a little to sta'b'd. If God were merciful, she might lay alongside, instead of crashing us, and slip by, grazing our scuppers. Men, mostly "holding on," were standing about her deck and a big, bearded, Yankee-looking lad was fighting the wheel.

Darkness and Big Dan shouting an order.

Then another voice, young stentorian, calling down the storm "Abijah, Abijah, here I be, Abijah. I'm a-coming."

It was Old Larry and, as he called, he gathered himself and leaped straight out into the sea. It was as though he were boarding that mysterious schooner.

Big Dan had seen, and I thought he would crush my arm with his grip.

"He jumped," the skipper croaked. "My God! He boarded her!"

Was that the ghost of the *Horton*? She cleared us which if not an illusion was a miracle of seamanship. Was she there? If not what had Dan and I seen? I dare not say, but certain it is that no schooner ever again reported her ghostly visitations.   □□

The Strange Obsession
of Hiram Marble

by Lowell Ames Norris

Hiram—followed by his son, Edwin—devoted their lives to digging 200 feet down into Dungeon Rock. Today, 100 years later, their purpose has been achieved.

In the Lynn Woods Reservation within the city limits of Lynn, Massachusetts, a few miles north of Boston, there is an eternal memorial to everlasting faith.

It is called Dungeon Rock and is in the midst of this reservation, which is open to the public from May to October. But before another spring arrives the wildness of the spot and its picturesque beauty may be gone forever with the possible intrusion of the interstate highway which may run through the reservation.

Dungeon Rock is a weird, man-made tunnel which extends down some 200 feet into living rock. The stairway leading to the tunnel has rotted away. But visitors may glimpse, through the iron-barred door beneath huge rough boulders, the beginning of the tunnel. They can see the vast grout pile of stone chips made by human hands over a period of thirty years and pay tribute at the grave of Edwin Marble.

The tunnel was laboriously cut out at the rate of one foot a month by the hands of Hiram Marble and his son Edwin. They were endeavoring to reach the treasure hoard of Freebooter Tom Veal, who, tradition says, was entombed by an earthquake with his shining doubloons and a beautiful mistress. . . .

Most men seek buried treasure to add to their own wealth. Hiram Marble and his son sought this treasure to perpetuate a community ideal —to make possible a free public reservation where people could enjoy nature in all its charm and natural beauty.

The Marbles have been dead nearly a hundred years. Edwin sleeps in a grassy plot, tucked in by rocks, on the sunny side of Dungeon Rock. The bottom of the underground passage in Dungeon Rock is flooded with water and the treasure remains undiscovered, but the ideal for which the Marbles lived and died has become an actuality. Dungeon Rock is now the crowning feature of the Lynn Woods Reservation and there are groves, drives and a lake, just as Hiram Marble planned . . .

All in all, it makes an amazing story which outrivals the most ingenious plots of fiction.

It had its beginning back in the late summer of 1658 when a sinister-looking ship, painted black, anchored one night off the Saugus River just before sundown. It flew no flag.

Immediately the word was passed around—"Pirates." As curiosity grew, a boat with four men put off from the ship and rowed up the river.

Next morning the ship had departed, but later a note was found fastened to the door of the iron foundry asking for shackles, handcuffs, hatchets and other iron goods. An adequate supply of silver coins was promised if these completed articles would be left in a secret place. This was done and the payment was speedily forthcoming.

Then come tantalizing gaps in the manuscript. Presently the mysterious "four oarsmen" again appeared. They landed in a secluded portion of the Lynn shore which even today is known as "Pirates' Glen." Once there, they erected a hut and apparently settled down. But their fancied security was of short duration. A British man-of-war made its appearance.

Her skipper landed men who made a surprise attack upon the "oarsmen." Three of them were captured and later hanged. The leader, Captain Thomas Veal, escaped.

Veal, the chronicle continues, made his way inland several miles to the north and found shelter beneath a huge ledge now known as Dungeon Rock. Here he is said to have lived—an odd change in the life of one who had been roving the seven seas and looting ships. Now he made shoes. The old narrative does not offer any explanation or tell us how he managed to make his peace with "Authority."

All we do know is that there was once a cave under the rock, that somebody lived in it, and that a tempest or an earthquake or some sudden convulsion of nature brought about a great fall of rock that completely closed the entrance to the cave and buried it many feet below the surface.

Tradition has it that Joel Dunn, a woodcutter, was in the cave quarreling with Veal when suddenly there came a sullen rumbling roar and a series of crashing growls as rock ground rock and the earth shook beneath them.

The woodcutter knew no more until he was picked up the next morning by another woodcutter who found him lying by the side of Dungeon Rock, which was strewn with fragments of rocks and torn branches. The fallen trees, upheaved earth, and ejected stones showed evidences of a terrific storm and an earthquake.

"These wordes didde make much talk," reads an old manuscript. "They didde holde Ioell Dun to be one not much given to lying. Bot he was giuen to another wickedness which do sometimes bring up strange phantases . . . Wee doubt not yat Ioell did abide in ye woods all night," concludes this chronicle, "in which yat dreadful earthquake didde occur."

Contradicting this report is yet another in which mention is made of the death of Thomas Veal beneath Dungeon Rock.

For some years, the ill-omened spot lay in the midst of a dense forest, shunned by men and almost forgotten. Then Hiram Marble of Charlton, Massachusetts, was given an interesting revelation of the future by a clairvoyant.

"You will dig for pirate's money," she told him, "and you will find—". She hesitated.

"What?" demanded Marble, laughing.

"The pirate himself, sir," she continued, "or rather what is left of him together with a treasure."

"That is interesting," he said, concealing his disbelief. "Where is this money I'm to dig up?"

"Somewhere along the sea shore," she answered him. "I think the spot lies less than twenty miles from Boston."

Soon afterward, in 1852, Marble heard the strange story of Dungeon Rock and of the pirate hoard. He decided it was true and determined to search for it. So sure was he that the treasure lay buried in its depths that he purchased the surrounding land, called Dungeon Pasture, from the City of Lynn and began to drill a passage through the solid rock. He worked under the direction of "spirits" which spoke from the other world through a local medium or clairvoyant. One spirit purported to be that of Thomas Veal himself, who was seemingly not averse to having his long-buried store unearthed.

Marble made several false starts, but each time messages from the "spirits" informed him that he was digging in the wrong direction and he started anew. Eventually the tunnel was commenced, and, at the cost of immense labor, driven forward and downward to where the supposed cave and its precious contents were. There were discouragements aplenty.

The rock is extremely hard porphyry and every drill hole had to be made by hand. Blasting was dangerous because every charge of black powder had to be tamped home and lighted with the crudest homemade fuse. The chips and debris had to be carried out by hand—a fatiguing task. Many times Marble was tempted to give up.

Then would come another heartening message from the "spirit world" and he would resume his effort to wrest the secret from the rock. Some of the notes from regions beyond have been preserved.

My dear charge, begins one alleged "spirit" response from Veal who had evidently been questioned by Marble on what his next step would be, *you solicit me or Capt. Harris to advise you as to what to next do. Well, as Harris—supposed to be the leader of the pirate gang—says he has always the heft of the load on his shoulders, I will try and respond myself and let Harris rest.*

Ha! Ha! Well, Marble, we must joke a little. Did we not we would have the blues, so do you, some of these rainy days, when you see no living persons at the rock save your own dear ones. Not a sound do you hear save the woodpecker and that little gray bird (a domesticated canary) *that sings all the day long, more especially wet days, tittry, tittry, tittry, all day long. But, Marble as Long* (a deceased friend of Marble's) *says, don't be discouraged. We are doing as fast as we can. As to the course, you are in the right direction, at present. You have one more curve to make, before you take the course that leads to the cave. We have a reason for keeping you from entering the cave at once.*

Moses was by the Lord kept 40 years in his circuitous route, ere he had sight of the land that flowed with milk and honey. God has his purpose in so doing, notwithstanding He might have led Moses into the promised land

Above: Assistant Park Superintendent H. Hood (1.) shows the author the entrance to the 200 foot tunnel. Below: Alleged entrance to the pirate's cave, filled in by a premature blast last century.

in a very few days from the start. But, no, God wanted to develop a truth.
And no faster than the minds of the people were prepared to receive it.
Cheer up, Marble, we are with you and doing all we can.

Your guide
TOM VEAL

Only one more curve!! Probably a distance of only twelve feet down into solid rock. Only one more curve to be broken off, bit by bit, piece by piece, by the ten fingers of a man sustained by faith and eternal hope. It took thirty days to penetrate a single foot into a passage seven feet wide and seven feet high. Every night bucket after bucket of broken stone was carried wearily up the long slope into the open air.

There were many curves. Somehow the instructions of the spirits bore no fruit. Marble labored eighteen long years, day after day, forgetting everything but the rock that lay in front and the treasure that lay behind the rock. Never doubting; always believing. When, on November 10, 1868, death stilled the bruised, battered fingers, his son Edwin, an even more ardent Spiritualist, took up the work.

In 1925, I personally met a few of the old-time residents who knew both Hiram and Edwin Marble. They vividly recalled the long years when the tap-tap-tap of a chisel could always be heard in the vicinity of Dungeon Rock and muffled blasts roared all day. When in 1886 all work ceased, folks said the woods were strangely silent.

One of those who knew Hiram well was George C. Blakely. He met him first near the close of the Civil War. Marble seemed to take particular interest in him.

"He was beginning to grow old when I knew him, with a flowing beard, bright eyes and he was always willing to talk. Many times I have recalled his faith, perseverance and efforts to accomplish what he called his life's work."

Blakely recalled one trip he made with Marble down a shaky ladder with only a lighted torch. As Marble worked his way down, he told his companion how the spirits directed his chisel. At that time, he told me, Marble only had twelve feet to go and then he would have money to build his park—the woodlands were to be laid out in groves and drives and forests. Blakely was silent for a moment.

"Well, Marble had his wish come true," he said. "His park which we thought a dream has become real. I'm glad of it. He deserved it." □□

Was She Buried Alive?

by Harold W. Castner

There were a lot of questions raised by the "strange doings" in the house of the Howe family of Damariscotta, Maine, but the strangest one of all concerned young Mary Howe . . .

One of the early emigrant families to arrive in the Massachusetts Bay Colony was the Howes—an unusual and talented family. Time and space will not permit the enumeration of their accomplishments in the Colony, except to mention that it was one of them who built the famous Wayside Inn, at Sudbury, Massachusetts, which was later restored by Henry Ford. Elias Howe was another member of this family who demonstrated considerable genius by inventing the sewing machine.

After the War of 1812, Colonel Joel Howe Jr. (whose father was the original Howe in this country) resigned his commission in the Massachusetts Militia and migrated to The District of Maine. He came to what is now the town of Damariscotta and purchased land presently on Elm and Hodgdon Streets.

Colonel Joel Howe's family consisted of four boys and five girls. They were Daniel, Edwin, Emily, Joel III, Lorenzo, Sally, Mary, Janette and Josephene. They were all what could be called intelligent people, and all had inherited a conspicuous interest in science and invention. This narrative, however, will be chiefly confined to daughter Mary and son Edwin.

All events and circumstances here related are based on authentic accounts and records from several sources, as well as personal conversations with persons who were present. I interviewed at least fourteen of the older residents of Newcastle and Damariscotta, Maine, and there is no variation in their respective accounts of the strange events which took place after the year 1880.

As time passed, Colonel Joel Howe Jr. died. The family moved across the street and established "Howe's Tavern," with Joel Howe III as proprietor. This became a popular tavern in stagecoach days and many distinguished guests are noted in the old "Hotel Register" that is still preserved. President James K. Polk was a guest while he was inspecting the lighthouses along the coast. (This tavern, in turn, became "The Plummer House"; an apartment house; The Joseph Melville King Memorial Hospital. It is now "Clark's Apartments.")

The Howe family became ardent believers in spiritualism. Mary was an enthusiastic believer, as well as Edwin and Lorenzo, but the boys divided their interest between spiritualism and invention. They devised a machine which they claimed would produce perpetual motion, and also a mold to make counterfeit half dollars.

Mary was classed as a "medium," and frequent "seances" and "trances" were held at the tavern. People came from miles around, many to observe the strange doings, while others (my own grandmother included) went to "see the show."

Mary Howe's enthusiasm knew no bounds. One day she conceived the idea that she could fly, so she stood at the stairs and "took off." Spreading her arms and mumbling strange incantations, she jumped into space and, although she landed in a heap at the bottom of the stairs with a broken ankle and was badly bruised, her faith was in no way shaken.

Many years later, when the old tavern was being remodeled for "The Plummer House," many wires, pipes, and strange devices were found, including the cradle used for rocking the Howe children and the previously mentioned mold for making half dollars. These are preserved to this day by the great-grandchildren of Charles Crooker who did the remodelling.

Eventually, the Howe family moved farther up the street and lived in the house of Mrs. Milliken Jones, now known as the George Alva Chapman House. The seances continued, with Mary presiding. In the hope of obtaining converts, everyone was welcome to ask questions or hear the voices of the departed.

I do not propose to discredit spiritualism, but I sometimes wonder if the voice of old "Grandpa Snazzi," which was so clear at the seance, might not have been Edwin moaning through one of the ingenious pipes which might be considered as "props" to the "act."

There were, however, many weird things that defied explanation. My grandmother went by invitation to many of these seances, with other ladies of the neighborhood. She told me that at one of the meetings a guest had a relative visiting New York City. Mary was asked when he would return. In the silence of the darkened room, Mary began mumbling and, in a muted voice, said: "I can see him clearly. I see many lights! Wait! He will not return! When all those lights appear, he will die!" Several days later word was received that he had died of heart failure at the exact time the lights were first turned on to illuminate the new Brooklyn Bridge!

There was much said about this strange coincidence throughout the community, as there were many who did not doubt the magic of spiritualism.

One of the most interesting and unexplainable practices of these mediums was "going into trances." They became unconscious and, apparently, were in a state of suspended animation. They would be laid on a couch with warm stones placed about the body to replace the loss of body heat. There they would remain for a week at a time, with no respiration, no apparent heart beat and, in some ways, seemingly dead. But there were no physical changes to their bodies. After a time, they would come out of the trances and show no effects of this strange interval of apparent death.

In 1882, Mary died. Or did she? Dr. Robert Dixon pronounced her dead and ordered the authorities to see that she was buried. She had gone into trances many times before—a great number of people had visited the house to see her thus, while Edwin acted as a sort of "master of ceremonies" during open house.

It was the summer of 1882. Mary went into one of her—by now—usual trances. She laid there for a week. Edwin welcomed all visitors and explained the use of and reason for the warm stones. Another week passed, and since so many had viewed Mary, it finally came to the attention of the authorities. Dr. Dixon was ordered to go to the house and give his medical opinion. After carefully examining Mary, he pronounced her dead!

From all appearances her heart had stopped beating; respiration had ceased entirely. But although she had lain there two weeks or more, there was not the slightest indication of rigor mortis. Her cheeks remained warm and flexible. Edwin continued to insist she was simply in a trance.

Dr. Dixon's pronouncement created considerable excitement throughout the whole community. In fact, it became the sole topic of conversation and newspaper men and reporters came to describe the story. They found evidences of death—but equally positive indications of life. It became a profound mystery.

At that time, my aunt, Laura Castner, was a young woman employed by *The Twin Village Herald & Record*, a newspaper which was published in Damariscotta by the Dunbar brothers, Kendall and Everett. At the close of one day, Everett leaned over the "slab" and said: "Laura, everyone has been up to see Mary Howe except you and me. Suppose we go up after supper?" My aunt reluctantly agreed. In later life she told me a detailed account of the visit.

She said they were cordially greeted by Edwin, who conducted them into a little room where Mary lay on a couch, with warm stones around her. She appeared to be in a state of suspended animation. Edwin demonstrated many evidences of life by showing that her cheeks were a natural color and pliable. He discreetly raised her skirt and exposed her lower legs, inviting my aunt to examine them. She told me, years later, that the legs were in a perfectly natural state, flexible and warm. She noted a stove nearby with a brisk fire yet, although the doctor had said Mary had been dead for over two weeks, there was not the slightest odor from the body.

By this time the doctors had demanded that the authorities seize

The George Alva Chapman House in Damariscotta, Maine. It was in this house that Mary Howe went into a trance during the summer of 1882 and it was from here that she was taken to Glidden Cemetery to be buried.

and bury the body. There were many arguments pro and con. A great number insisted that they were going to bury a woman alive. At all events, a group consisting of the sheriff, a minister, and an undertaker went to the house and, over the violent protests of Edwin, prepared the body and carried it away.

The next difficulty they encountered was that no one could be found to dig the grave. It was finally done, however. Then, the undertaker's assistant would not help lower the body into the grave. Eventually the sheriff, the undertaker, and the minister lowered the body to its final resting place and filled in the grave. Mary Howe was consigned to Mother Earth.

After the burial, there were many who were afraid to pass the cemetery. Others insisted they heard moans and groans and saw dim lights. Many children were afraid of the place, but Mary Howe has lain there these eighty-odd years, and if she was, as claimed, in a trance, she would naturally have suffocated after burial.

Thus passed from this earth, Mary Howe. Whether she was buried alive or dead will undoubtedly forever remain a mystery.

AUTHOR'S NOTE: I searched the Glidden Cemetery in Newcastle where Mary was buried, but was given to understand that hers was an unmarked grave. Recently, some trees were uprooted and revealed some hidden stones. I looked them all over in hopes of finding a clue. Furthermore, it did seem strange that she was not buried in the Hillside Cemetery which is almost directly opposite where she lived in the Chapman House. However, I think I have a plausible reason.

Originally, this Hillside Cemetery was small. It was the Benjamin Metcalf Yard. Benjamin Metcalf was one of the factions who believed Mary should not be buried and that may be the explanation of why they had to take her body over to the Glidden Cemetery. □□

This has *to be the strangest tale that YANKEE Magazine ever published and, by popular request, we published it twice, once in the April issue of 1940 and again in March, 1963. Incidentally, if you have ever wondered how men might travel for hundreds of years to distant stars, well . . .*

Frozen Death

by Robert Wilson

Illustration by Margo Letourneau

Worthy of Poe in one of his most darkly imaginative moments is the story recounted in a 100-year-old clipping from an ancient, and now extinct, Vermont newspaper.

Yet this tale, stranger than fiction, today is accepted by eminent American physicians as antedating their "discovery" of the new "frozen death" treatment for cancer, the drug habit and other serious afflictions of mankind.

The clipping, contained in an old scrapbook owned by Elbert S. Stevens of Bridgewater Corners, Vermont, describes the adventures of an unnamed traveler who witnessed members of a snow-bound Vermont hamlet entering into a frozen sleep-death, and four months later watched their Lazarus-like resurrection.

In 1939, Drs. Temple S. Fay and Lawrence W. Smith of Philadelphia announced before a meeting of the American Medical Association in St. Louis, the discovery of a new therapeutic treatment of serious organic diseases by freezing. They told of stripping several women patients, covering them with cracked ice, and freezing them for a period of six hours. Their bodily functions thus suspended, the subjects slept for five days, and when awakened were refreshed and without any memory of their harrowing experience. Subsequent accounts related remarkable alleviations of pain through the treatment.

Their attention attracted to a practice of this treatment in Vermont over a century ago, the doctors investigated, and apparently accepted the startling story as true, since in a recent address given at Providence, R. I., Dr. Fay told the story, attributing the animal-like hibernation to a scarcity of food in Vermont during the long winters.

This story, accurately entitled "A Strange Tale," is as follows:

"I am an old man now and have seen some strange sights in the course of a roving life in foreign lands as well as in this country, but none so strange as one I found recorded in an old diary kept by my Uncle William that came into my possession a few years ago at his decease.

"The events described took place in a mountain town some 20 miles from Montpelier, the capital of Vermont. I have been to the place on the mountain and seen the old log house where the events I found recorded in the diary took place and seen and talked with an old man who vouched for the truth of the story and that his father was one of the parties operated on.

"The account runs in this wise. January 7—I went on the mountain today and witnessed what to me was a horrible sight. It seems that the dwellers there who are unable either from age or other reasons to contribute to the support of their families are disposed of in the winter months in a manner that will shock the one who reads this diary unless that person lives in that vicinity.

"I will describe what I saw. Six persons, four men and two women, the man a cripple about 30 years old, the other five past the age of usefulness, lay on the earthy floor of the cabin drugged into insensibility, while members of the families were gathered about them in apparent indifference. In a short time the unconscious bodies were inspected by several old people who said: 'They are ready.'

"They were then stripped of all their clothing except a single garment. Then the bodies were carried outside and laid on logs exposed to the bitter cold mountain air, the operation having been delayed several days for suitable weather.

"It was a night when the bodies were carried out and the full moon occasionally obscured by flying clouds, shone on their upturned, ghastly faces and a horrible fascination kept me by the bodies as long as I could endure the severe cold.

"Soon the noses, ears and fingers began to turn white, then the limbs and faces assumed a tallowy look. I could stand the cold no longer and went inside, where I found the friends in cheerful conversation. In about an hour I went out and looked at the bodies. They were fast freezing.

"Again I went inside where the men were smoking their clay pipes but silence had fallen on them. Perhaps they were thinking of the time when their time would come to be carried out, for in the same way, one by one they at last lay down on the floor and went to sleep.

"I could not shut out the sight of their freezing bodies outside, neither could I bear to be in darkness, but I piled on the wood in the cavernous fireplace and seated on a shingle block passed the dreary night, terror stricken by the horrible sights I had witnessed.

"January 8.—Day came at length but did not dissipate the terror that filled me. The frozen bodies became visibly white on the snow that lay in huge drifts about them. The women gathered about the fire and soon commenced preparing breakfast. The men awoke, and conversation again commencing, affairs assumed a more cheerful aspect.

"After breakfast the men lighted their pipes and some of them took a yoke of oxen and went off toward the forest, while others proceeded to nail together boards making a box about 10 feet long and half as high and wide. When this was completed they placed about two feet of straw in the bottom. Then they laid three frozen bodies in the straw. Then the faces and upper part of the bodies were covered with a cloth; then more straw was put in the box and the other three bodies placed on top, and covered the same as the first ones, with cloth and straw.

"Boards were then firmly nailed on top to protect the bodies from being injured by carnivorous animals that made their home on these mountains. By this time the men who went off with the ox team returned with a huge load of spruce and hemlock boughs which they unloaded at the foot of a steep ledge, came to the house and loaded the box containing the bodies on the sled and drew it to the foot of the ledge near the load of boughs.

"These were soon piled on and around the box and it was left to be covered with snow which I was told would lay in drifts 20 feet deep over this rude tomb. 'We shall want our men to plant our corn next Spring,' said a youngish-looking woman, the wife of one of the frozen men, 'and if you want to see them resuscitated, you come here about the 10th of next May.' "

Turning the leaves of the diary, the old man recounts, he came to the following entry: "May 10.—I arrived here at 10 A.M. after riding about four hours over muddy, unsettled roads. The weather here is warm and pleasant, most of the snow is gone except here and there there are drifts in the fence corners and hollows. But nature is not yet dressed in green.

"I found the same prairies here I left last January ready to disinter the bodies of their friends. I had no expectations of finding any life there, but a feeling that I could not resist impelled me to come and see.

"We repaired at once to the well-remembered spot at the ledge. The snow had melted from the top of the brush, but still lay deep around the bottom of the pile. The men commenced work at once, some shoveling, and others tearing away the brush. Soon the box was visible. The cover was taken off, the layers of straw removed and the bodies, frozen and apparently lifeless, lifted out and laid on the snow.

"Large troughs made out of hemlock logs were placed nearby filled with tepid water, into which the bodies were placed separately with the head slightly raised. Boiling water was then poured into the troughs from kettles hung on poles nearby until the water was as hot as I could hold my hand in. Hemlock boughs had been put in the boiling water in such quantities that they had given the water the color of wine.

"After lying in the bath about an hour, color began to return to the bodies, when all hands began rubbing and chafing them. This continued about an hour when a slight twitching of the muscles of the face and limbs, followed by audible gasps showed that life was not quenched and that vitality was returning.

"Spirits were then given in small quantities and allowed to trickle down their throats. Soon they could swallow and more was given them when their eyes opened and they began to talk, and finally sat up in their bath tubs.

"They were taken out and assisted to the house where after a hearty meal they seemed as well as ever and in nowise injured, but rather refreshed by their long sleep of four months.

"Truly, truth is stranger than fiction."   □□

Newfoundland's Great Air Disaster of 1981

by William E. Mason

It was meant as a fantastic promotion stunt but it resulted in some amazingly accurate predictions of things to come!

W hen readers of the *Boston Globe* opened their papers on the morning of January 1, 1881, they were surprised to note that the date on the first page and three pages that followed was "Jan. 1, 1981."

Believing, no doubt, that a glaring typographical error had occurred, they became further mystified by the headlines which covered a variety of subjects—science, politics, economics, engineering, aviation (the first plane had not yet flown) and other topics. And all the stories were dated "1981."

One headline near the top of Page One read "Mid-Air Collision Over Newfoundland." The story recounted in considerable detail how two aircraft traveling in opposite directions had crashed headon over the stormy North Atlantic, hurling passengers and their baggage into the sea and telling of rescues after parachutes dropped them to the surface of the ocean.

The *Globe* writer called the aircraft involved in the Jules Verne-type story "cars" and named them "Messenger Bird," traveling from Boston to London, and "The Duke of Wellington," bound from London to Boston. A "derangement" of the steering apparatus of the "Messenger Bird" was given as the cause of the mid-air crash. The "engineer" explained, the story said, that the "plates of the electric battery were of impure zinc, and hence the current was not sufficiently strong to move the rudder instantaneously."

All persons in both "cars" were saved, thanks to "automatic life parachutes," the story went on, adding that the "Duke of Wellington" was able to resume its journey after slight damage was repaired, but the

Predicting the future in the fields of science, politics, economics, engineering, and aviation, the 1981 edition of the Globe is now a collector's item.

tunnel built beneath Boston Harbor . . .

"Messenger Bird" needed extensive repairs, including new "wings" and "battery plates of pure metal."

No wonder the story caused consternation among the readers of the infant newspaper. The fictional account was printed twenty-two years before the Wright Brothers made the first flight of a piloted, power-driven, heavier-than-air machine at Kitty Hawk, North Carolina.

As the *Globe* subscribers read on they found themselves engrossed in one of the most fantastic journeys in fictional journalism ever conceived. The air crash "story" and many others were included in a four-page supplement to the *Globe's* regular edition. Today it is a collector's item.

Globe Historian Willard DeLue tells how that fantastic issue of the paper came about. The newspaper at the time was only nine years old, having been established by Gen. Chas. H. Taylor March 4, 1872. The publisher, beset by terrific competition for circulation, constantly sought means of having his paper talked about. As a result, readers were often regaled with stories that did not always adhere strictly to fact.

DeLue says that Gen. Taylor often placed advertisements in trade journals soliciting ideas for making his newspaper known to a greater clientele. And goodly sums were paid many individuals who came up with ideas for nineteenth century newspaper promotion.

Consequently, the almost unbelievable accounts of fictional happenings built up a tremendous readership and the *Globe* prospered.

The identity of the person who dreamed up the New Year's Day edition of the *Globe* and had it dated "1981," a hundred years ahead of its time, is lost in the mists of the past. At any rate, records show that the scheme was linked with an advertising idea involving a product known as "St. Jacob's Oil," a concoction of A. Vogeler & Co. of Baltimore, Maryland.

"St. Jacob's Oil," DeLue explains, "was offered as cure-all for rheumatism of every type and painful disease of every kind." It is noted, says DeLue, that scattered throughout the fantastic articles in the *Globe* was mention of "St. Jacob's Oil" and readers were constantly reminded of the "wonderful cures it has worked."

The special issue of the *Globe* that day carried the information that extra copies of the issue could be had for three pennies. But, requests for copies were not to be sent to the newspaper but to the Vogeler company in Baltimore. This, no doubt, was done to prove to the advertiser the pulling power of the *Globe*.

As a result more than 1,000,000 persons sent three cents each for copies!

The old *Globe* told of a mass air journey taken by "30,000 Harvard students to Egypt" for a two-week holiday. This was many years, it must be remembered, before an airplane was even flown—and a great many more years before mass flights in huge airliners became a reality.

"Election Troubles in Central Africa" was another headline in a day when that continent was quiet, primitive, and backward. It remained for the 1950's to actually produce political turmoil and anti-government riots among African nations, yet the *Globe* envisioned such happenings eighty-odd years before.

Gen. Taylor's paper at the time dreamingly bragged about its great new press, "stretching far out toward Dock st along Washington st" which, it said, was capable of producing 300,000 papers an hour. If the writer of that fantastic article could have lived another twenty years, he would have seen *Globe* presses doing that very thing. Today, in contrast, the *Globe*'s battery of presses in its Dorchester plant, rising three stories high, can produce 150,000 ninety-six-page papers an hour, or the equivalent of 2,000,000 eight-page sections an hour.

The *Globe* of 1881 carried a story of the non-existent "Kingdom of Jerusalem." Seventy-seven years later the state of Israel was created—today one of the world's newer, thriving nations.

Locally, the issue of the *Globe* told about a new tunnel built beneath Boston Harbor when the only means of crossing to East Boston was by slow ferries. It remained for the twentieth century to produce the Sumner and Callahan tunnels which now link the two sections of the city.

The *Globe*'s writers envisioned the joining of all North and South America into one state. The last decade has seen the establishment of the Organization of American States, encompassing nations of both continents.

Commenting upon the union, the *Globe* article said "The year 1980 will forever be memorable in the annals of the American Republic, and therefore of the world, in point of population, wealth, commerce and all that makes up the sum of power.

"We are now an indissoluble Union of 139 independent states, embracing a little over 800,000,000 people, speaking five distinct languages, besides 111 marked varieties of United States (or English as the old writers used to say)."

Continuing, the article forecast: "If the application of Brazil, Chile and Peru to be admitted to the Union, which comes before Congress at the January session, shall be granted, as seems probable, we shall speedily be a nation of over 1,000,000,000 inhabitants.

"There is, indeed, no reason why they should not be admitted and the admission of Canada in 1903, Cuba in 1910 and Australia in 1914."

Also described in the 1881 *Globe* was an excursion by air of 5000 "rosy-cheeked, merry, fun-seeking school boys and girls" from Boston for a week-end in Florida. "The aerial barge 'Hope,'" the story related, "safely conveyed and returned the visitors with no accident and in good time."

At another look into the future, the *Globe* could see in its memorable 1881 issue the day when railroads would no longer be used for the transportation of passengers. Editorial comment which was made about trains that day appears all the more remarkable today because the Boston & Maine Railroad has actually taken the first steps toward ending all passenger services and other roads want to do the same. "Railroads are still useful, though in limited ways," the *Globe* wrote. "The day of their employment for the transportation of passengers and perishable freight has evidently gone forever."

The *Globe* suggested that aerial transportation of freight would not only be faster but less costly. It did say though that "Bulkier and imperishable articles can still be carried more economically by terrestrial than by aerial transportation lines."

"Coal," the story continued, "for instance is in so little demand compared with a few years ago that there is no need of despatch, and it can be moved by rail a few cents a ton cheaper than by aerial cars."

The paper went so far as to say that some financiers recommend "giving up all the railroads in this country as useless encumbrances" and foreseeing the day when air transport would fill all needs.

Publisher Taylor, apparently proud of the special edition that startled New England, editorialized that New York editors "could no longer regard Boston journalism as being asleep."

The journalistic stunt captured the imagination of editors across the country and editorial praise was so profuse that the *Globe* immediately could see beneficial result in the way of circulation—which soon rose to the highest any New England newspaper had ever enjoyed. □□

Dudleytown
Never Had
a Chance

by Joseph A. Owens

. . . All that's left of Dudleytown is history, and that's mostly material for a collection of strange and tragic stories. Nobody goes up there anymore, except strangers and tourists, and they don't know any better . . .

In the charming hills and valleys of western Connecticut there lies the remnants of Dudleytown, a town which breathes no more. Dudleytown rose spectacularly, produced a number of distinguished people, died tragically.

Nature has buried nearly all evidence of past life in the little hamlet. Only traces of once-massive foundations of fine homes, a school, and a church are left. These stone ruins are cloaked almost completely from view by brush and weeds. In the old cellars there can be found the last remains of sturdy timbers decayed by time and exposure.

Not yet erased are the routes of the community's main arteries, Dudleytown Road and Dark Entry Road. Narrowed by disuse, the carriage trails are nothing more than foot paths through the abandoned town.

Since the last inhabitant packed up and left about fifty years ago, Dudleytown, niched into an eminence overlooking the village of Cornwall, has been undisturbed, save for an occasional adventurous hiker or explorer.

It will remain quiet and peaceful in the center of old Dudleytown for years to come. No one is eager to rebuild the fallen town, for in death Dudleytown bequeathed to history material for a collection of strange stories. These tales are more familiar to the men and women living and working in the shadow of the "curse-stricken hill."

Cornwall realtor Frank Cole readily admits the area holds good potential for new homesites, but dutifully reminds, "There is the matter of the legend, too."

At the General Store, Carter Monroe asserts his whole-hearted belief in reports that many Dudleytown residents mysteriously became mentally ill. He further notes, "Something caused the town to fold up."

That "something," reveals retired businessman Frank Breen, is considered to have been an execration from the throne of England, an evil cast upon the town's founding family, the Dudleys, in the 16th century. Two Dudleys lost their heads for plotting to overthrow the king, and a third schemer in the family, the Earl of Leicester, narrowly escaped the same ignominious fate. A direct descendant of this ambitious and lucky fellow, William Dudley, figured the New World offered more opportunity and less temptation than his birthplace.

He planted roots in the seaside town of Guilford, Connecticut, across the sound from Long Island. From the Guilford Green, Abriel and Barzillai Dudley marched off to the French War. They did not return. Instead, these hard-fighting soldiers bought a piece of land in Cornwall Township. Soon two other members of the clan, Gideon and Abijah, joined them.

The quartet hunted deer, logged, and raised buckwheat. The settlement grew with the coming of the Joneses, Pattersons, Carters, Tanners, Dibbles, and Porters—solid families all. They called it Dudleytown. Working together, they converted the former Mohawk Indian hunting ground into a jewel of a community.

Farming was the chief occupation until discovery of iron ore in nearby Salisbury. Charcoal was needed for the furnaces in Salisbury, so Dudleytown men sank their axes into the pine, oak, maple and chestnut trees about them. Thus these hardy people prospered. Life in Dudleytown was good, and not unlike life in other New England communities of the day.

And they were people of achievement. One of the town's daughters, Mary T. Cheney, left to teach school, was courted and won by Horace Greeley, founder of the New York *Tribune*, and unsuccessful candidate against General Ulysses S. Grant in the presidential race of 1872.

This was not Dudleytown's only reach for the White House. Samuel Jones Tilden, who in 1876 tallied one less vote in the electoral college than Rutherford B. Hayes, was the grandson of Dudleytown's Major Samuel Jones.

In the field of law, Deacon Thomas Porter bade good-bye to his posts as Selectman and Captain of the Militia to go north. He became a judge in the Vermont Supreme Court.

His son, Ebenezer, born in Dudleytown, won recognition in educational circles as president of Andover Seminary. He refused the president's chair of several colleges.

Another native, William Jackson, grew up to become a minister, preached the gospel for fifty years in Dorset, Vermont, and before he died founded a society for the training of preachers.

To Dudleytown's enduring credit is a long list of eminent people with direct ties. One of General Washington's advisors, General Herman Swift, was an early resident. So was Nathaniel Carter, whose son founded one of the country's first foreign mission schools.

For every success there was a calamity.

Abiel Dudley went through his earnings and wound up a pauper, out of touch with reality.

Gershon Hollister was murdered in William Tanner's home and the

[314]

subsequent investigation robbed Tanner of his mental powers.

Lightning killed General Swift's wife and, shortly after, the General became demented.

Few families were spared heartache. Deaths surrounded by unusual circumstances and cases of mental disorders gave rise to the story that the people of Dudleytown had been cursed.

As the story spread, the pendulum began to swing against Dudleytown. No new families moved in. By late in the 19th century a muscular man of Polish extraction (his name has been obscured by time) was the only resident. He too left.

An Irishman named Brophy moved in with his family and a flock of sheep, picking up where the Pole had left off. Brophy lost most of his sheep in the rugged country; his two young boys went into Cornwall one night, stole sleigh robes, and were never seen again, and consumption took the life of Brophy's wife. He remained alone in Dudleytown until his house caught fire one night. Helplessly Brophy watched the flames wipe out all he owned.

Everyone in the area thought this would be the final chapter for Dudleytown. However, fate had at least one more cruel act to perform.

Dr. William C. Clark of New York City discovered Dudleytown, loved its solitude, and built a sturdy residence from hemlocks he felled himself. He and his wife spent vacations in their cottage, using the streams and pools for swimming and fishing. One summer Dr. Clark was called back unexpectedly to New York. Upon his return a few days later, he found his wife had lost her mind.

Since then the lowlanders have hesitated to climb the hill and walk among the overgrowth of this ghost town. "Strangers, not local people, go up there and poke around," reveals Mrs. Lillie Wehmeyer, operator of a gift shop across the highway from Dark Entry Road.

Not only do people within walking distance of Dudleytown's borders stay out of the bygone town, they also tactfully avoid discussion of possible practical causes for Dudleytown's fatal decline. There are at least three. The Dudley brothers selected a poor location for the town; the Salisbury iron mine closed with the introduction of the Bessemer steel process and Dudleytown lost its chief buyer of timber; and by logging the hillside Dudleytown men invited spring rains to wash away the rich top soil of the farm areas.

Still, "cursed before birth" is the epitaph man has written for Dudleytown. □□

The Ghost Shaft of Bristol Notch

It all started back in the late 1700's when a curious old man appeared in Bristol. He ordered a supply of food and then disappeared into the woods

by Curtis B. Norris

Devil's Pulpit looms high and brooding on South Mountain in Bristol, Vermont. No sermons were ever preached from its precipitous heights, yet a congregation of fanatics dug steadily, greedily, frantically at its base for over a hundred years.

They were treasure seekers. Hundreds of them sought New England's most famous silver hoard in a once-hustling area known now only to lumbering bears, curious hikers—and a ghost boy and dog.

It all started back in the late 1700's when a curious old man appeared in Bristol. He ordered a supply of food and then disappeared into the woods. People wondered at his curious foreign accent, which none could place, but he was soon forgotten in the busy activities of frontier life.

Then, a short time later, some boys came across the man prying among some rocks in the woods. When they persisted in questioning him, he became threatening and the boys reported the incident to their parents. Angry neighborhood fathers soon descended upon the old man and told him that he was, in effect, a trespasser, and that unless he gave an accounting of himself he would have to leave the neighborhood. The old-timer saw he had no choice and told his story with reluctance.

He was Spanish, he said, and his name was DeGrau. His father had discovered a rich vein of silver here years ago while prospecting. The father returned the year following his discovery with proper equipment and a large mining party which included DeGrau, then a small boy.

They managed to secure a huge fortune that summer, although they were hindered by Indian attacks and wild animals. They acquired so much silver, in fact, that they were unable to move it out with them when winter threatened.

For a hiding place, they selected a cave near their diggings which was shaped like an old-fashioned brick oven. After their tools and the treasure were carried into the cave, the entrance was walled up with flat rocks. Mud and earth were then plastered over the rocks, and a coat of moss finished off the job.

The fortune was securely hidden. The miners departed to their distant homes planning to meet back there the following year. No one was to return without the rest of the group.

For one reason or another, the complete group could never get together at the same time. The treasure gatherers died off one by one until only the younger DeGrau was still alive.

[317]

DeGrau embellished his tale with details which lent an authenticity few would deny. He told of traveling a mile and a half to the river to get alders, which were then burned into charcoal for the mining operations. He mentioned women in the party and how the body of one had been sunk into a pond 100 yards west of the mine to protect it against wild animals.

The Spaniard's tale spread rapidly through Vermont and neighboring states. Meanwhile, DeGrau continued his search, prodding here, prying there, never losing hope. He was certain he recognized all the old landmarks and that they verified the location of the mine.

But finally, after a fruitless year had passed, he became discouraged and left. He was never seen again.

Soon after his departure, a strange and ancient bowl was found under a nearby rock. Some dismissed it as being an Indian relic, but the more credulous identified it as Spanish and it caused much excitement.

A flock of treasure seekers began to flood the area. Many of them, guided by the fortune-tellers and clairvoyants who were so influential in New England at that time, were blackened with grime and black powder.

Up to around 1840, the digging had been done on an individual basis, but in that year a dozen elderly and middle-aged men descended upon the area. They organized on a stock system, promising to return $100 for every dollar invested when the treasure was found. They took in meat, butter, any provisions—for all was legal tender.

The leading spirit in the enterprise was one Simeon Coreser, "a man of little education but of great persuasion." He was 60 years old when he arrived in Bristol. Although a man of great strength, he ruptured himself early in the work.

Coreser went around the area and talked, and gained recruits. He was described as a stout, shaven man with coarse, heavy features and a florid complexion. His eyes twinkled with merriment as he told listeners an endless supply of anecdotes. And apparently his honeyed tones drew many more recruits to the diggings.

Eventually the stock venture failed, perhaps when Coreser ran out of anecdotes, and two brothers named Hoyt, from California, moved into the area. The country reminded them of the ravines and gulches of their home state. They toiled all one summer and left a huge excavation "big enough to bury a house in."

Others struck out on their own after the elusive silver—one here, another there. Perhaps hundreds of shafts were chipped and blasted for the next hundred years in this area, which today is known as Bristol Notch.

The Ghost Shaft is the most westerly of the old diggings and drops almost vertically for about 50 feet. Originally it headed off in a horizontal direction for more than a hundred feet under the base of towering South Mountain.

According to a local story, a young boy fell into this shaft years ago and perished before he was discovered. The bones of his faithful dog—who would not leave his master—were found above the entrance of the shaft. This reporter has visited the scene, and while a Middlebury student (in 1951) spoke with persons who claimed to have heard feeble cries and the howl of a dog near the site on a dark night.

Three other deep excavations were dug between the Ghost Shaft and South Mountain, all within a few yards of each other. One of them descended vertically for over 100 feet before it started out horizontally under the mountain.

The Ghost Shaft is visible today, but countless other shafts are covered by rockslides from the mountain. Perhaps the treasure—if there is one—is also, although treasure seekers still visit the area.

A visitor 75 years ago wrote of the diggings that "for half an acre all around the surface is literally honeycombed with holes a few feet in depth, where generation after generation of money diggers have worked their superstitious energies . . ."

Now, much of the early work has been covered or destroyed by nature's landslides and man's dynamite. But many, many traces remain deep in the woods of Bristol Notch. The only sounds in this area of haunting but gloomy beauty today are those of wildlife and the babbling of a mountain brook as it descends from one clear pool to another.

I recently climbed up to this wild area of ledges, holes, cliffs, natural caves, and mine shafts, accompanied by two guides. To reach it, we traveled miles down a dirt road, left the car at a lonely location, and trudged uphill for about half a mile until we reached the ancient site.

We couldn't help but be impressed by these relics of a hundred broken dreams. The Ghost Shaft looked gloomy, and I half expected to see a spectral hound materialize in the gathering dusk. I felt uneasy, but awed.

Is there a buried treasure, a fortune in hidden silver, awaiting discovery in haunted Bristol Notch?   □□